Sniping in the
Great War

For ex-Sergeant sniper Harry Furness,
whose dedication to, and belief in, his craft
has never wavered, and whose friendship
I value greatly.

Sniping in the Great War

Martin Pegler

Pen & Sword
MILITARY

First published in Great Britain in 2008 by
Pen & Sword Military
An imprint of
Pen & Sword Books Ltd
47 Church Street
Barnsley
South Yorkshire
S70 2AS

ISBN 978 1 84415 755 6

A CIP catalogue record for this book is
available from the British Library.

Typeset in Ehrhardt by Phoenix Typesetting, Auldgirth, Dumfriesshire

Pen & Sword Books Ltd incorporates the imprints of Pen & Sword Aviation,
Pen & Sword Family History, Pen & Sword Maritime, Pen & Sword Military,
Wharncliffe Local History, Pen & Sword Select, Pen & Sword Military Classics,
Leo Cooper, Remember When, Seaforth Publishing and Frontline Publishing.

Contents

List of Illustrations

The first true snipers.

Men of 'C' Coy, the Cameronians in trenches at Houplines.

A scout regiment telescope and carry case.

Captain K.W. Brewster of the Royal Fusiliers.

A neophyte British sniper wearing the simplest of camouflage.

Instructions issued to British snipers for the use of loophole plates.

The dead Hun.

A poorly constructed British trench in 1914.

The Queen of the battlefield.

A Martin Galilean magnifying sight in its box of issue.

The Barnett or Ulster sight with its carry pouch.

A Gibbs optical sight.

A Mk I Lee-Enfield.

If there was one thing the German army was not short of in 1914, it was sniper plates.

The value of camouflage was not clearly understood at first.

Sniper training school, early 1916.

SMLE fitted with a French A.PX Mle. 1907/15 scope.

Australians being instructed at a sniper school.

Hesketh Vernon Hesketh-Prichard, photographed in 1910.

A fine example of a commercial 8mm German Mauser sporting rifle.

Austrian snipers using a rare carbine variant of the M1895 Mannlicher rifle.

American snipers undergoing training with a British officer of the King's Royal rifles.

US Army snipers in full Ghillie suits.

November 1918, the first US Marines snipers to graduate from the training school at Quantico.

Some of the sniper OP camouflage offered by the Royal Engineers' Special Works Department.

SMLE with PP scope and mounts.

Two of the most common forms of Gew. 98 bases, offset and partially offset.

SMLE with Whitehead mounts and the popular Winchester A5 scope.

SMLE with the ugly but functional Evans mount and base.

The Austrian Mannlicher M1895 with Kahles scope.

During the retreat of 1918, a German machine-gunner with light Maxim 08/15 works in conjunction with a sniper.

The sniper sniped.

A typical British observation post with camouflaged box periscope.

The Pattern 1914 sniping rifle with Aldis scope and carry case.

Ninety years on, this relic Mauser Gew 98 sniping rifle was found in a quarry near Miramont on the Somme.

Acknowledgements

I would like to offer my thanks to the following museums and individuals: the photographic staff at the Imperial War Museum; the National Firearms Collection at the Royal Armouries, Leeds; the School of Infantry, Warminster; Springfield Armory National Historical Site; the Australian War Memorial; the South African Museum of Military History; the Canadian War Museum; the Director and staff of Le Historial de Grande Guerre, Péronne; Jon Haslock and the Museum of the Great War, Albert; Messrs W. Evans of London, Fultons of Bisley, Monsieur Jean Verdel and Ibrahim Attalik. I must also thank Malcolm Johnson for 'Sniper Sandy'; Peter Smith for the loan of many books and Lovat photos, Clive Law for much Canadian material, Harry Furness for so much information, Dr Robert Maze and Dr Geoff Sturgess for photos of some of their wonderful collections and Simon Deakin, for his great help with photography and checking text. Finally, to all of the Great War veterans, now long since passed away, whose stories led to this book being written.

Preface

Although I had been a competitive rifle-shooter since my teenage years, my knowledge of the subject of sniping was virtually non-existent until kindled by interviewing Great War veterans during the late 1970s and 1980s. During that time I was fortunate to meet and speak to a large number of these retiring men, some of whom had remained obstinately silent about their experiences for sixty-odd years. Why they chose to talk then, and to me in particular, is a mystery, but possibly they realised that time was soon going to draw a veil over their generation and its experiences, and many certainly believed the truth in the saying that those who forget the past are often condemned to repeat it.[1] I was thus able to record on tape the accounts and experiences of soldiers of every possible social status and military rank.

Of all their stories (and many were very remarkable indeed) it was a tiny number of specialists – the snipers – who I found the most enigmatic. My shooting knowledge at least enabled me to appreciate the level of dedication and patience it took for them to become snipers and to survive those emergent years. They became experts in their field in an age when the Army did not even acknowledge that the art of sniping existed. This head-in-the-sand attitude remained embedded in the High Command psyche until the closing stages of the war, and it says much for the determination of that small but enthusiastic band of sniping proponents that the British Army was able to meet the Germans on equal terms by the middle of the war and be the dominant sniping power by the end of it.

The questions that initially intrigued me were: from where did sniping originate, and how did it evolve into the combined art and science that it had become by the early twentieth century? When I began searching libraries I found little published on the subject. Vernon Hesketh-Prichard's fascinating *Sniping In France* existed, and Herbert McBride's *A Rifleman Went to War*, but precious little else, barring a few instructional leaflets and lecture course notes found in the Imperial War Museum and MOD Pattern Room Libraries. But eventually one or two obscure books surfaced: F.M. Crum's *Scouting and Sniping*, privately published and purchased at an eye-wateringly high price, was a valuable addition to my library, as were a couple of Second World War memoirs, but that, apparently, was it, in terms of available literature.

I was fortunate though, for my job as curator of firearms at the Royal Armouries Museum gave me access to the firearms (both military and commercial) that enabled the technological evolution of the modern rifle to begin. Thus, by returning to the rifle's roots – the introduction of firearms into Europe in the mid-fifteenth century – I was able to form an accurate idea of how a constant striving for improved accuracy on the part of European gunmakers eventually shaped modern rifle development. For it was commercial gunmakers who created the technology that enabled the military rifle to be realised.

It must also be remembered that it was not the military, but the hunting fraternity, to whom the term 'sniper' is owed. Until the twentieth century, the commonest term referring to accurate shooting with a musket or rifle (in a military context) was 'sharpshooter' – borrowed from the original German, 'Scharfschütze'. The term 'sniping' seems to have its roots in game-bird shooting in India, where it was in use in the mid-eighteenth century by British officers, who used it as a generic hunting term – 'going sniping in the hills' – but at this time it had no military connotations whatsoever. Given the reluctance of most democratic governments to spend money equipping their armies, the sporting gunmakers and sports shooting fraternity are to be thanked for their huge contribution to the development of firearms.

There are gaps, of course, for rarely is it possible to be specific about how and when a particular technological development occurred. Normally it happens not through the brilliance of a single individual but as a result of the combined efforts of a number of people, working in different places and over a long period of time, but certainly one exception was the development of the practical flintlock mechanism by a French gunmaking family called Le Bourgeouys in Lisieux around 1615–20. While they did not invent the flintlock mechanism, they perfected the lock, and this must rank as one of the most important technological developments of the age, as it is from this period that a truly efficient form of priming mechanism was to emerge. By this date, the benefits of using rifled barrels was well-known (although they remained rare and expensive), for rifling as a science had been understood for some considerable time. It involved reaming out the interior of the barrel with a set of spiral grooves – something that had to be done with utter precision if the barrel was to function efficiently. On firing, the musket ball 'gripped' the rifling grooves as it passed up the barrel, which imparted 'spin', providing it with gyroscopic stability.

Apart from problems with loading (too much force ramming the ball down would deform it and ruin its ballistic properties) and the difficulties of keeping the grooved barrels clear of fouling, the rifle had one property that made it outstanding in a world where the average military musket had an aimed range of no more than 80 yards: it had an effective range of around 300 yards.

The rifle's march of progress was also assisted by the Industrial Revolution of the early eighteenth century, when, for the first time, water and steam power were harnessed to power mass production, enabling rifled barrels to be manufactured cheaply on an industrial scale. Naturally, the gunmaking industry benefited both financially and technically, as more sophisticated weapons could be made in larger numbers and with greater precision than ever before.

Despite this, as far as the British Army was concerned, the rifle was nothing more than a backwoods curiosity, used by some colonials for hunting. But with the advent of the American War of Independence in 1776, these same backwoodsmen bloodied the British Army sufficiently to make its chiefs – albeit reluctantly – form a rifle company to counter the rebel marksmen. This force was equipped with breech-loading rifles designed by their commander, Captain Patrick Ferguson of the 70th Foot, who, somewhat ironically, was killed by American riflemen later in the war.

Although Ferguson's contribution was small, it did raise many questions about the potential use of riflemen on the battlefield. Thus, in a sense, the sniper ethos was born.

Chapter One

The Genesis of the Rifle

Aside from its use during the American War of Independence, the rifle was of little more than passing interest to the eighteenth-century military mind, for the traditional method of fighting was – and had been almost since the introduction of the firearm – that of linear warfare. This tactic involved the use of long lines of soldiers, normally three deep, loading their smooth-bore muskets as fast as possible and firing at the enemy from ranges of between 100 yards to virtually point-blank. The carnage was frightful and the most disciplined troops were generally the victors, as it was foremost a test of nerve, not shooting. What was the point in the wholesale issue of rifles when their additional range counted for nothing when employed in traditional linear warfare? Although Denmark and some of the more forward-thinking German states adopted the rifle in the early eighteenth century, few other European powers saw the need to re-equip their armies expensively simply to fight traditional warfare.

In England, the introduction of the Baker rifle in 1800 was a landmark in firearms development, as it was to foreshadow a very slow shift in attitude away from the old tactics. Initially, the use of these rifles was limited to the newly formed rifle companies of the 95th and 60th Regiments, which served with distinction in the Napoleonic Wars. And yet the overall contribution of these riflemen was a minor one and the service issue of rifles generally remained a low priority for the British Army. Nevertheless, the qualities of the Baker rifle in skilled hands made it greatly feared, as recalled by an unnamed French officer:

I was sent out to skirmish against some of those in green – grasshoppers, I call them – you call them Rifle Men. They were

behind every bush and stone, and soon made sad havoc amongst
my men, killing all the officers in my company, and wounding
myself, without [our] being able to do them any injury.[2]

Crucially, the rifle regiments had to devise new tactics that enabled
them to make the most of their new weapons: so skirmishing, scouting
and the deliberate shooting of the enemy to harass or frighten him
became accepted. It did not endear the riflemen to their opponents,
however, and stories of sharpshooters being captured and immediately
executed exist from this period onwards. But the slow introduction of
the rifle onto the battlefield continued, and by the 1830s, its ability to
outshoot any other service arm made it the must-have technology for
all European armies.

Despite the success of the rifle regiments in every European force,
it was not until the 1840s that the British Board of Ordnance finally
gave way to the inexorable march of progress and began issuing rifles
to all line regiments. This was partly due to the fact that rifles were
now commonplace in military use and France – the traditional enemy
– had already issued rifled muskets to its troops. The French had once
again led the field in firearms technology, for the design of a simple
conical bullet (by one Captain Claude Etienne Minié in 1845) wiped
out, almost overnight, all technical objections to the rifle from the
smooth-bore diehards. Slow loading, exacerbated by fouling, meant
that bullets had always been supplied slightly under bore size, which
led to poor accuracy due to gas escaping past the bullet (known as
windage or blow-by). But at a stroke, Minié solved these problems: for
his conical bullet, which resembled a lead sewing thimble, had a
hollow base in which sat a metal cup; as the propellant charge was
fired, the blast of hot gas struck the hollow base, forcing the cup
upwards and into the interior of the bullet, enabling its sides to expand
against the rifling. This at once gave the soldier an unassailable advantage in range and accuracy over his smooth-bore-equipped enemy.

The Minié was further assisted by another small but vital improvement, which had coincidentally happened within a few years of the
invention of the bullet. Flintlocks had their disadvantages, particularly
when used in wet or windy weather, when the priming charge either
became waterlogged or simply blew away. The mechanism was also

relatively fragile and having a good supply of flints was vital (a fine quality flint needed replacing after twenty to thirty shots, a poor one after ten). Black powder was notorious for its hygroscopic properties, absorbing moisture like blotting paper and a loaded flintlock needed unloading and recharging on a daily basis if it was to fire reliably. But in 1805, thanks to the obsession of a dour Scot named Alexander John Forsyth, a new form of priming mechanism was produced: the *percussion lock*. As usual, Forsyth's success owed much to pioneering work done by others, but his genius was in harnessing the violent explosive power of fulminate of mercury to create a fast-acting priming compound that would reliably fire a main charge without recourse to flints, priming pans and powder. He did not actually produce the percussion cap in its final incarnation – for that was probably the work of a British inventor named Joshua Shaw, who created the now familiar 'top hat' percussion cap in 1822 – but Forsyth's pioneering work made the percussion ignition system viable and it had been almost universally introduced into military service by 1845. For the rifleman, it was an incredibly important innovation: no more plumes of priming smoke giving away their positions, virtually no misfires due to dampness or bad flints, and at last he had the ability to carry a loaded rifle for a week or more without the ingress of moisture. There could no longer be any practical objections to the adoption of the rifle and the first British Pattern 1851 'Minnie' rifles were seeing service in the war against Russia in the Crimea (1854–56), some 17,000 eventually being issued.

The Crimea was, in many ways, to be a proving ground for the later methods of warfare adopted in 1914–18, as trenches, mining and countermining, artillery bombardments and sniping all had their roots in the conflict. The issue of accurate rifles to soldiers who were confined to cold, wet, trenches, suffering bombardment from Russian heavy mortars, foreshadowed the conditions faced six decades later in France. However, some satisfaction was gained by British soldiers from the fact that they could, and did, use their rifles with good effect to shoot at an enemy who, only a few months previously, would have been beyond the effective range of a smooth-bore musket. At a stroke, the issue of the 'Minnie' rifle changed that, to the utter consternation of the Russian troops:

We dismounted from our horses and watched with curiosity
these strange things [. . .] even the artillerymen could not name
them, suggesting that these bullets [. . .] were aimed at our
artillery's cartridge boxes but were in no way meant for us [. . .]
we looked death right in the eyes. But after a few seconds we
learned from experience the significance of these 'thimbles'.[3]

There were also a few British officers who were more than interested
in the tactical effects of the new rifles. One Lieutenant M. Green used
his own Jacobs rifle[4] to shoot through the embrasures of a troublesome
Russian field gun at the unheard-of range of 800 yards, with the result,
according to an observer, that: 'in a very short time his fire caused the
gun to be withdrawn from the embrasure.'[5] Perhaps of greater significance for the future science of accurate shooting was the presence of
Lieutenant Colonel D. Davidson of the 1st City of Edinburgh Rifles.
Davidson was a hunter and an experienced target shooter who had
made a particular study of the use of optical devices for long-range
shooting. He took a keen professional interest in the soldiers' use of
the new rifled musket while in the trenches before Sevastopol, later
writing that:

One soldier was observed with his rifle carefully pointed at a
distant embrasure, and with his finger on the trigger ready to
pull, while by his side lay another with a telescope directed
at the same object. He, with the telescope was anxiously
watching the movement when the [enemy] gunner should
show himself, in order that he may give the signal to fire.[6]

The two British riflemen had discovered that long-range shooting
(alas, Davidson does not indicate the range) could be successfully
accomplished by the use of a telescope, even when the target was too
distant for the shooter to see clearly, and this use of a spotter and a
shooter pre-dates their general adoption for sniping by over half a
century. Davidson went on to produce and fit a wide range of telescopic sights to sporting and military rifles. And yet, however effective
these impromptu sniper-posts may have been, their scattered use
during the Crimean campaign achieved little and the tactical use of

rifles was still limited to their traditional use in linear warfare. Possibly the only benefit, from the point of view of the ordinary soldier, was that the enemy could be engaged at much greater distance than hitherto, thus limiting the likelihood of cavalry breaking into the infantry ranks, and the fact that they were, for the first time, taught the rudiments of range estimation. Prior to the issue of rifles, soldiers were merely ordered to raise and fire their muskets. The word 'aim' was not considered relevant. After the issue of the Pattern 1851 rifle NCOs, while still responsible for commanding men to fire, were instructed to teach men basic range skills, although only to 500 yards.

The American Civil War

But it was not to be on the battlefields of Europe that the rifle would come into its own as a sharpshooting weapon. The outbreak of civil war in America in 1861 was to herald a new era in the use – both tactical and individual – of the rifled musket.

Both sides – North and South – were predominantly armed with rifles, although large numbers of smoothbores were still employed, particularly by the Southern Confederates, who lacked the manufacturing capability of the industrialised North. But if weapons technology had advanced almost by a quantum leap in the previous two decades, tactics had not. Linear warfare was still the order of the day and the hopeless attacks by massed formations against well protected rifle-equipped enemy units turned many battles into bloodbaths. Despite the ranges at which rifles could now be used (500 yards was perfectly feasible for aimed shooting) 85 per cent of all combat during the American Civil War was to take place at distances of less than 250 yards.[7]

The rules of combat may well have remained at eighteenth-century levels had it not been for the introduction of a new and specialised form of soldier: the sharpshooter. As a result of a collaboration between Caspar Trepp, a Swiss professional soldier serving in the Union Army, and the firearms inventor, target shooter and supreme egotist, Colonel Hiram Berdan, the idea of a regiment of sharpshooters, raised specifically to act as scouts, pickets and skirmishers was mooted. It appealed to the US Army, although doubtless this might have had something to do with Berdan's promise to raise and equip the 1st US Regiment of Sharpshooters at his own expense, but it did display a willingness on the part of the Union command to embrace a novel idea. Such was the response to Berdan's call for men that, in the event, two regiments were formed, totalling some 1,800 men.

Crucially, neither Berdan nor his men were willing to accept the issue Springfield rifle, and the story of Berdan's battle to force the reluctant US Board of Ordnance to furnish his men with their weapon of choice has been the subject of more than one book. Suffice to say that they wanted – and eventually got – the Model 1859 Sharps rifle, which was certainly the best long-range breech-loading weapon then available. It ranked equal in accuracy with the Enfield Pattern 1853 rifle and the rare and incredibly expensive Whitworth target rifles.

There were, perhaps, only 200 Whitworths in Confederate hands,[8] and most of their sniping was done by men shooting commercially made Enfield P53 rifled muskets – highly regarded on both sides. In terms of performance, the Sharps, Enfield and Whitworth rifles had little to choose between them: the muzzle-loading P53 and Whitworths were very similar in form and function, although the .45-calibre bullet of the latter was considerably smaller than the .577-inch Enfield bullet (the Whitworth being noted for its particularly punishing recoil) but both were capable of 1,000-yard-plus shooting. In the hands of expert shots, torso hits on targets at ranges of 800 yards were commonplace: indeed, Union General John Sedgwick was shot in the face by a Confederate marksman probably using an Enfield at a range of about 800 yards. For sharpshooters, a major drawback was that, to load these rifles meant standing in full view of the enemy, thus presenting a truly excellent target to anyone who happened to be needing one. The Sharps' advantages were in its breech-loading system, for aside from its rate of fire (five shots could be fired to every one from a rifled musket), it meant that a man could lie in total concealment and reload without exposing himself to enemy observation.

There had been concerns that the .52-calibre bullet of the Sharps, with its preformed combustible cartridge, would prove underpowered compared to the large charges used by the muskets, but this was not so. In fact, unlike the undersized ball of the musket, the breech-loading system enabled the bullet to be a very tight fit in the breech and this produced what was called a 'forced ball' effect, with no loss of velocity through gas escaping past the bullet, which was such a commonplace problem in muskets. It provided considerably more velocity to the bullet and enabled the Sharps to shoot at similar ranges to those of the Enfield. There are many accounts of a Sharps' bullet killing two men with one shot, and at Fredericksburg, a detachment of Berdan Sharpshooters so effectively outshot the Confederates that the rebels arranged an unofficial truce.[9]

It was, in part, the effectiveness of such rifles that was to bring about a change in attitude among the military, in terms of deciding which weapons to re-equip their troops with. In the wake of the evidence, even the most stubborn traditionalists could not ignore the clear advantages that the breech-loading system possessed over the old muzzle-loader.

Training and Combat

Although the Union Army was the first to raise and train sharp-shooters (the 1st Regiment USSS being formally approved on 15 June 1861) the Confederacy was not slow to appreciate their value, and by the spring of the following year, they received Congressional approval to raise and begin training sixteen battalions of sharpshooters.

It is interesting to note the men employed as snipers on both sides were generally of higher education and intelligence than those of the infantry, and were noticeably more reluctant to be told what to do, or blindly accept a situation they deemed unreasonable. This was evidenced when, in the wake of the failure of Berdan to persuade the Ordnance Department to have the promised Sharps rifles delivered, the entire regiment threatened to refuse to go into combat. As a result, they soon gained a reputation for being 'cussed'. As one veteran said, with a hint of pride: 'It appears [. . .] [the Sharpshooters] are hated by all that have to deal with us.'[10] They were, in short, individuals, united by *esprit de corps*, but who took no truck from anyone. This attitude was to be a common feature among snipers of later generations, who regarded themselves, with some justification, as better trained and more skilled than their infantry counterparts. It was not an attitude that endeared them to the common soldiery though; neither was the fact that they were excused from onerous routine duties, such as guarding supply lines and fatigues.

Matters were further complicated by the dress of the new units, which sensibly did not follow the normal convention of Union armies – that of a blue sack coat and sky-blue trousers. Instead they had distinctive, but above all, practical, green tunics and trousers and a black 'Hardee' hat, which was soon rejected in favour of a varied assortment of slouch hats or the comfortable peaked kepi. Indeed, the demands of being a sharpshooter soon led to the men adopting almost any form of dress they chose. When inspected by a staff officer in late 1862 the 1st USSS were castigated as being 'perfect slouches and slovens in appearance and of whom it can be said that hardly any two are uniformed alike'.[11]

Much of their work in combat was unseen by the infantry: a common future factor for all sharpshooters and snipers. Working as skirmishers or pickets, they were often the first to meet the enemy and they did so out of sight of their own armies. The story of the training and tactical use of these regiments of sharpshooters are of particular interest to students of the history of sniping, for it is from this date that the use of the sharpshooter begins to break from that of light infantry rifleman to a new form of battlefield specialist. This is not to say that their use on either side during the American Civil War was solely limited to covert long-range shooting, far from it. Both North and South employed their sharpshooters as regular line infantrymen whenever required, albeit with shooting skills considerably above those of the ordinary soldiers, yet it was this gradual evolution of training and tactical use away from the accepted methods of the infantry that was to help turn sharpshooter units into specialists, and to foster a belief among the men that they were an elite on the battle-field. Paradoxically, it was also to begin to lead to them becoming marginalised and ostracised by the mainstream of regular infantry-men. The only times that a sharpshooter would perform in front of an audience was when one was required to deal with a visible enemy, such as an artillery spotter or another sharpshooter. In these cases, the shooting often took on the appearance of a carnival, with men cheering if the target was hit, or the enemy signalling misses with flags if the shooting was poor.

At Petersburg in 1864 one rebel sat sipping his coffee and chewing a hard tack biscuit. A Berdan sharpshooter called: 'I say Johnny, time is up, get into your hole.' To which the response 'all right' was made, but the man did not move. The rifleman responded: 'Just hold that cup still, and I will show you whether it is alright or not.' A second later the cup was smashed by a bullet, sending the Confederate diving for his trenches, to the jeers and laughter of others who witnessed the event.[12] While it may have been light relief to the onlookers, it was not a game to the sharpshooters, many of whom died in fierce no-quarter duels with their opposite numbers, and counter-sniping, as it later became known, was to become a vital part of the sharpshooters' duties. How effective these men were is difficult to judge, for records were not kept of the tallies of snipers on either side, but some evidence of their deadly nature can be gleaned from the comment by a Union Army engineer who wrote that:

> the least exposure above the crest of the parapet will draw the
> fire of his telescopic Whitworths, which cannot be dodged.
> Several of our men were wounded by these rifles at a distance
> of 1,300 yards.[13]

While in trenches opposite Charlestown, the Union Army lost ten men a day to Confederate sharpshooters, roughly the same rate as that experienced by the Allies in the early months of the First World War. Of course, the effectiveness of the sharpshooters endeared them even less to the enemy and, as had happened in the American Wars of Independence, there was evidence that captured sharpshooters were often immediately put to death. Union Major C.A. Stevens recalled the relief of a number of Confederate sharpshooters taken at Devil's Den, Gettysburg, when they realised that they had been captured by their counterparts, the 1st USSS, as they 'fully expected to be hung as snipers'.[14] As a consequence, the wearing of badges signifying that an individual belonged to a sharpshooter regiment began to fall out of favour. For the Confederates, this was not such a problem, as they wore the usual grey or butternut clothing issued to all southern troops, but the Berdan men, with their distinctive green uniforms could do little to hide their origins, although, as the war progressed, many opted to wear a mix of civilian and Army clothing that was practical but less distinctive.

With the cessation of hostilities in 1865, the armies of the North and South were disbanded, along with their sharpshooters, but the knowledge of what had been learned lingered in the minds of many professional soldiers who stayed on in the Union Army. While the further training of sharpshooters ceased, improvements in weapons and the tactics for using them more effectively were to continue apace. In particular, the war had witnessed the death knell of the old musket, for by 1870 new breech-loading Springfield rifles were being introduced in the US and they adopted their first magazine-fed bolt action rifle, the .30-calibre Krag Jorgensen in 1892.

The introduction of the radical new Dreyse rifle, with its self-contained cartridge, during the Danish–Prussian War of 1864 had a profound effect on military thinking, as the Prussians used their new bolt-action rifles to horrible effect, sweeping Danish soldiers from the battlefield before they could even move close enough to engage.

In breathtakingly rapid succession (bearing in mind they had clung to the muzzle-loading system for almost two centuries) Britain adopted the .577-calibre Snider breech-loading rifle, then the single-shot .450-calibre Martini. Most other nations adopted similar large-calibre, single-shot rifles over the next few years. However, one factor often overlooked in the face of the great strides in improving military rifles since the 1870s was the advances made simultaneously in the development of ammunition.

The Cartridge

For centuries, the projectile for a musket was a simple lead ball, and without doubt, the most significant invention in the history of the use of black-powder firearms was Captain Minié's simple, conical bullet. However, this alone was not sufficient to meet the demands of the rapidly expanding firearms industries of Europe, for the muzzle-loading Minié was in use only about three decades before the new generations of bolt-action rifles began to appear.

Elsewhere, across Europe, advances in weapons design and construction showed in the development and issue of a whole new breed of long arms. Prussia had rearmed with the Dreyse bolt-action single-shot needlefire rifle, and in combat during the Franco-Prussian war (1870–71) they outshot the French by a ratio of 3:1, inflicting enormous losses on them. As a result of this mauling France soon equipped its Army with a similar design, the Chassepot rifle, but both sides had learned that the killing power of these weapons was far beyond anything they had experienced before on the battlefield.

Foreign observers could not ignore this progress and thus began the great arms race of the late nineteenth century.

Other significant advances in ammunition had appeared at around the same time, however. Colonel Hiram Berdan had patented a centre-fire cartridge in early 1866,[15] inspired in part by the increasingly popular demand for breech-loading rifles and by the need for development of his own highly successful breech-loading design, the Berdan 1st Model Infantry Rifle. Coincidentally, and almost simultaneously, across the Atlantic a British officer, Colonel Henry Boxer, had patented a practical, self-contained, centrally primed brass cartridge in early 1867.[16] Made of brass foil with a separate riveted steel base, these new cartridges – although primitive – were a huge leap forward in ammunition design. At a stroke they had solved the problems inherent in using fragile paper cartridges and separate priming. The killing power of these new Berdan and Boxer cartridges was tremendous, and the heavy .45-calibre swaged Martini-Henry's bullets used at Rorke's Drift had each been capable of killing two or three native Zulu warriors before becoming non-lethal through loss of velocity, despite achieving only very moderate velocities of under 1,000fps.

Despite technological advances in ammunition manufacture, there were still two serious drawbacks facing any firearms designer in the last quarter of the nineteenth century. First, any weapon had to be designed around a cartridge that was loaded with black powder. This propellant was a woefully inadequate chemical combination of salt-petre, sulphur and charcoal that absorbed moisture, created huge amounts of smoke when fired (300 times its own volume) and left behind a sticky, highly corrosive residue that remorselessly attacked iron and steel unless cleaned off immediately. Its burn rate was also comparatively slow, generating low chamber pressures and bullet velocities. To counteract this, increasingly powerful charges were being used in rifles and this often resulted in such high velocities that the soft lead bullets were unable to grip the rifling as they moved up the bore. A solution was found to the inherent problems of black powder by a French chemist by the name of Marcel Vielle. In the 1860s he been experimenting with new chemical propellants, in particular one called *nitro-cellulose*. He found that a mix of 58 per cent nitroglycerine, 37 per cent nitro-cellulose and 5 per cent mineral jelly produced a virtually smokeless propellant that generated far high chamber pressures than black powder. By 1885 he had perfected it. In practice, the new powder was initially quite unstable and several French military magazines were damaged by explosions, but such minor problems were soon solved and 'nitro' was to become the predominant propellant for all subsequent small-arms.

Trials of the new powder so impressed the French government that in 1886 they ordered the wholesale adoption of a new rifle, the 8mm Lebel, to replace their old service rifles. Some weapons historians have argued that in adopting the Lebel, France actually steered Europe on a course that resulted in the arms race that prepared the ground for European war. Other countries followed suit almost immediately: Austria adopting the Model 1885 Mannlicher, Britain the magazine-fed .303-inch Mk I Lee-Metford rifle in 1888, Germany the excellent Mauser Model 1888, Italy the M1891 Carcano and Russia the M1891 Mosin-Nagant. All these rifles were well constructed, accurate and magazine-fed. They used the now universally accepted rotating bolt mechanism to chamber and fire the new smokeless ammunition.

The second major problem, that of the inability of solid lead bullets to perform properly, was taken particularly seriously by a serving Swiss soldier, Major Eduard Rubin, who reasoned correctly that the old bullets were both inefficient and unnecessarily heavy. It was fortunate that manufacturers had, by the 1870s, finally solved the problems associated with producing brass that could be spun or lathe turned, and were producing cartridge cases that were strong, durable and reusable. Rubin utilised this technology to develop a copper-jacketed, lead-cored bullet that could be made in a much smaller calibre than normal (his design was of 7.5mm, when, typically, bullets were of 11mm or .450 calibre). With its thin, hard, copper jacket, the bullet was able to grip the rifling efficiently and this provided greater range and accuracy as velocities soared, with bullets now commonly reaching speeds of 2,500 fps or greater.

And so, by 1900, most countries of any military significance had adopted the new smokeless ammunition, older rifles being converted to accept it. The bullets in use were mostly copper or nickel jacketed of .30 inch (8mm) in diameter, but true to form, the French took a different path. They circumvented the complex Swiss patents relating to jacketed bullets by producing lathe-turned ones, which they used in all of their small-arms throughout the First World War.

The Boer War

The conflict that had been simmering in South Africa for more than two decades finally erupted into war in late 1880, lasting just over a year. It was not *real war*, as the Europeans imagined it, but a series of clashes with irregular Boer *kommando* units – detachments of mounted troops who knew the country intimately and could travel rapidly across it. These ragged soldiers, to the astonishment and chagrin of Her Majesty's Army, soundly defeated the Regular Army at the battles of Laing's Nek and Majuba Hill, forcing Britain to sue for an embarrassing peace.

Fighting was to erupt again in 1899 and this time was to last for three years. The Boer *kommandos* did not usually attack frontally against the well disciplined British defensive squares, but preferred warfare as a series of hit-and-run raids. Crucially for the British soldiers – used to fighting poorly equipped natives – the Boers were armed with the latest bolt-action rifles and they certainly knew how to use them. When pitched battles were fought, the British found them-selves outshot by an enemy they seldom saw. Lieutenant F.M. Crum, a subaltern serving with the 60th Rifles, and himself an excellent shot, understood very quickly the danger of this new form of warfare, where 'the invisible, galloping crack-shot Boer, with the modern quick-firing long-range rifle, was thoroughly at home'.[17] Taught volley fire and shooting only upon command, the British infantrymen had little idea of how to take on an enemy at long range. Moreover, the Boers were tanned from long hours in the sun, wore dull coloured clothing and were often bearded, thus the important white facial 'disc', taught to soldiers as a vital mark for judging distance, was totally invisible (at 50 yards a man's features are clear, at 100 the facial features are visible but indistinct, at 200 the face is a pale blur). Moreover, the Boers had used their rifles from childhood to kill game, often in very difficult terrain:

> We were taught never to waste a bullet. Small game was approached as closely and silently as possible and despatched with a single shot. If a springbok or deer ran, we learned to shoot as they passed. Woe betides a man or boy who missed with his shot for the approbation of all would descend upon his head.[18]

The British soldiers, with their light-coloured helmets and white belts, were perfect targets for the Boers, who could (and did) force the dispersion of entire companies of infantrymen with the use of no more than half-a-dozen carefully placed sharpshooters:

> We could shoot them from five or six hundred yards, usually from a place of concealment that we had chosen before dawn. We had plenty of water and our horses were always close by, in the event of our needing to make a swift retreat. In this manner, we could pin down large numbers of British soldiers, preventing their officers from commanding or supplies from reaching them.[19]

There were, of course, many excellent shots within the ranks of the British Army, and there exist accounts of some fine shooting, Crum recalling one cavalry trooper who dismounted and shot three Boers in quick succession at considerable range. However, the mounted troops suffered in being issued with the Lee-Enfield Mk I cavalry carbine, its 20-inch barrel not made for long-range shooting, despite the rear-sight being optimistically graduated to 2,000 yards. Nor were troopers or infantrymen instructed in the finer points of long-range shooting. Even experienced shooters like Crum had problems calculating distances in the featureless veldt. He once recalled that, upon spotting a Boer group, he was soon at odds with his commander over the actual range: 'Major Greville thought it was 1,200 yards. I put it at more.'[20]

The Boers learned that the reliance of the ordinary soldiers upon the experience of their officers and NCOs made them particularly vulnerable if their chain of command was broken. As a result they targeted commanders, for once the men were leaderless, there was little chance of the Boers facing any organised or effective response. This tactic was proven by the debacle of Spion Kop on 23–24 January 1900. An initially successful assault by the Lancashire Fusiliers had driven the Boers from a hill, but the lifting fog of dawn revealed that the British were occupying a shallow depression surrounded by higher peaks on three sides, all of which were filled with Boer riflemen who began to subject the troopers to constant sniping. Thirst and lack of ammunition helped sap the will of the Fusiliers, who were huddled in shallow, inadequate trenches and unable to take shelter from the enemy artillery, rifle fire or merciless sun:

> Corpses lay here and there. Many of the wounds were of a horrible nature. The shallow trenches were choked with dead and wounded.[21]

After sixteen hours, the men were withdrawn, having lost 243 killed and 1,250 wounded or captured. The Boers suffered only sixty-eight dead and 267 wounded, much of it as a result of artillery fire. It was a frightening foretaste of what was to come, but the success of the Boers was hushed up for fear of upsetting the public. Indeed, many NCOs and officers who fought through the Boer campaign were to recall the horrible feeling of being under such accurate and sustained rifle fire, and some of them, Crum included, were to become responsible for sniper training on the Western front in 1915 and after. Crum himself received a bullet in the arm from a Boer sniper and was fortunate to survive the encounter, one which, quite understandably, he never forgot.

1914: A Sharp Learning Curve

August 1914 was to see the start of a conflict greater than any in the history of mankind. Some 65 million men would be under arms and the quantities of weapons, munitions and supplies required to wage the war was beyond the imagination of even the most prescient of soldiers or politicians. It required leaders of vision, perspective – and no little faith – to comprehend the enormity of the events unfolding, and it has to be said they were few in number. It is a historical fact that many senior officers commanding the British Army in 1914 (French, Roberts, Smith-Dorrien etc.) were old-school colonial and cavalry soldiers who had fought across the empire, believing that subduing native peoples (by whatever means possible) was the key to military victory and political power. But the fighting that began in Europe in 1914 was to prove to be a very different form of warfare.

Britain had not been involved in a European war since Napoleonic times, and there lingered an unrealistic Victorian attitude that waging war was still the preserve of an 'officer and gentleman' – an attitude upheld for generations within the British public-school system. It had been exemplified as far back as the American Revolutionary Wars, when a British officer, Lieutenant Patrick Ferguson, had written of having a mounted American officer in the sights of his rifled musket. He did not shoot him, later commenting that: 'I could not bring myself to shoot so inoffensive an individual so coolly going about his duties.'[22] This was either a shame, or a blessed relief, depending on your point of view, for the officer in question was George Washington. But this story underlines the overwhelming attitude prevalent among the officer class that war should be, as Lieutenant Julian Grenfell[23] wrote, 'a great sport'. Any fighting against a civilised enemy should be by fair means not foul, with certain ethical standards maintained.

Thus, in 1914 it was expected that the war would be somehow noble, with dashing cavalry charges and the brave fallen soldiers clutching at their breasts while making heroic last-minute gestures towards their flags. After all, for a century, there had been no reality for the public to believe otherwise. While this may have been fine in sentiment, it was, of course, to prove utterly fatuous in a war fought on an industrial scale with machine guns and high explosive. Further, in the British Expeditionary Force, it was axiomatic that private soldiers clearly possessed no brain of any measurable size, and they existed primarily to obey orders and be shot at when required. They certainly could not be relied upon to do the simplest task, unless supervised, and the concept of a ranker being trained to shoot any of his superiors – even if they were the enemy – was an anathema, along with the entire concept of sniping.

The Germans, however, were not imbued with such an outdated sense of social correctness and their Light Infantry – known as *Jägers* – had been employed to great effect from the mid-eighteenth century. By 1914 the German Army was training and equipping snipers as fast as it could, and as far as they were concerned, any British soldier, NCO or officer who fell to the shooting of a sniper was one less enemy to worry about. In preparing for war, Germany had made exhaustive plans for the equipping, supplying and movement of troops and these even extended to the acquisition of suitably equipped rifles to enable sniper units to be formed.

Where conducting large-scale warfare was concerned, in most respects, Britain was at a grave disadvantage, having a small Regular Army thinly spread around the globe. The British Army also lacked suitable artillery and there were no contingency plans for the mass transportation of troops; and battle tactics were firmly rooted in the Victorian age. Needless to say, there was no provision whatsoever for the formation, training or equipping of snipers. Besides, the concept was utterly alien to the BEF when it arrived in France in mid-August 1914 and the first regular soldiers to come under fire were bemused by the constant harassment they suffered from German riflemen. Private Frank Richards wrote of his frustration in the first few weeks of the war:

> We were safe from sniper fire only as long as we crawled on our bellies [. . .] but when we got to the end [. . .] we would have to jump out of the ditch and we knew full well that the enemy would be waiting.[24]

The BEF could ill-afford the ceaseless haemorrhaging of men through sniping, which, on average, cost between twelve and sixteen men per day, per battalion. And yet, at the time, this tally was simply put down to the enemy possessing a large number of 'good shots' – sniping not being comprehended as a specific form of warfare. In particular it was the loss of irreplaceable good officers and NCOs that was so hard for the Army to bear – the rank and file were still generally regarded as expendable, as evidenced by battalion war diaries and newspapers of the time, which were full of detailed information regarding losses of commissioned officers, whereas the ordinary soldiers were given scant coverage:

> Lieutenant F.L. Pusch DSO[25] [. . .] who had only come up from the entrenching battalion a few days before, was sniped and killed at once. He had gone with his orderly to pick up a wounded man in a trench, and both were hit by the same bullet. [Other ranks] Four dead and seven wounded were that night's total.[26]

It was generally accepted that three seconds exposure above a trench was sufficient to result in a shot from a German rifleman. One unfortunate officer in the West Kent Regiment unwisely rose above the parapet and was hit simultaneously by two shots from different snipers.[27] Meanwhile, the term 'sniper' became common currency from this period, but in a generalised way, for it covered any form of aimed rifle fire. To a certain extent it was the fearsome efficiency of their own snipers that was to bring about the Germans' own nemesis, for their effectiveness created a ground swell of opinion among British field commanders that some means to retaliate had to be found.

Unlike the German Army, whose sniping was promoted as a cohesive programme throughout the entire Army corps, the history of British Army sniping in the formative years of 1914–15 was primarily one of individual effort. It took almost two years of war and exhaustive lobbying by soldiers like Hesketh-Prichard, Crum, Fremantle and others, to bring about a change in attitude on the part of the British Army High Command. And even then, there were many senior officers who, until the end of the war, refused to accept the usefulness of employing snipers, regarding them as unmitigated nuisances. As late as 1916 there came from GHQ a suggestion that front-line snipers served no useful purpose and that sniping sections should be disbanded.

This was certainly not the case as far as the line officers in the trenches were concerned, and fortunately, within the corridors of power and the higher echelons of command, there were also some very senior officers without whose support no schools of sniping would ever have been formed. Winston Churchill was a quiet but strong supporter of Hesketh-Prichard, as was the legendary Arthur Conan-Doyle, whose opinions often held greater influence for politicians than those of field commanders. There were Regular Army men too, like General Sir Charles Monro and his MGGS, General Lynden-Bell, both of whom were utterly convinced at a very early date of the need to train British snipers. And so too were many line commanders (for example, Lieutenant General Sir Richard Haking, commander of XI Corps, and Lieutenant Colonel Bartholomew, of the 10th Infantry Brigade), who wholeheartedly supported those few who were determined that some form of official training be adopted.

Of all the people involved in the early efforts to have snipers accepted into the military establishment, the name most frequently connected with the subject is that of Vernon Hesketh-Prichard. Born of upper middle class parents, with all of the privileges bestowed upon his class, his life story reads like that of the hero in a Victorian novel: big game hunter, competitive shooter, athlete, cricketer. Then there was F.M. Crum – also a man of very respectable social standing – possessing all the traits expected of his class: a keen Baden-Powell scout, a hunter, and a professional soldier. He had fought through the Boer War and had been on the receiving end of sufficient Boer marksmanship to make him a keen exponent of skilled musketry training and sniping for the British Army. There were also a plethora of others, many not so well known, the officers and NCOs who began to teach in the makeshift schools of sniping. Men such as Lieutenant George Grey, King's Prize winner at Bisley and one of the first sniper instructors, with Lieutenants N. Hands, and W.B. Curtis, both fine competitive shooters and future instructors. Then the numberless NCO instructors – that backbone of the British Army – whose knowledge and dedication were to be the moving force behind the training of hundreds of snipers. Sergeant Major Betts, Armourer Sergeant

Carr, Sergeants Blaikley, Hicks and Slade, generously seconded from their front-line regiments, who provided much of the practical teaching for the Schools of Sniping. They were ably assisted by Territorials (the 'Sunday Afternoon Soldiers') like Donald Cameron, a highland stalker, Lovat Scout and expert hunting shot, upon whose shoulders much of the day-to-day fieldcraft training of the First School of Sniping and Scouting fell.

Fortuitously, there were many enlightened battalion commanders who had witnessed, from the opening months of the war, how potentially deadly the menace from German sniping was. Consequently, they adopted any means possible to help combat the problem, often organising and supporting their own quasi-official unit snipers in the months before any official training was available. In the formative years of 1914–15 there were dozens of now forgotten infantrymen, who used their modest shooting skills to try to beat the Germans at their own game. Men like Company Sergeant Major Fairall[28] of the Queen Victoria's Rifles, who took a steady toll of Germans from the earliest months of the war, until himself shot by a sniper; and soldiers such as Private P. Blessing[29] and Sergeant J.K. Forbes,[30] who did the best they could with virtually nothing in the way of training or special equipment, but who went out day after day into No Man's Land, and whose life expectancy was inevitably brief. And there were many others whose names are now lost to history.

So how was it that by mid-1916 Britain and her Commonwealth allies had managed to turn the tide in the stealthy war that was being waged in No Man's Land? The answer is a complex tale, encompassing elements of technological advancement in weapons and optical science, a near obsessive desire to beat the enemy on the part of a few very dedicated men, the accessibility of a first-class gunsmithing trade in England, and most importantly of all, an extraordinary personal effort by the men behind the rifles, who excelled at what they were trained to do, and frequently paid the ultimate price in the process.

In reality, what they actually did was mostly shrouded in secrecy and only their fellow snipers ever understood quite how much effort and courage was involved: the interminable hours of being either baked, soaked or frozen, the eye-watering strain of observation, the cat-like patience, the boredom – sometimes dispelled by a brief moment of heart-pounding activity. For those men there were no fanfares and very few medals. After all, whoever witnessed their small acts of courage? Only one VC was ever awarded to a sniper during the entire war and a handful of DCMs and MMs, in part because awarding medals was official recognition that, somehow, sniping was an acceptable military pastime. Most snipers' final destination was usually a simple grave, quickly dug behind their trenches, or an anonymous burial on the battlefield.

The attitude in Germany, however, was vastly different, as sniping was quickly capitalised upon and recognised as a vital part of the war effort. Snipers were lauded in the press and the Iron Cross – both first and second class – was regularly awarded, with as many as 15,000 being issued to snipers. Of course, this war of stealth did not solely belong to the Commonwealth or the Germans, for almost all the combatant nations fielded their own snipers in greater or lesser numbers. The French, Italians, Austrians, Americans and other countries who fought in that conflict also produced their own share of highly trained and brave men, and this is their story too.

Chapter Two

The Tools of the Trade

France

In 1914 France was still using its venerable 8mm Fusil d'Infanterie Modèle 1888 Lebel rifle, which was already an outmoded design that used an old-fashioned tubular magazine. Moreover, the bolt of the rifle was long and the bolt handle awkwardly placed, making loading and cocking a cumbersome and slow procedure. Further, the tube magazine was slow to reload, and if dented would result in the cartridges jamming. Early in the war the Department d'Ordnance realised that the Lebel was nearing the end of its service life and introduced the Fusil d'Infanterie Modèle 1907/15 Transformé, a rifle-length version of the better designed Modèle 1890 Berthier carbine. Small numbers were introduced but for most *fantassin*[31] the Lebel was the weapon of issue for the duration. Its heavy barrel, which was 7 inches longer than the Enfield, made the weapon both weighty and clumsy, and the length – worsened by the fitting of its long tapered bayonet – made it a very unwieldy weapon for trench fighting. To be fair, it was not a bad weapon, being strongly built, and a standard rifle was expected to achieve a test-group of 3.8 inches at 200 yards – adequate but not exceptional.

But France was fortunate in having a moderately large pre-war optical industry. Indeed, French field glasses (in widespread use from the 1860s) were much favoured by British officers for their image clarity. There had, of course, never been any requirement for an optical sight to be produced for infantry use, but in the face of France's terrible blooding in the early months of the war, and the serious casualties suffered at the hands of German snipers, the French commanders were soon convinced by their field officers that some method of retaliation was vital. That the Lebel should be chosen was automatic – there was simply nothing else suitable since manufacturing production, already overstretched, was unable to countenance the design of any new rifle, and the Berthier was in short supply.

Yet some form of suitable sight was required, and the Army looked for anything that might do the job. Pre-war, a telescopic sight had been developed by the Atelier de Puteaux (Puteaux workshop), near the Bois de Boulogne in Paris, which was based on the popular commercial German hunting telescopes. It was a 2 x brass bodied scope, with a focusing ring just in front of the ocular lens, fine wire cross-hairs, and a standard elevation drum on top of the body. It was known as the A.PX Mod. 1896 and was available commercially, being fitted with mounts to any suitably modified sporting rifle. Some British Enfield rifles had been fitted with these scopes very early in the war, and at least one example is still in existence. The French Committee d'Armes Militaire felt that it was sufficiently close to their requirements to make a tolerably effective sniping scope, but nothing had been done to design a suitable mount for the Lebel, so work began in late 1914 to find a system that could be easily fitted.

While this was in progress, the Army also acquired a few American Winchester A5 scopes, but whether this was by special arrangement or simply through commercial purchase is not known. These were fitted to a number of Lebel rifles by means of a machined metal plate clamped around the front of the receiver and screwed to the rear by means of a lengthened trigger-guard screw. The bases were commercial tapered dovetails, as were commonly used on Winchester scopes. These were fielded very early in 1915 but their numbers must have been minimal. There is some evidence that sporting rifles were used for sniping, *la chasse* being as fundamentally important to the French rural psyche as it was to the German, and while few of these weapons would have been optically equipped, there were certainly enough good-quality rifles in circulation to provide a more accurate sniping weapon than the standard-issue Lebel. Meanwhile, in late 1914 the French ordnance workshops began work in earnest to try to turn the A.PX sight into a workable sniping scope, but it was to be a slow process.

French Ammunition Development

France had a curious reputation where its weapons were concerned, for in the eighteenth century it had been a world leader in the design and production of firearms, yet by the twentieth century it had somewhat lost direction, designing quirky weapons that seldom lived up to expectations (the truly awful Chauchat light machine gun being a fine case in point).

The new 8mm ammunition France adopted in 1886 is a good example of the unhappy fusion between old and modern, for the 8 x 50mm cartridge was based on the old round-nosed 11mm black-powder cartridge, a common European type that had seen widespread use from the late 1870s until the demise of black-powder-loaded ammunition in the late 1880s. Yet the new cartridge was loaded with the new smokeless Nitrocellulose powder, itself the result of French experimentation and, more importantly, it was soon to be produced with an entirely new type of pointed, tapered bullet designed by Captain Désaleux in 1898, called the 'Balle D'. Tests showed that these pointed bullets provided a much smoother airflow and the taper, or *boat-tail*, at the rear resulted in a swirl of air that reduced drag and aided long-range performance. Concerns over the lethality of these smaller bullets proved unfounded, for after considerable testing on pigs and condemned prisoners (a very pragmatic French solution) it was proven that far from being less efficient when striking a human body, if anything, the new bullets created more severe wounds, as the design raised the terminal velocity.

The Balle D bullet adopted in 1899 was 198 grains in weight and generated 2,380 fps. Moreover, it was uniquely made of lathe-turned 90/100 brass. It seems ironic, therefore, that this new ammunition was to raise as many problems as it solved when used in the new generation of military firearms. While round-nosed bullets were fine for tubular magazines, the new 8mm cartridge was very pointed and the tubular magazine design of the Lebel resulted in incidents of the bullet striking the primer of the cartridge in front and detonating it. Worse still, the heavily tapered and bottlenecked case, when used in any modern military rifle employing a box magazine meant that any more than a three-rounds capacity, required the magazine to be almost banana-shaped to allow for the curve of the ammunition, which was both impractical and unsightly. However, the requirement for huge quantities of ammunition meant that the French Army had little option but to continue to use it and there was no doubt that, despite its exterior design limitations, its performance was certainly more than adequate, as evidenced by the interest German ammunition designers were to take in it.

Germany

From the very first days of the war Germany was fielding trained snipers equipped with telescopic-sighted rifles. They took a steady (and draining) toll on the British and French, both of whom failed to comprehend how the enemy managed to maintain such a high level of accurate shooting: indeed, most contemporary sources refer to men being killed simply by 'stray' bullets.

In 1914 the use of optically-sighted rifles in warfare was unheard-of and few in the BEF understood exactly what they were facing. At every level the Germans were far better prepared for a sniping war, and the reasons for this were complex, as much the result of different sets of social conditions as they were pure military pragmatism. From the eighteenth century the creed of the *Jäger*, or hunter, had been deeply embedded in the German psyche. These men – stalkers, hunters and gamekeepers – learned their craft in vast forests and private estates and thus, for many German youths, the mastery of hunting skills was almost a rite of passage: thus they grew up with an intimate knowledge of firearms, stalking, observing, patience and good shooting.

Target shooting, too, was a highly popular sport and competition was encouraged among the large number of pre-war military reservists. Behind America the most modern and powerful industrial nation in the world was not, in fact, Britain, but Germany. The Germans had been planning long and hard for war and to that end had considered many aspects of the type of warfare they knew would inevitably come. Not only did this planning help minimise the massive logistical problems they faced (for example troops and supplies were quickly rushed to the front by special railway links) but the weapons for conducting the war were among the best and most advanced in Europe. Thanks to a massive expansion of the Krupp works, German artillery was plentiful and well supplied with shells, and their highly effective use of the MG-08 Maxim gun in the early stages of the war (German battalions each had eight Maxim guns compared to the British two) was a painful lesson to the British and French of how careful planning and an appreciation of the tactical nature of the new warfare was leading to a radically new form of fighting. In contrast, Britain was woefully unprepared in strategic, tactical and *matériel* terms.

When it came to the infantry rifles issued to line regiments, the combatants were fairly evenly matched, for they were of largely similar types and calibres. The German Mauser Gewehr Model 1898 in 7.92 calibre was an improved version of the old Pattern 1888 rifle, with a rotating locking bolt that was world-famous for its strength. It had a five-round box magazine and was clip-loaded. However, for the first few months of the war, it was not supplies of Gew. 98 sniping rifles that were to assist the Germans in dominating No Man's Land, but large quantities of commercial sporting rifles, almost all of which were fitted with telescopic sights. These commercial rifles played a vital part in providing the German Army with its unchallenged sniping superiority in the first year of the war and they were predominantly manufactured by Mauser, Walther and Männlicher.

As Germany was preparing for war a call was made to all patriotic men who possessed good, optically equipped hunting rifles (*Jagdgewehre mit Handelsüblichen Zeilfernrohre*), to hand them over to the Army for the duration of the conflict. So much importance was placed on this that a senior officer, the Duke Freiherr der Graf von Ratibor, was given the task of organising the collection and issue of these weapons. From the start of 1915 it became an offence in Germany to own a scoped sporting rifle of model 88 or 98 configuration, and the mayors of local communities were instructed to ensure all such weapons were handed over.[32]

These guns were available in a wide range of calibres, but by far the most common chambered the standard 8mm round-nosed Mauser cartridge. Their barrels were comparatively short (22 to 26 inches) and of relatively thin-walled construction to keep weight down. A light barrel was not a problem, for long-range shooting was not a prerequisite for this type of rifle, as game shooting was undertaken at a maximum of around 200 metres. Indeed, this early limitation of range was borne out in an official document issued to snipers in 1915, which stated plainly that: 'The weapons with telescopic sights are very accurate *up to 300 metres*.'[33] (Author's italics.) Stocks were usually of fine walnut, with chequering to aid grip, and the trigger, which was normally a double-set type, was adjustable for pull and they weighed between 6 and 9 pounds. Exactly how many were provided prior to the outbreak of war is a moot point: Hesketh-Prichard estimated some 20,000 rifles were in military hands by December 1914[34] but this number may have included the newly introduced military pattern sniper rifles as well. A more conservative estimate is that perhaps 8,000–10,000 commercial rifles were supplied, which if true, was still 8,000–10,000 more than the British Army possessed.

Naturally, Germany could not expect to wage a long war by equipping its snipers solely with borrowed commercial rifles, and Army commanders were well aware of the limitations with regard to reliability that using sporting rifles long-term would impose on frontline snipers. In addition, their obsolete Model 1888 8mm ammunition, although still in plentiful commercial supply, posed a problem for an Army that was equipped solely with rifles that used the new, more powerful 7.92mm cartridge, and it had to be made clear that commercial rifles issued to snipers at the start of the war were not safe to fire the new ammunition. Each rifle was therefore to be marked with a small engraved plate stating 'Nur fur Patrone-88, Keine S-Munition Verwenden'. (Only to be used with 8mm ammunition, not suitable for S-Ammunition.) That they were used to good effect was of little doubt, for accounts of the heavy fighting of 1914 are littered with references to the effectiveness of German snipers:

Armentières, September 1914. By noon Armentières was in British hands but concealed German snipers continued to cause casualties for days afterwards [. . .] We remained in the house for a few days [. . .] indeed bullets used to come in through the window as the enemy's snipers knew we were in the house. I lost one of my chums here named Scott,[35] a proper Irish Paddy [. . .] and many the good time we had had together in peacetime. He was shot by a sniper through the head.[36]

It is, of course, impossible to determine whether the German riflemen were simply marksmen using standard rifles, or snipers equipped with scoped rifles, but comments about the levels of shooting at dusk and dawn would seem to indicate widespread use of the latter.

German Optics

By far their most important advantage that the Germans possessed was the telescopic sights to which they had unfettered access. Between them, Germany and Austria led the world in the manufacture and supply of high-quality optical instruments.

In 1884, at the town of Jena, the Austrians had established the Glastechnisches Laboratory, later to become the renowned Schott Glaswerke. Indeed, it was the Austrian technicians who had, in that same year, perfected the science of producing achromatic glass, which was free of blemishes and the chromatic aberration that resulted in irritating blurred vision and rendered useless much commercially produced optical glass. Hunting being a national sport, there had long been a demand for optics in the form of telescopes, and from the mid-1860s also binoculars and early telescopic sights. Some of the best silicon dioxide (quartz) for lenses was available in Austria and by means of a heating process, in which it was mixed with calcium and an alkali, it became liquefied, then was allowed to cool. This cooling process had to be perfectly controlled to prevent bubbles, curvature or imperfections occurring, which would ruin the glass. It then had to be ground and polished, an exacting and very slow process entrusted only to skilled lens workers: but in this area Germany and Austria had probably the largest workforce in the world.

Early sporting rifles of the 1860s had fixed brass-bodied scopes, zeroed to perhaps 150 or 200 metres with limited elevation adjustment and a very narrow field of vision of about 2 or 3 degrees. This was actually a fundamental problem in the use of the early scopes on anything other than a static target, for if the quarry were moving, then the narrow field of view through the scope meant it would rapidly pass out of sight of the shooter, unless he were skilled enough to follow it quickly. On a fast-moving target, such as a running deer, it was well-nigh impossible to make a running shot using a telescopic sight and the small diameter of the tubes suffered from both poor magnification and poor vision in lowlight conditions. But it was not long before the optical industry was forging ahead in both design and development of telescopic sights that were far more advanced than those then in use in Britain or America, and by the turn of the century a more modern design of telescope was beginning to appear.

The Germans pioneered the use of multiple lenses, known as an erecting cell system, and they also began to improve both the magnification and lens sizes, resulting in better light transmission and a wider field of view. The actual number of optical manufacturers is difficult to calculate, but on the outbreak of war there were certainly ten companies producing good quality telescopic sights.[37] The new breed of sights had strong one-piece tubular steel bodies, of any diameter between 20 and 28mm (although 26mm or 1 inch was the common average) with a bell-shaped ocular end to which a leather eye-cup was normally fitted to prevent unwanted ingress of light. The lenses that were fitted provided increased magnification, commonly 3 x or 4 x, and being of larger diameter, they gave enhanced light gathering properties. This provided the shooter with a clearer sight picture, better field of vision, and greater magnification than earlier types. In practice, the ability of these scopes to be used at greater ranges than was really required for small game hunting meant they were more technically advanced than was required for this sport, but they proved perfect for military use.

Of course, no optical sight was of any practical use on a rifle unless it was firmly anchored to the weapon, so early on, the German rifle and scope manufacturers had turned their attentions to solving these problems in an entirely practical way. They favoured slotted metal pads that were screwed or soldered (often both) to the receiver and Knox-form on the barrel. These bases provided an immovable mounting point for the scope, and, moreover, permitted the scope to be mounted over the bore, to provide the best line of sight for the shooter. Some were partially offset to the left, but never in the extreme manner later adopted by the British. The telescopes had to be quickly detachable, so the preferred method was the use of hooked feet, known as claw mounts, that locked into the slotted bases. As the initial requirement was for hunting, the scopes themselves needed to be quickly detachable, so as to be kept safely out of harm's way until required, and the claw system proved excellent in this respect, as telescopes could be detached and then refitted without needing to be re-zeroed. In addition, the front and rear mounts were normally bridged or bored through, enabling the shooter to use the iron sights instantly if the situation required it. This simple method of overbore mounting with easy access to iron sights was to provide the German snipers with a priceless advantage in the sniping war.

German Ammunition Development

Throughout the late nineteenth and early twentieth century the military rifle bullets in use were solid lead, heavy, with long parallel bodies, flat bases and round or conical noses. These, it was believed, provided the best combination of stability and knock-down power, but German cartridge manufacturers had been playing with their bullet designs for some years and tests using the new, pointed, Balle D bullet, adopted by the French, had proven that it was undoubtedly more efficient by a considerable margin than the traditional round-nosed design. Thus the old M1888 Mauser bullet, which weighed 226 grains and produced a velocity of 2,093 fps was immediately outclassed by the new *Spitzer* (pointed) bullets adopted by Germany in 1905. Lighter at 154 grains, they generated an impressive 2,880 fps and testing also proved that by adopting a tapered tail, or *boat-tail*, it further reduced turbulence as well as radically increasing its range (in the case of Maxim machine guns, this enabled their maximum effective range to be increased from 2,700 to 3,800 yards).

This ballistic improvement created a new problem, however, for the increased chamber pressure and hot gases behind the bullet caused heat erosion that led to unacceptably high rates of barrel wear. In infantry rifles, with their slower rate of fire, this was not such an issue, but it was to be a serious problem for machine guns. The new pointed bullets were referred to by the German Army as S-Munition (Spitzer ammunition) and it was to become the standard for the duration of the war. But the German Army was conscious that under some circumstances special ammunition would also be needed, in particular for aerial use, and it embarked on the design of a number of bullets for specialist purposes. In the course of the war the Germans produced not only the Spitzer ball, but armour-piercing, tracer, incendiary, explosive, and heavy ball projectiles. Of these, there were two of specific interest for snipers: the heavy ball and armour-piercing bullets.

The heavy ball (officially the schweres Spitzgeschoss or s.S.Patrone) weighed 197 grains and was slightly slower at 2,575 fps but had much increased penetrative power. It was, however, introduced only in the final months of the war and small numbers saw service, although some certainly did reach snipers, as will be shown later on. It was to become a very important cartridge for sniping in the Second World War.

Much more freely available was the 178 grain armour-piercing round, known as the Spitzgeschoss mit Stahlkern (S.m.K), which was able to defeat almost any armour of the period, and from mid-1915 this was soon issued in limited quantities to snipers. An S.m.K bullet exited from the muzzle of a rifle at 2,600 fps, with a pressure behind it of a little over 18 tons per square inch, and a German technical paper produced in March 1915 stated that tests with these bullets showed it was capable of penetrating 4.5mm (3/16ths of an inch) of high-quality chrome-nickel armour-plate at a distance of 1,400 metres, assuming the plate stood vertically. Later tests showed that, at the closer ranges typical for trench warfare, its performance would enable it to punch through 11mm (almost ½ inch) of plate at 100 metres when set at 90 degrees, and 6mm (¼ inch) if the plate were angled at 60 degrees.[38] As at this stage in the war, Britain had virtually no protective armoured plate for trench use, and what was available was often borrowed scraps of ordinary boiler plate, the performance of these S.m.K bullets did not bode well for the British snipers. Corporal Bill Skipp recalled just such a makeshift sniper position that his battalion set up early in the war:

We had a sniper's post, which was just a sheet of metal two inches high and a foot wide – just a hole big enough to put the end of a rifle through. We had two boys, they were orphans, they'd been brought up together. They were standing in the trenches and one said, 'What's this George, have a look through here.' And no sooner had he approached it than down he went with a bullet through his forehead . . .[39]

The *Scharfschützen* Gewehr 98

Soon after the introduction of the Gewehr 98, work had begun on adapting and fitting commercial patterns of mounts and scopes to create a military-issue sniping weapon. This was to become known as the *Scharfschützen* Gewehr 98 (Sharpshooters rifle, Model 1898). The system for selection of a rifle for conversion was on the basis of test firing, all service rifles were expected to provide accuracy of one minute of angle (1moa) at 100 metres. This equated to a 1-inch group at 100 yards or 2 inches at 200 and so forth, but all rifles that could achieve better grouping than this were put aside for conversion. Perhaps one rifle in 100 might be deemed suitable and for this reason sniping variant Gew. 98s will not be found with consecutive blocks of serial numbers, and there is no evidence this practice changed through the war, weapons being selected purely on the basis of shooting performance. The mounts and scopes were supplied by commercial contractors to the factories in batches, the work being undertaken only by skilled armourers, many of whom were peacetime gunsmiths. Scopes, rings and mounts would be sorted and loosely matched, each component then being stamped with an identical number (often but not exclusively with the last digit of the weapon's serial number) to ensure that the selected components would remain together.

Telescopic sights were normally 3 x or 4 x with a range drum on the upper body and most had a focusing plate, held by a screw, which enabled the focus to be adjusted for an individual shooter's eye (although a few manufacturers, such as Dr Walter Gerard, had a knurled ring in front of the ocular lens that performed the same function). The system for mounting to the rifle was almost universally of the 'claw mount' type, using a block mount at the front and a similar mount on the rear receiver. There were three primary forms of mount: double claw mount, single claw mount, or claw and stud, and the method of securing the scope to the rifle may be offset, bridge, or a combination of both, always permitting the shooter to access the iron sights. The quick-release mechanism incorporated either a press-stud, spring catch, or rotating lever that unlocked the rear mount and enabled the entire scope to be lifted free of the rifle. Naturally there were variations on a theme, as employed on some C.P. Goerz scopes with a semi-turret front mount and studs rather than claw feet, but mainly the system was the tried and tested one, which had worked well on thousands of sporting rifles.

Prior to assembly, every scope would be fitted into its rings, which were normally split and clamped with a small screw, (some scopes had one-piece rings that were an interference fit requiring low temperature solder to secure the scope body in place). The rings and bases would then be hand-fitted to the rifle, often requiring the feet of the claw mounts to be carefully filed to ensure a perfect fit. The base pads were then soft-soldered into place on the rifle using a jig, and the mounts and rings carefully lined up to ensure they were perfectly parallel to the axis of the rifle. This was a lengthy task, as the scope had to be stripped of internal fittings prior to soldering, then reassembled to check accuracy. Once satisfied, the armourer would drill and tap the holes in the Knox-form and rear receiver and fit the pads, which would also be soldered into place and final fitting done. The whole assembly was then collimated to the bore. If, at the final stage, a mistake was made and went unnoticed, it would produce an irreparably poor shooting rifle. Properly done, however, once assembled, this mounting system was rigid enough not to require the rifle to be zeroed every time the scope was dismounted – always the Achilles heel of any optical system fitted to a rifle.

Some indication of the care taken and craftsmanship involved can be seen from the fact that all visible screw heads on genuine German sniper rifles are either in line with, or at perfect right angles to, the line of the bore. In fact these screws are frequently covered with a layer of solder, in part (one suspects) to prevent unwarranted tampering in the front line. Doing this was a laborious task that provided no end result other than being very pleasing to the eye, and the work involved is out of all proportion to the requirements for the rifle. It was, though, indicative of an age when craftsmanship was considered as important as the practical result.

There was one problem inherent in using these mounts, and that was the difficulty in providing lateral (windage) adjustment. As the rear base was often fixed solidly to the receiver, the only method of moving the scope left or right was by means of a winding screw on the base of the rear mount. This was turned by means of what was, effectively, a small clock key, and it provided a limited amount of movement, literally by flexing the body of the scope against its front mounts: hence the requirement for the rifle to be set up as accurately as possible in the first instance. Too much adjustment could twist the scope body out of line, or more commonly, jam it firmly into its bases as the front claws were forced out of alignment in their slots. To circumvent this, some scopes, notably Austrian ones, had the adjusting screw on the front, while the rear of the scope could be adjusted by a sliding dovetail.

Once scopes were mounted the rest of the rifle was reassembled with careful fitting of the receiver into the stock to ensure its bedding was as solid as possible. The bolts were invariably modified by means of bending the cocking handle so that it curved downward, to prevent it striking the scope body when cocking the rifle. Doing this raised a secondary problem though, for it provided insufficient clearance between the shooter's fingers and the side of the stock, so most (but not all) *Scharfschützen* Gew. 98 have a machined hollow on the right of the receiver to give extra clearance for the fingers. The requirement for this was dependent on the type of scope fitted: some examples merely have a hollow ground on the outer face of the arm of the bolt with the stock unmodified.

Each rifle was then test fired at ranges of 100, 300, 500 and 600 or 800 metres and the range drum accordingly marked up to a maximum of 1,000 metres. Each scope was engraved or stamped with the serial number of its rifle, and it would remain with that weapon for its service life. The hand-fitting invariably meant that scopes were not interchangeable unless returned to an armourer and reassembled from scratch. Scopes were supplied in fitted leather cases, with instruction leaflet, lens brush and windage adjustment key, with a set of leather lens covers and normally a soft leather eyepiece.

The Mauser set-up was superior in almost every respect to the sniping rifles that Britain and the Commonwealth were able to field during the war and this meant that in 1914 the German sniper was the best equipped and best trained on the battlefield.

Germany's staunch ally, Austria-Hungary, was also able to field good snipers, for Austria of course possessed its excellent home optical industry as well as a good basic rifle upon which to mount their own telescopic sights – the 8mm Repetier-Gewehr Modell 1895, otherwise known as the Steyr-Mannlicher M95. It was an unusual rifle in sharing with the Canadian Ross a straight-pull bolt action, the bolt locking home with a turning bolt-head in much the same manner as an artillery breech-block. In other respects it was of typical late nineteenth-century design, with a five-round box magazine and heavy long barrel, which made it a good rifle for conversion for sniping, and Austria employed a considerable number in their long campaign in the mountains and valleys of the Italian border.

German Sniper Training

From the outset the German Army commanders could see no reason they should not employ as many of the skilled hunters as snipers as they possibly could. They selected men on the basis of sound marksmanship, the ability to keep a steady nerve under fire, or sometimes simply because they had requested sniper duty, as did eighteen-year-old Mannfried Gossen:

> I was always an excellent shot and had hunted with my father. I watched with envy as some of my comrades were given telescope rifles. Eventually I plucked up courage and asked the Sergeant if I could try one. It was a good sporting rifle, a Mauser and after some instruction on the telescope, I took it into the line and within a day I had my first kill.[40]

For the German soldiers, training was quite basic, as sniping rifles were initially issued only to the senior NCOs of each company, who were given sniper training and expected to disseminate the information to their men – a method that did not always work well. While most NCOs took to sniping with alacrity and learned a great deal through experience, not all were capable of passing this information on, and a few regarded the duty as merely a useful means to escape the normal mundane trench routines from which snipers were excused and undertook almost no sniping themselves:

> My Sergeant took no part in our duties and I learned everything by practice and by talking to comrades who did the same. If we had better instruction in those early months, we would have been much more efficient.[41]

In the first months of the war this system sufficed, but in the wake of the rising demand for snipers things soon changed.

Understanding the scale of the German Army is a clue to the reasons for this change in doctrine with regard to sniper training. On the Somme alone there were about 190 divisions, each comprising two brigades, within which were two infantry regiments and one dragoon regiment. In total, each fielded nine fighting battalions (three per regiment), each with four companies of 250 officers and men (about 1,000 men per battalion): thus a line regiment had between twenty-four and thirty-six snipers working per battalion at any time, although this number could and did vary considerably. By simple calculation, assuming an average of thirty snipers being fielded per battalion on the Somme front alone (25 miles long), there would be 5,130 snipers operating: roughly one for every 800 yards of front.

It took time for the German Army to organise new training schools close to the front lines, but by late 1916 it was estimated that thirty were operating along the Western Front alone. There were also several large infantry training schools in Saxony, Hesse, Bavaria, Prussia, and near Berlin. These provided a sound course in rifle handling and shooting, telescopic sight adjustment and maintenance, camouflage, observation and fieldcraft. The courses appear to have lasted between ten and fourteen days. Although German snipers were taught to work together, in practice it appeared that most preferred to work alone, possibly due to their ability to roam at will and to their hunting experience:

> In the line I worked with a comrade who had binoculars, but often when I was in No Man's Land or concealed behind the lines I worked on my own. I believed there was less risk of discovery if I was alone.[42]

Great Britain

Britain's pre-war Regular Army had initially been equipped with the .303-inch Charger Loading British Mk I Lee-Enfield. However, in a remarkably far-sighted move, from late 1903 the Board of Ordnance decided to re-equip troops with the new Mk I, Short, Magazine Lee-Enfield[43] rifle (hereafter referred to as the SMLE). It was a fairly radical concept, not because of its mechanical operation – for it used the same turning bolt-action common to practically all military rifles of the period – but because it was considerably shorter in length than any other rifle then in service, being a compromise between a carbine and long rifle. This was partly due to painful lessons learned in the Boer War, where cavalry armed with short carbines were outshot by Boers, and the length of the original Lee-Metford and charger-loading Lee-Enfields was found to be a hindrance to troops mounted on horseback. So too was the charger-loading system that had to be retro-fitted to early rifles to enable them to be loaded using five-round ammunition clips. The new rifle's barrel length was reduced from 30.2 inches to 25.2 inches and had a machined charger bridge to facilitate easier loading. It also acquired a very distinctive bayonet lug, or stud, which gave its muzzle a faintly pugnacious air. Of course, a major consideration in adopting the SMLE was one of cost, for the Enfield factory required two production lines to make the rifles – a waste of both skilled workers' time and money, particularly when the manufacture of a single rifle involved no less than 1,505 separate machining operations. At maximum output, the BSA factory alone was producing 10,000 rifles per week in 1917, barely keeping pace with demand.[44]

The new design would streamline manufacture, as well as proving suitable for all branches of the service. The Enfield was to become the workhorse of the British and Commonwealth armies for the duration of the war (and well into the next one) and its strength lay not the fact that it excelled in any single field, but that it was perfectly competent for whatever purpose it was put to, and this was to include its many guises as a sniping rifle. It was to become probably the best and most recognisable rifle of the war. What has now been largely forgotten was that its introduction at the time raised a storm of protest from both the English gun trade and target shooting fraternity. They believed the shorter barrel was not up to scratch as a military weapon and that the short barrel would badly affect accuracy, as well as dramatically increase the recoil. The Board of Ordnance's Small Arms Committee, however, remained unmoved, insisting that it was infinitely more practical from the point of view of production and handling, was lighter, barely affected by increased recoil, and suffered from no discernible loss of accuracy. The latter point was not strictly true, for the SMLE was never to prove to be as accurate as the earlier Enfields at long ranges, but following tests in early 1904[45] it was quietly improved when it was found that altering the depth of lead into the barrel provided a positive improvement in accuracy. As a combat rifle it was to prove exemplary, but as a sniping weapon it was to have its detractors and fair share of shortcomings. Apart from minor mechanical differences, both of the rifles of the two main combatant powers were similar in both form and function and beautifully manufactured to very high standards. Fitted into fine walnut stocks, neither the early war production Mauser or the Enfield rifles would have disgraced the gunroom of a British or German country house.

British Ammunition

In view of the work being undertaken in Germany, Britain's Small Arms Committee had also taken a long hard look at the service .303-inch ammunition. The original design had already undergone several improvements, for in 1892 the old black-powder-load had been replaced by new smokeless cordite propellant, and this upped the velocity from 1,850 fps to 1,970 fps. More importantly, the Mk VI cartridge, with its old round-nosed 215 grain bullet, had proven too unstable at extended range, so in October 1911 a new, lighter, 174 grain spitzer bullet – the Mk VII – was approved for service.[46] In practical terms, this meant that from the outset of the war the Mauser rifle bullet had a modest range advantage over the Enfield, although in the forthcoming trench warfare, this was not to prove so damaging as it might have done. In practice the Enfield ball ammunition was not short of power, being able to penetrate 9 inches of bricks, 14 inches of mortar, and 18 inches of packed earth at 100 yards – almost identical performance to the Mauser.

What Britain really lacked was special purpose ammunition. Pre-war the Government had employed the giant Austrian ammunition company, George Roth, to design and supply an armour-piercing bullet, which sensibly retained the characteristics of the ordinary ball .303 ammunition to ensure unaltered range and performance. Roth duly produced a 174 grain bullet with a steel core, but in tests it proved little more effective than the ordinary ball round and was inaccurate at long range. In mid-1916 the Kynoch company came up with an improved design, the 170 grain Mk VII P, but this too proved problematical, being difficult to manufacture as well as being inaccurate, due to the hard core preventing the thin copper envelope of the bullet from gripping the rifling sufficiently. The simple answer lay in fractionally increasing the diameter of the bullet jacket. This solved the problem so effectively that the .303 Mk VII S cartridge was to remain in service for almost forty years. However, they were not issued in any quantity until late 1916 and snipers (assuming they even knew of their existence) found them virtually impossible to obtain. Incendiary and explosive ammunition was available, but only for aircraft use and these were never issued to infantry.

Thus, throughout 1914 and early 1915, Britain was to face the German snipers with nothing more effective than its service rifle, and ball ammunition. No thought was given to the supply of special-purpose ammunition to snipers, and the number of men who died as a result of this lack of foresight must surely have run into hundreds.

Canada

Uniquely, in the case of the Canadian soldiers who entered the war in early 1915, their fighting was not to be done with the ubiquitous

SMLE but a Canadian-designed and manufactured rifle, which was unusual not only for its mechanical function but also for the amount of criticism that was flung at it. The history of the Ross rifle is worthy of a chapter in itself, but space permits only a brief description here.

The Ross was designed by Charles Ross, the ex-Etonian heir to one of the largest fortunes in Britain, and owner of the vast 350,000-acre Balnagown Rossshire estate in Scotland. Although he patented his first rifle action while still at Eton in 1893, of more interest was the rifle he developed the following year, which was to become the Model 1897 Magazine Sporting Rifle. It was a straight-pull design, very similar to that of the Austrian Mannlicher, and it used a rotating bolt housed in a sleeve, the bolt handle being integral with the sleeve. Inside the sleeve were helical spirals that travelled inside rails machined on the inside of the sleeve, which was a delicate and expensive process. The bolt head had solid opposing locking lugs, rather like those on the breech of an artillery piece. When the bolt was pushed forward the helical spiral rotated inside the sleeve, turning the bolt-head and locking the lugs on it into machined grooves in the receiver. The system was very strong, but complex to manufacture and it relied on very close machine tolerances and scrupulous cleanliness to ensure proper functioning.

The Ross rifle may well have remained a limited-production oddity had not Canada become embroiled in the Boer War, where her soldiers were fighting with outdated single-shot Martini and Snider rifles, and desperately needed a new weapon. Ross offered his rifle for Canadian service use, but unlike many other contemporary inventors, he had the financial backing to be able to develop and manufacture his weapon. He had already established a factory in Hartford, Connecticut, where they produced completed rifles for the American sporting market, as well as parts for the British gun market. These were supplied to Charles Lancaster and Company of London, who assembled and finished them, generally, it must be said, to a higher standard than the American-made rifles.

As far as calibres were concerned, most were chambered for the very potent .280-calibre Ross ammunition introduced in 1906. At a time when British military ammunition was barely producing velocities of 2,000 fps the .280, with its 140 grain bullet, was capable of a dazzling 3,000 fps. Many other Ross sporting rifles had been chambered for even more powerful commercial hunting calibres, such as .354-inch, .370-inch and .450-inch Nitro, and while it was very tempting for Canada to adopt a more advanced cartridge for military use, there was no way it could countenance such a drastic measure in the face of Britain's use of the dependable .303, so all military-made Ross Mk I and Mk II rifles were chambered for the .303 calibre.

The rifle offered to the Canadian forces was the Model 1901, and ever the opportunist, Ross offered to build a factory at his own expense in Canada to make the new weapon. There were problems though, for during rifle trials in August 1901 the Ross had fared very badly compared with a Mk I Lee-Enfield, which had fired 1,300 rounds without mishap, whereas the Ross quickly overheated and jammed continually. It was found that, while largely due to manufacturing problems, the Ross's poor performance was exacerbated by using low-quality military production ammunition. While this was not a problem for the hunter or sporting shooter (who would buy the best commercial cartridges), it certainly was where military application was concerned.

In the wake of these tests there had been considerable Conservative political opposition to the adoption of the rifle, but Ross had the personal support of the Minister of Militia, Sir Charles Borden, as well as the Government, which could see the financial sense of turning the production of rifles over to private enterprise. The Minister was faced with a dilemma: for supplies of Enfields could not be guaranteed by Britain and it could take months or years to find and fund a commercial company who could tool up to provide sufficient rifles. Yet the Ross, while not deemed acceptable for military service, could be manufactured in large numbers within a comparatively short time by a Canadian company whose director had considerable experience of firearms design and manufacture. Understandably Borden took the decision to adopt the Ross and in March 1902 he authorised the construction of a factory on the Heights of Abraham. By 1903 the Ross Rifle Company was in business.

The rifle adopted was the Rifle, Ross Mk I, with a 28-inch barrel and fine target sights calibrated to 2,200 yards, adjustable for both elevation and windage. This was not fanciful on Ross's part, for he believed that high-quality iron sights were the key to accurate shooting and in this he was correct. The rifle was initially plagued with reliability problems – bolt stops failed, springs broke, and during rifle practice in August 1906, a bolt flew back into the face of Sergeant Major W.J. Bowdridge, blinding him, and giving rise to widespread tales of Ross rifles being dangerous to fire – a myth that lingers to this day.

The first deliveries of Mk Is took place in September 1905,[47] far too late for the Boer War, but in the nick of time for the First World War. The Ross was an exceptionally accurate weapon and soon gained a large following among target shooters, where it began to dominate the long-range target shoots. At Bisley, in 1911, and the Camp Perry competitions in 1913, the Ross virtually wiped the board. The rifles were rapidly modified, becoming, in quick succession, the Mk II, then the Mk III, which, among a plethora of changes, had modified rifling chamber tolerances, safety and extractor designs, trigger, sights, stock, buttplate and even barrel bands. It was this rifle that was carried into France in late 1914 by Canadian troops.

Its subsequent failure as an infantry rifle is not really the topic of this chapter, but suffice to say that, in the prevailing trench conditions, the Ross rifles performed badly. This was unfairly blamed by Ross on poor ammunition quality, but was due to the rifle's inherently weak extractor and the poor design of the bolt stop. In addition, the inability of soldiers to keep the vulnerable locking lugs free of mud led to excessive force being applied (something soldiers are noted for where care of weapons is concerned) to open or close the bolt, thus exacerbating the problem. The result was the withdrawal of the Ross as an infantry rifle in September 1916, troops being supplied with the SMLE.

The Sniper's Ross

For sniping purposes, the Ross proved to be a very good rifle indeed, particularly as it was the only pre-war rifle in Allied service to be provided with a telescope sight. Prior to 1914, the use of telescopes on sporting rifles in Canada was far more prevalent than in Great Britain, the distances and opportunities for hunting being greater and the type and number of game animals being larger than in Europe. Many Ross rifles had been fitted with German-made scopes and a number found their way to France in 1915 with their owners, the most notable probably being the Zeiss-equipped .280-calibre Ross rifle owned by Lieutenant L. Greener, nephew of W.W. Greener, the gunmaker, and used by him for sniping – he accounted for fifty-four Germans prior to his death.[48]

The Canadian militia had been interested in adopting some form of optical sight with which to equip sharpshooters and had examined a number of alternatives, including British Periscopic Prism Company, German Zeiss, Bock and Gerard, American Winchester, and Warner and Swasey, and also the French APX Mlle. 1896. That the Warner was chosen was, to a great extent, a matter of expediency as much as practicality, for obtaining the required number (500 were ordered) was a matter of some urgency and the Warners were available, 250 Model 1913 scopes being supplied between April and July 1915, the balance in October 1916. The Warner was a prismatic scope, which necessitated its body being both bulky and heavy, but it provided the greatest magnification power of any military scope of the day – 5.2 x albeit with only a 4.5-degree field of view. Excepting the weight (the scope and mount weighed a hefty 2½ lbs in total) there were other drawbacks with the system, for in common with other optical sights used by the Allies, it was offset to the left, making it awkward to use. Worse still, it suffered from extremely short eye-relief, the ocular lens requiring a heavy rubber eye-cup fitted to protect the eye socket from recoil. Not for nothing did McBride comment that shooting the Ross could 'make a flincher out of a cigar-store Indian'. Tales of the eye cup having to be peeled away from the firer's eye because of suction, while doubtless exaggerated, have the ring of truth to them, for all Ross eye cups have holes in them to prevent them adhering to the shooter by suction.

Meanwhile, the body of the Warner was prone to ingress of water misting up the mirror and optics – by no means unique to scopes of this period – but made worse on the Warner because of its box-like construction and multiple screw fittings. There were troubles, too, with the scope mounting plate on the left side of the receiver, which carried the full weight of the scope, as well as transferring the recoil force through its mounting screws on firing. This often loosened them, or caused premature wear on the dovetail fitting, for which the cure (mentioned by McBride) was to tap tiny pieces of razor blade into the gap, wedging it solid, much to the disgust of the armourers, as it proved almost impossible to remove. The rifle and scope combination was viewed with mixed feelings by the Canadian snipers, McBride writing that:

> it might not rate so high now but at that time, it was better than any other I had ever used. One of the best features was that it could be mounted and used without interfering with the iron sights. It is my opinion that when compared to others we had at that date and time, it was a pretty good sight. The one I used gave good results and was fully as accurate and reliable as the Winchester A-5 type. This latter model was particularly hard to 'keep up'.[49]

The Ross rifle itself suffered from a number of shortcomings as well, one being the warping of the woodwork on the fore-end, which adversely affected accuracy, normally solved by sawing it off leaving the barrel free-floating forward of the first barrel-band. With this combination Canadian snipers were to become the most aggressive and successful of the early part of the war.

Chapter Three

Early Days

The wealth of technical improvements that had occurred in the design and development of the military rifle over the previous two decades were probably of little interest to the Regular Army soldiers of 1914. Although their rifles were theoretically accurate to 2,000 yards, long-range shooting was still the preserve of the competitive shooter, of whom there were very few within the Regular Army. Other ranks were still trained to volley fire only on the command of their officers or NCOs, but it is true that the men of the BEF excelled at it. Certainly, they were famed for their fifteen-rounds-a-minute aimed rapid fire, which had proved so effective at the start of the war that German field commanders often reported being held up by massed British machine guns. It certainly proved devastating for dealing with the extended lines of advancing Germans they faced in the early months of the war. Trumpeter J. Naylor recalled:

> The officer, cool as anything was saying, *At two fifty* [. . .] *at two hundred* [. . .] And then he said, *ten rounds rapid*! And the chaps opened up – and the Germans just fell down like logs. I've never seen anything like it [. . .] the fire discipline of those troops, I've never forgotten that, I was so impressed.[50]

For the Germans on the receiving end of such concentrated fire, it was a horror that survivors would not easily forget. Most of the German soldiers were young volunteers full of patriotic fervour, but so enormous were their losses that, by the late autumn of 1914, some German regiments had all but ceased to exist: the 247th Infantry Regiment was known as the 'Regiment of the Dead', while the soldiers of the 207th Reserve Infantry Regiment, which went proudly into battle wearing pre-war Prussian-blue uniforms, their peacetime student caps on their heads and singing *Deutschland Uber Alles*, were totally annihilated by British rifle fire. Not for nothing did German troops refer to this period of fighting as 'the Massacre of the Innocents'. Over 20,000 Germans were killed or wounded in the fighting for Langemark alone and by the end of the year some 800,000 Germans (almost exactly the number of men in their pre-war Regular Army) had become casualties.

Certainly, the tenacity of the Allied defence had been a surprise to General von Falkenhayn, but despite the failure of the Schlieffen Plan the German High Command was not unduly concerned – the BEF had lost some 50,000 regular soldiers, one-fifth of its total pre-war standing, and the *Entente* had been forced back to a point where, it was believed, a little more effort would surely drive it into the sea.

But with the onset of winter the inconclusive see-saw fighting across northern France had to stop, as both sides were forced by nature into a near cessation of hostilities. Trenches were dug, in part to provide shelter from enemy fire, but also as necessary protection from the bitter winds and cold that swept unhindered from Eastern Europe. What began as a series of temporary shelters was about to turn into a near-permanent front line, which eventually stretched 425 miles from the Belgian coast to the Swiss border. It would result in a form of troglodyte warfare of a type unimaginable to even the most far-sighted politicians and Army commanders. It soon became the perfect breeding ground for many new and terrible forms of warfare: enormously destructive high explosive shells, deep mining involving hundreds of men and tons of high explosive, aerial bombardments, poison gas, flame-throwers and – almost dwarfed amongst it all – the employment of men with rifles and telescopic sights.

Early Trench Sniping

In trying to understand how the trench deadlock came about, it is important to appreciate the different doctrines employed by the combatant armies. From the outset, German commanders believed there would be a long-drawn-out war and they chose their defensive lines with particular care. As far as Germany was concerned, all captured territory was now German and would remain in their hands indefinitely, so the concept of giving up any captured ground was not to be even remotely contemplated, and where this was done it was only as a result of tactical expediency. In accordance with this belief, the German trenches that began to appear in the autumn of 1914 were established predominantly where they had a strategic advantage. This invariably meant the high ground, as any visitor to the old battlefields will quickly appreciate. Geographically this was useful from the purely practical standpoint – in wet weather the rain ran down into the British and French lines, and the flooding meant continual work for the British soldiers and their shallow trenches left them very vulnerable to sniping:

> One morning Stevens and I were watching a man fix a hand-pump; the trench at this point took a sharp turn to our right front and we were on the corner. It was Berry [. . .] he had his boots socks and puttees off [. . .] and his language was delightful to listen to. Suddenly he slipped on his back in the water and we burst out laughing. Then suddenly Stevens too dropped down into a sitting position with his back against the back of the trench; but this was no laughing matter. A sniper on our right front had got him right though the head. No man ever spoke who was shot clean through the head. Some lived a few seconds [. . .] Stevens[51] lived about fifteen minutes.

From a tactical point of view, the trenches provided German marksmen with a superior view over British lines, often enabling them to enfilade the Allied positions. Moreover, the German lines were excavated with care and line regiments actively encouraged sniping. Their *Jägers* were to prove adept and were permitted free rein to work anywhere along their entire regimental frontage, making their own hides and choosing their preferred vantage points. In this they were aided by the fact that, as a matter of course, sniper posts were placed at regular intervals along the trenches with concealed loop-holes and observation platforms. The trenches were deep, well equipped, and where ground conditions permitted, dugouts were excavated to a great depth – often 30 or 40 feet – and were virtually shellproof. The

Germans were therefore content to reinforce their newly won positions and settle on a well-thought-out defensive strategy – at least until they could prepare for a new offensive to drive the enemy back to the coast.

From the British and French perspective, the ground held by Germany in 1914 had merely been misappropriated from France and was in the possession of the enemy only temporarily. They believed, initially at any rate, that by Christmas 1914 the *Boches* would be driven out and the land restored to its rightful owners. Thus the Allies were destined to be perpetually prepared for offensive action, and this led to the adoption of a different tactical doctrine: that of waging a perpetual offensive, and this affected the construction of trenches.

The British and French always regarded trenches as nothing more than temporary, affording protection to the troops until such time as they were able to advance. The result was that, in 1914 and through the early months of 1915, British trenches were poorly constructed, being far too shallow and having insufficiently thick parapets. But a German Mauser bullet was capable of punching through 10 inches of bricks (the average thickness of a house wall) at 100 metres and almost 20 inches of earth-packed sandbags or 5 feet (almost 1.5 metres) of earth banking. Even hardwood, in the form of a railway sleeper, could be penetrated to a depth of 8 inches. Few soldiers were used to the power of these high velocity bullets and the appalling effect they had on the human body. They assumed that taking shelter behind a brick wall or layer of sandbags rendered them immune from harm, but they were wrong. Earth or sandbags may have slowed down the bullet but they did not stop it being lethal, particularly at the typically short ranges that separated the trenches:

> The hardiest soldier turned sick when he saw the effect of the pointed German bullet, which was apt to keyhole so that the little hole in the forehead where it entered often became a huge tear, the size of a man's fist on the other side of the stricken man's head.[52]

Worse still, in the early months of the war the trenches were frequently dug in straight lines. This provided almost no shelter from shelling, as any explosion in the trench would send its blast laterally along it. In addition, any sniper who was able to enfilade the trench could fire up and down it at will, the men having nowhere to hide. Hard experience soon showed that a system of bays and traverses was far safer. Furthermore, trenches were seldom deep enough, making it too easy for a man to stand upright in an unthinking moment, thus exposing his head. This made life hell for the taller soldiers, who had to spend every waking moment hunched to ensure they were not visible: for a second's forgetfulness literally mean death. And yet, in Flanders, the water-table was only a foot or so beneath the ground, making deep trenches impossible to dig. This resulted in the construction of miles of shallow trenches using tens of thousands of sandbags reinforced by wire and timber to provide cover, although these could not withstand shellfire and were frequently insufficient to even stop close-range rifle fire.[53] Consequently, the German engineers in Flanders took to building reinforced concrete pillboxes, that were all but indestructible.

Initially, few British officers understood the importance of providing protection from aimed rifle fire, shells being the main concern of GHQ, which totally ignored sniping but which instructed that no unit should ever dig trenches within 200 yards of a road, as it would be too easy for artillery to pinpoint them. Yet, according to the soldiers in the line, it was not artillery but aimed rifle fire that was their greatest worry, as noted by Captain J.C. Dunne:

> October 1914. A (Company) dug by platoons: Stockwell [. . .] made no parapet, he argued that the occupants would be less visible. In time to come the front Companies were to be troubled by snipers in isolated barns and buildings; C (Company) was also under inescapable enfilade from Rouges Bancs, which was only 350 yards away [. . .] for most of the deaths were from rifle fire, shells caused comparatively few.[54]

At this period the British tended to refer to *any* aimed fire as being from 'snipers', although this clearly could not always be the case: prepared as they were, the Germans probably fielded no more than a few thousand snipers along their entire front, although they had many excellent riflemen in the ranks as well, and they accounted for a large number of the British casualties.

Further south, on the Somme and in Artois, the chalk lent itself to digging. As winter closed in, British soldiers excavated deeper and more solid dugouts to house themselves, while the Royal Engineers began constructing more efficient forms of trench networks: deeper, with wooden duckboards on the floor, drainage sumps for water, proper fire-steps and thicker sandbag parapets.

In responding to the German sniper menace, the British troops were hidebound to a certain extent by King's Regulations, for in tune with the Army's obsession with neatness, they were instructed to lay sandbags in regular rows, with headers and stretchers, just as if they were bricks. This was unfortunate, for it meant that the layers of perfectly packed and laid sandbags made the insertion of any form of concealed sniper loophole impossible, for it would stand out like a sore thumb:

> At this time [. . .] concealment was nearly impossible in the form of the parapet then in use. Many of our units took an actual pride in having an absolutely flat and even parapet, which gave the Germans every opportunity of spotting the smallest movement. The parapets were made of sandbags beaten down with spades, and it is not too much to say that along many of them a mouse could not move without being observed by the most moderate-sighted German sniper.[55]

Hesketh-Prichard noted in his diary:

> Alas, we lost another fine young officer [. . .] he jumped up and without my noticing, peeped over [the parapet] on my left. There was a crash and a smack and I realised he had been hit. The bullet had passed through a rotten sandbag and hit him low down in the head. He died as he fell, without a groan or a word. The bullet had come from a well concealed loophole 250 yards on our left.[56]

For the men under this wearing rifle fire, the need to strike back became paramount and many tried to beat the Germans at their own game. One of the most common methods adopted of returning fire was to leave a very narrow gap between the sandbags on the parapet, but it was a dangerous practice:

> We got used to standing in a fire trench and trying to aim through a tiny hole, just big enough to get a rifle through. We used to watch for German snipers. When a German fired, you might see a little spark come out of the barrel, and you'd fire through that tiny hole. I remember when Lenny Passiful[57] my best friend said 'Let me have a go, Smiler' and [. . .] put his rifle through that tiny hole. I saw him fall – I was in the trench close by him and put my arm out and I caught him. His rifle stuck in the hole, but the sniper had got him, right through that tiny little hole. I laid him down and stayed with him until help came. Well I said to Lenny, 'You're very lucky, you've got a Blighty one! I'll write to your mum in England.' He never got back to Blighty. He's buried in Béthune Town cemetery. A few years ago I went to France, to Béthune, and I laid a wreath on his grave. I think of him most days.[58]

As the armies settled down to see the winter through, it gradually became evident that the casualties inflicted on the British soldiers were following a regular pattern that could not simply be explained away by the usual response of 'stray bullet'. Head shots were the most common form of death and in the shallow trenches that had originally been constructed, Private Arthur Barraclough recalled that:

> You might have a quick peep over the top, just for a moment, but you wouldn't if you'd any sense at all. We lost fellas [*sic*] during the daytime just because they forgot or were careless for a moment.[59]

Neither was the situation helped by the attitude of some officers, who believed that any display of cowardice under fire on their part was a bad example to the troops. As a result, many paid with their lives for acts of foolish bravery, such as leading attacks armed only with their walking sticks or refusing to take shelter under heavy fire. A considerable number simply appeared to doubt that snipers were a significant threat, despite the fact that officers and NCOs were primary targets. So too were Forward Observation Officers – the eyes of the artillery – who were particularly vulnerable, occupying, as they did, advanced posts in the front lines, from where they could direct battery fire. Sadly, some warnings regarding the deadly efficiency of German marksmen went unheeded:

> A gunner major, tired of remaining with his battery [. . .] decided one day to reverse the roles. He would observe his battery's fire from the front-line trenches. In spite of all the warnings of the officers of another company of my regiment, who were on the spot, the Major insisted upon observing from the dangerous bit of trench. What was more [. . .] he deliberately stood up on the fire-step and surveyed the enemy's trenches. He paid for his nonchalance with his life. There was the sudden, mysterious 'crack' of a striking bullet. It had got him clean through one eye, and he fell dead without a word.[60]

Major Patrick Butler, whose artillery unit served in Flanders from the earliest months of the war, was well acquainted with the effects of German sniping:

> Sniping, both from the enemy's side and from our own, went on all night and it was very wearing. Particularly dangerous places were marked with crude signs saying 'Danger sniper' and the men soon learned not to ignore these terse warnings.[61]

Loophole Plates

Accounts by British soldiers from this period illustrate their frustration at identifying German sniping positions (from which they could be shot without hindrance) only to lack sufficient means to deal with them. Frequently mentioned are the use of loopholes and sniper plates, with which the Germans were well furnished. These were

The first true snipers emerged during the American Civil War. Here, 'California Joe' (real name Truman Head) of the 1st US Regiment of Sharpshooters stands behind Colonel Hiram Berdan. Joe holds an M1859 Sharps rifle with double set triggers.
(Vermont Historical society)

Men of 'C' Coy, the Cameronians in trenches at Houplines, Ypres December 1914. The impromptu sniper's plate sitting prominently on the skyline gives some indication of the unsophisticated nature of sniping at this time.
(Author's collection)

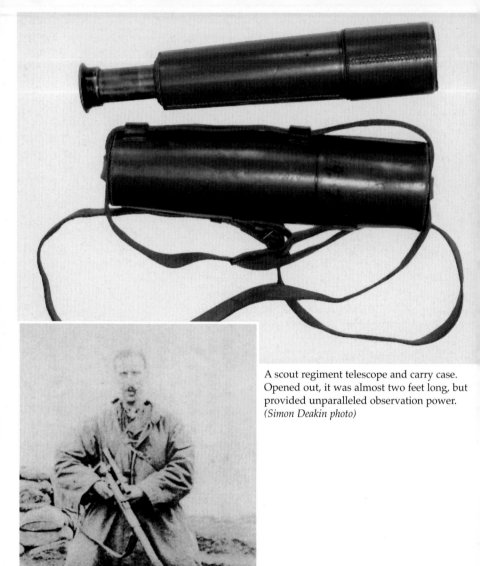

A scout regiment telescope and carry case. Opened out, it was almost two feet long, but provided unparalleled observation power. *(Simon Deakin photo)*

Captain K.W. Brewster of the Royal Fusiliers in early 1915 with a commercial Ross rifle. He has fitted what appears to be a German-manufactured telescopic sight. *(Photo via Harry Furness)*

A neophyte British sniper wearing the simplest of camouflage, a sniper's hood. It would be ideal for sniping from a trench, when the rest of the body was protected from view. *(IWM photo)*

Instructions issued to British snipers for the use of loophole plates.

LOOPHOLE TO BE USED BY SNIPERS ONLY.

The greatest care must be taken to prevent this loophole being located by the enemy.

As little movement as possible.

As quiet as possible.

See that the background is blinded.

Never leave the shutter open.

See that the disguise of the aperture does not get shifted or out of date, or blocked with new wire or obstacles.

Do not fire from the loophole too often.

Do anything you can to mislead the enemy as to the true position of the loophole.

NOTE.—When handing over to a new Regiment loopholes should be specially handed over with a range card and any information as to the habits of the enemy, etc. If possible the Commanding Officer should give special orders to prevent O.P.'s or Sniper's Loopholes from being "given away."

The dead Hun. An extremely lifelike dummy manufactured by the Royal Engineers' Special Works Park. *(Daily Mail)*

An extremely poorly constructed British trench, in 1914. It would have proven a death-trap if a shell landed in it and a sniper could shoot down its entire length with impunity. *(Author's collection)*

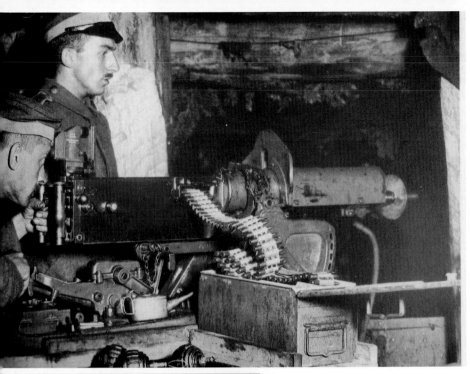

The Queen of the battlefield. A German Maxim 08 machine gun, in a bunker. These were prime targets for snipers, as evidenced by the armoured jacket. *(Bundesarchiv)*

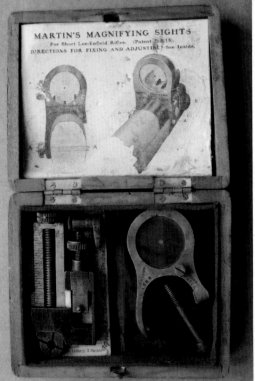

A Martin Galilean magnifying sight in its box of issue. *(Dr R. Maze collection)*

The Barnett or Ulster sight, with its carry pouch. This type of sight had magnifying lenses both front and rear. *(Dr R. Maze collection)*

A Gibbs optical sight showing the painted reticule on the front lens and the aperture rear sight. *(Dr R. Maze collection)*

A MkI Lee-Enfield with a typical target aperture sight fitted. These sights were particularly popular with Australian and New Zealand snipers. *(Dr R. Maze collection)*

If there was one thing the German Army was not short of in 1914, it was sniper plates. This photo was taken on the Flanders front late in that year. *(Author's collection)*

The value of camouflage was not clearly understood at first, but the sniping schools soon realised its vital nature. Here a British rifleman in service greatcoat and cap poses next to a sniper wearing a camouflaged robe. *(IWM photo)*

niper training school, early 1916. A ovat's instructor points out concealed opholes to a mixed bunch of snipers. lthough their scopes are dismounted, e leather carry cases can be seen ung on the shoulders of several men. WM photo)

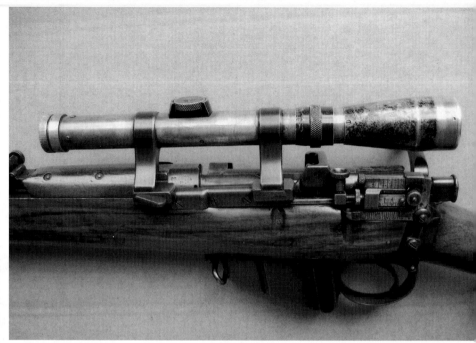

An SMLE fitted with a French A.PX Mle. 1907/15 scope. The fine workmanship indicates this was done by a good London gunsmith, but no further details are known. The aperture sight is also visible. *(Dr R. Maze collection)*

Australians being instructed at a sniper school. The Lee-Enfield being casually held by its muzzle (hardly good practice on a range!) is fitted with a Zeiss prismatic telescopic sight. *(IWM photo)*

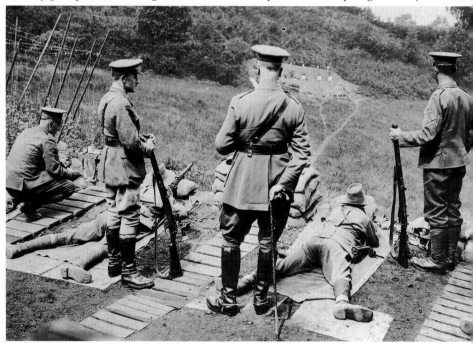

produced in their tens of thousands for general issue to all front-line units and they soon became a fundamental part of the sniper's arsenal, and illustrate the degree of thought that had been given by the German Army to providing a workable environment for their riflemen and snipers. These loophole plates took many forms, early ones sometimes being very large and they were constructed from nickel steel with a swivelling disc in the centre, through which observation, or a shot, could be made. Detecting them was not easy either, for, unlike the British trenches, the German lines had an unkempt, ragged appearance that was quite deliberate:

> The German trenches presented quite a different appearance from ours – ours being beaten down [. . .] until they made as clear a line as a breakwater. The German trenches were deeper, with much more wire in front, and from our point of view looked like the course of a gigantic mole which had flung up uneven heaps of earth. Here and there a huge piece of corrugated iron would be flung upon the parapet [. . .] here and there lay great piles of sandbags, black, red, green, striped. It was said the Germans used the pink ones to look around, because they approximated to flesh colour [. . .] [they] made the outline of their parapet as irregular as possible, with corrugated iron, coloured sandbags, dummy plates, biscuit tins, barbed wire and so forth, among which they concealed the sniper's loopholes. Our own parapets were often absolutely level [. . .] so that the slightest movement behind them was bound to be instantly detected. I think their [the German] trenches good, and easier to take cover in when one is firing from them. Their tops are more serrated, and with different coloured sandbags.[62]

The Germans also understood the requirement for snipers to be able to observe the enemy in safety:

> Our trenches were very deep and lined with wood. The fire-step had loopholes cut into the sandbags for us [snipers] that were angled. We could not fire straight ahead, and that made

it impossible for the French to see where we were shooting from. We were well supplied with periscope viewers.[63]

Certainly, in the early months of the war, the Germans were so confident of their superiority that their sniper plates were often simply propped on the parapet:

> The early German shields were huge cumbrous steel plate, defying any attempt to hide them. They used to stand brazenly on the German parapet, sometimes right against the skyline, so that the loophole was plainly visible when the protecting panel was swung open.[64]

In some instances, this arrogance proved the downfall of some German snipers, for the BEF was not bereft of good shots, and many men who were adept with a rifle were ordered (or took it upon themselves) to beat the Germans at their own game. In this they were aided by the enemy's mistaken belief that they faced virtually no capable opposition when it came to sniping:

> I try to get the men to dig like hell, for the Hun sniping is very severe. During the night the Germans had entered a line of a ditch and hedge about 300 yards in front [. . .] We employed the best shots to pick off any who showed themselves. Davis [he became the RSM] 'who is a beautiful shot' was got [*sic*] to snipe at thirty or forty in a part of their line: 'Saw a few drop'.[65]

Many private soldiers were also good shots and became unofficial company snipers, but with no telescopic rifle sights or training, it was often a case of enthusiasm overcoming skill, working under conditions that would have had their German counterparts convulsed with laughter. Private Barraclough recalled his early days as a company sniper:

> I'm a bloody fair shot so they put me on this stunt. You dug your own trench just big enough so that you could fit in [. . .] I used to build up my position, use any old bricks or owt [*sic*]

like that, and then you just lay down. Sometimes I used to get
a brick and throw it away from me just to attract somebody to
have a shot, and I'd be ready with my rifle. I didn't like the job,
it were a lousy job just lying there if it were wet or cold.[66]

The fact he survived his early sniping exploits can only be put down
to luck and a dearth of experienced German snipers opposite him, but
others were less fortunate. Company Sergeant Major John Fairall had
been a pre-war King's Prize winner at Bisley and was regarded as one
of the best shots in the Army. Incensed at the toll the Germans were
taking on his men, he began tracking down and shooting any enemy
snipers that were spotted along his battalion lines. After stand-to in
the mornings, he would stride about the trenches, asking if anyone had
been shot at, and where they thought the bullets had come from.
Observing with a periscope, he would try to pinpoint the snipers' lairs,
often drawing fire to do so. He established his own sniper platoon,
whose enthusiasm was matched only by their determination, and
despite suffering heavy casualties they managed to force the Germans
to reduce the level of sniping in their lines. Had telescopic-equipped
rifles been available, doubtless their success would have been even
greater, but alas, Fairall was himself to become the victim of a German
sniper's bullet, falling to a head shot as he looked through a loophole
one morning. Sadly it was to prove a typical end to the life of a man
who could have doubtless contributed much to the neophyte sniper
training programme that was then being developed. Other men were
detailed to become company sharpshooters simply because they
were marksmen, and while it was an unequal battle, a few did manage
to achieve respectable results, despite a dearth of any training. Private
P. Blessing[67] of the 2nd Royal Inniskilling Fusiliers was a fine shot.
His tally was not recorded but he became one of the regiment's most
senior snipers, until his unfortunate death through shellfire in 1917.

In reality, few BEF snipers or sharpshooters working in 1914 or
early 1915 were to make it as far as 1917. Indeed, the fact that any
snipers at all survived those early years of the war was remarkable, as
their attempts to tackle the Germans were frighteningly amateurish.
Of his regiment's attempts to field snipers in late 1914 and early 1915,
Private Richards wrote that a sniping post had been very roughly

constructed in front of the trenches and any man who fancied his chances could go out and use it:

> There were no hard and fast rules as regards sniping and although we had one recognised company sniper any man could go sniping if he wished to. I felt very sore after Stevens [was shot] and for a number of days I spent many hours in that sniping post. A man needed plenty of patience when sniping and might wait hours before he could see a man to fire at. I had amply revenged Stevens.[68]

One of the first priorities for the British was to find suitable steel plate from which to manufacture proper loopholes, and then to place them where they would be of the greatest use, of course easier said than done:

> There were very few loopholes in the British trenches, whereas the Germans had a magnificent system. I rarely found a loop-hole from which I could reconnoitre, and as every German sniper seemed to be supported on either flank by other German snipers, looking for him with one's head over the top of the parapet was simply a form of suicide.[69]

Initially, boiler plate was requisitioned from local dumps belonging to the Royal Engineers and cut into oblongs about 18" x 12". A 3" x 2" hole was cut in the centre but there was no attempt to put any form of swivelling loophole into the plate, a piece of sacking merely being hung over it to cover the aperture. Gradually this amateur approach was abandoned as properly manufactured plates began to appear, towards the end of 1914 and early 1915. These had a loophole which could be closed off with a rotating blanking plate and they were largely modelled on the German plates. There was a snag, however, for the unhardened boiler plate proved incapable of stopping the standard German ball ammunition, as Hesketh-Prichard found when he under-took some tests on them:

> The English plates [. . .] were easily pierced by the German

Mauser rifle, while the German plates needed a Jeffery .333 or .450, or the heavier elephant rifles.[70]

The best solution to defeat the German bullets was to place two plates one in front of the other, and up to mid-1915 this idea proved adequate in providing reasonable protection. But with the introduction of the new German K armour-piercing ammunition in mid-1915, even this proved inadequate at closer ranges:

> We had steel loopholes in our post, and the Huns' bullets would often clang off them. One day, a bullet come [*sic*] straight through the plates, it come right between us and scared us witless.[71]

As trench warfare settled into its dull routine in the winter of 1914/15 a gradual system for the proper supply of the plates and the construction of sniper posts was slowly being adopted by the British. Ever inventive, Prichard came up with a new design of sniper plate that he attempted to interest the authorities in:

> I am working on a new loophole now, which reduces the chances of being shot by 99 per cent. A bullet entering No. 1 loophole can only enter No. 2 loophole if fired from the direct front. And after a German has shot [. . .] he will grin and stop but all he will have done is to go through the first plate. Thus if you have a sniper fifteen yards away you can get him with safety . . .[72]

Aside from obtaining the proper rifles for sniping the next most pressing problem was in finding some means of penetrating the German loopholes, which utterly defeated the service .303 bullet. If they could see it a very few men were capable of putting a bullet through an open loophole plate, but until well into 1915, there was no method of satisfactorily dealing with an enemy sniper's position once it was located. Calls for artillery assistance were invariably ignored, as the shell shortages rendered the Royal Artillery almost impotent unless a serious crisis was under way. Shell rations of two or three rounds a day did not permit the searching for a sniper by a gun battery, no matter how troublesome he was, although this situation would improve dramatically as the war continued.

The only satisfactory method of dealing with enemy snipers was to pit British snipers against them and it is from this time that 'counter-sniping' began to become a priority. With few telescopic sights available to the British sharpshooters operating in the front lines, there was only one sure means of dealing with an opponent, and that was to get close enough to ensure a killing shot. This was no easy task, involving leaving the safety of the trench and crawling into a concealed, advanced observation post, or sap, from where the German line could be observed and enfiladed in daylight. Sergeant J.K. Forbes[73] was one of the earliest exponents of counter-sniping. A brilliant divinity student – who, nevertheless, believed strongly in the just cause of the war – he saw at first-hand the carnage caused by German snipers along his own battalion front. His story is a rare instance where the pioneering sniping work undertaken by a line infantryman was actually recorded, albeit briefly, in print.[74] An excellent competitive shot and stalker, he began stalking German snipers from his arrival in France in late 1914 and continued until his untimely death in September 1915. Upon arrival at the front, Forbes worked out a training plan to deal with the sniper menace. Thus, it was no surprise when he was selected to become the battalion's first Sniper Sergeant. His method of working was risky but fruitful:

Two points of our lines came in for his special attention. On more than one occasion he went beyond even the sap and crawled even into the brushwood at considerable risk to himself. But he seemed to know when the risk was worthwhile, and had a knack of knowing where the greatest possibilities were. At least two Germans fell to his rifle from this sap. The second place he favoured was a particularly dangerous locality at the junction of a communication trench [. . .] near Hooge village [. . .] the spot referred to was 'crumped' [shelled] incessantly, yet time after time J.K. went there to observe. He used to get over the parapet and lie in the open while he took in every detail of the German line.

Although the lives of these sniping pioneers were to be brief, the priceless lessons they learned were passed on to others, in Forbes's case with official blessing, for he was soon to form the regiment's fist sniping company. He picked sixteen men, all of whom he knew well, and whose characters he understood. He had, with typical thoroughness and extraordinary prescience, already prepared lectures on sniping covering subjects such as:

> ordinary observation [. . .] recognition of targets, scouting and visual training, and always paid special attention to developing the powers of observation and memory. Judging distance with great accuracy, and practice in approaching enemy positions [. . .] involving snake-like crawling then gave way to more advanced scouting work.' As his biographer further recorded, 'as time went on, studying the landscape for the purpose of finding suitable sniping spots formed part of his scheme [. . .] many days were spent on bulletproof sniping posts.

These largely copied the German defences, with loopholes inserted well forwards into the parapet, with room for the sniper to rest his elbows when observing or aiming. Gradually these evolved into properly excavated dugouts, with some form of seating, a camouflaged loophole, and most importantly, a covered entrance over which hung a large piece of cloth. This allowed entry to the position without the sudden distinctive glare of light from behind illuminating the open loophole – a sure giveaway to any enemy observing at the time. From 1915 the more-or-less permanent occupation of trenches also enabled senior officers, often ignorant of the facts of trench life, to see for themselves the problems faced by their men. This was a positive factor in bringing the sniping menace to the attention of higher echelons of command. In early 1915, Captain F.M. Crum was asked to escort his colonel around the lines:

> It was to be an educational trip for the Colonel. Wherever we had been in the front trenches, the tops of the sandbags were being constantly ripped by bullets, and periscopes being broken. Occasionally one of our men would jump up and take a snapshot

over the parapet, but for the most part our men were keeping well down. At one point we crawled to an isolated trench, sniped at as we went. Bullets were ringing on an iron loophole plate our men had inserted in the parapet, and the tops of the sandbags were constantly being ripped open. The Colonel put his periscope up. It was shot at once, and he got a knock in the face. Covered with mud, he turned to his men and said 'We mustn't let them have it all their own way.' But neither he nor I had any idea how this thing was to be stopped.[75]

Slowly there began to emerge, in the spring of 1915, a more cohesive programme in dealing with the German snipers, starting at battalion level. At its root were the untrained infantrymen like Fairall and Forbes, who had worked as snipers through the latter months of 1914 and who had learned a great deal about methodology and practice. The construction of early sniping positions in the British lines was to be the first move in the deadly game of sniper-chess that was being played along the front, but it was not enough to give the British the edge they needed, for to meet the Germans on equal terms, they urgently required the tools to do the job: proper steel plates, camouflage material, and of course, rifles with telescopic sights – and in large numbers.

Yet the situation was not entirely without hope, for Britain was not totally bereft of suitable equipment and there existed sufficient manufacturing technology to enable her, within a few months, to start producing rifles and scopes capable of taking on the Germans.

By early 1915 the trench lines had been well established across Flanders and France and the armies settled down to their invisible existence. There had clearly been no end to the conflict by Christmas and it was becoming obvious that this would be no rapid war of movement. Instead the soldiers made the best they could of the cold, wet, lack of comforts and incessant shelling and sniping. Simply keeping a rifle functioning was to prove a serious problem for the infantry and snipers, for the ever-present mud, often 2 or 3 feet deep meant that anything in contact with it would become instantly clogged:

October 1914. The old shelling and sniping went on all day. Rain and mud were now causing a lot of trouble with rifles and the supply of oil had given out. There was nowhere to lay or lean a rifle without it getting clogged with mud, or a plug in the barrel, which caused the barrel to bulge or burst when a shot was fired. D Company had but two ramrods to clear jammed barrels.[76]

While the private soldiers were generally limited solely to the use of the SMLE for sniping, there was more latitude permitted for officers. Some, who had hunted small game pre-war, brought their own rifles over with them. Lieutenant Greener had his .280-calibre Ross rifle and Lieutenant Oliver of the Durham Light Infantry used a similar rifle. For some years the author owned a Holland and Holland sporting rifle in .450 calibre (alas, missing its scope) that had belonged to an officer in the Coldstream Guards. Most of these rifles were equipped with telescopic sights, which gave them an added advantage, but their predominant function was to penetrate the enemy's sniper shields. Both Prichard and Crum left accounts of their effective early use – Prichard used a scoped Rigby (unfortunately not mentioning the calibre in his correspondence) as well as Jeffery rifles in .333 and .450 calibre, while Crum habitually carried a .333 Jeffery. They were certainly able to deal effectively with the German loopholes, but the problem was in obtaining sufficient rifles and scopes to make any appreciable difference. Hesketh-Prichard was writing to everyone he could who might be able to provide a suitable scoped rifle, or even a telescopic sight, and commented in a letter to his wife:

> I want to get all the telescopic sights for rifles I can. Very, very important. Every one I can raise will be of inestimable value. Try everyone you can. Many have given their telescopic sights to the Army, but there must be many who have not.[77]

Some officers were natural shots and they became extremely successful snipers. Lieutenant Julian Grenfell, a troop officer of the Royal Dragoons, was one such:

> He had recently been doing great work in knocking off German snipers, and had brought back from his last London

leave particularly for this purpose, a Lee-Enfield sporting rifle, with telescopic sights.[78]

Although few of these men had any sniping training, their ability to obtain telescopic-sighted rifles and their knowledge of hunting provided them with a positive advantage, particularly when the German snipers were not expecting any serious retaliation. However, the tendency on the part of many of the officers was to regard their sniping as an amusing game, and carelessness was often their downfall:

> I heard Julian [Grenfell] being hit. I heard a thump and he grunted. I looked round; he hadn't fallen; he was kneeling. I saw blood flowing from a wound in his temple. I turned back, got a bandage out and managed to get it halfway round his head, but he cursed me furiously and tore it off. Then clutching me with one hand and his precious rifle with the other, he staggered back towards the cutting [. . .] and when we got to the Red Cross orderlies, he collapsed.[79]

Ammunition for Sniping

While later in the war constant exposure to wounds and death taught most soldiers how lethal a bullet could be, in the years of 1914–15 there was a common belief that the terrible wounds that bullets inflicted on the human body were due to the fact that the Germans used what were commonly referred to as 'tampered' bullets. Of course, no soldiers were experts in the science of forensic ballistics and actually being able to tell the type of bullet used from the wound inflicted was impossible, as the energy generated by an ordinary solid ball projectile was immense. Nevertheless, this belief was to lead to one of the most enduring myths of the war, that of the use, by both sides, of forms of expanding or dum-dum bullets. Many veterans interviewed by the author still insisted that dum-dum bullets were routinely used and this was often repeated in print:

> Standing on the fire-step with the sergeant and another sniper, gazing over No Man's Land [. . .] it seemed impossible for

them to be seen by the Germans. A bullet sang between the officer and sergeant. Their companion slid down into the bottom of the trench with a hole in this head into which a man could have put his fist. 'Tampered bullet,' the sergeant said curtly.[80]

In reality the use of tampered bullets was extremely rare, especially by snipers, although there is some evidence they were used on a small scale by the infantry, although it was a court-martial offence if discovered:

> Bois Grenier. We could always tell when a man had been hit by an expanding bullet, which caused a frightful wound. Whenever one of our men got shot by one of these bullets, some of us would cut off the tips of our own bullets which made them expanding and then go on sniping with them. It would be very difficult to decide which side used those bullets first, but one of ours whom I knew very well never went sniping unless he had cut the tips of his bullets off.[81]

These modified bullets could take several forms, from simply having their tips cut off or filed flat, to being extracted from their cases and replaced back-to-front, with the base pointing forwards. With regard to altering the nose of the bullet, from the point of view of accuracy, any change of the bullet's position or shape would render accurate shooting impossible at any significant range. Reversing a bullet in its cartridge case was a slightly different matter. Exactly who discovered that doing this enabled it to penetrate a steel plate will never be known, but it was certainly the case that a bullet fired backwards was capable of punching through metal that would defeat a normal ball round. This useful property might well have been found during ballistic tests in Germany, and there were odd instances of German soldiers being captured with a clip of five reversed bullets in their pouches: indeed the author owns one such cartridge found on the Somme battlefield. Modifying ammunition in this manner was dangerous, as inserting the head deep into the cartridge could dramatically raise the chamber pressure generated on firing (albeit assisting the bullet to achieve a higher velocity) and may, in extremis, cause a breech rupture. Nevertheless, it is quite possible some were modified for the purpose of defeating early British loopholes prior to the introduction of 'K' armour-piercing ammunition. The penalty for a sniper captured with such modified ammunition would have been immediate death, but there were doubtless instances where its use was believed justified, in view of the unavailability of any armour-piercing ammunition. The truth was that there was never any form of expanding ammunition *officially* issued for infantry use on either side.

However, early in the war, some German snipers were using requisitioned commercial hunting rifles that chambered the old 8mm cartridges and many had access to hunting ammunition, which may have been soft-pointed:

> My first rifle was a nice Mauser sporting gun with, I think a Zeiss telescope. It was light and accurate to about four hundred metres. It fired the old 8mm hunting cartridges [. . .] sometimes these were difficult to get and once I asked my father to send me some from home.[82]

This account does not give much clue as to the type of ammunition used but even if it was soft-point, the numbers in question must have been tiny indeed. Besides, wear and tear on these fragile sporting rifles meant that by mid-1915 few, if any, were still serviceable, and the purpose-built Gew. 98 sniping rifles had largely replaced them.

With regards to service ammunition, all snipers knew that it was imperative to have high-quality cartridges, for if accuracy was to be maintained, all cartridges must be manufactured to near identical specifications. For this reason, a sniper or civilian target shooter would zero his rifle using only the ammunition supplied in a particular batch. Thus, if he had two or three identical boxes of cartridges marked with the same lot or batch number, then once the rifle was zeroed it would retain its accuracy for as long as that particular batch of ammunition was available. All military ammunition boxes were marked with a 'lot' number, indicating that it had been manufactured during one specific production run and that it was all, theoretically, identical. British and German snipers soon began to adopt their favourite brands of ammunition, and there were dozens of manufacturers to choose from, although some were reckoned to be better than others:

> Not all the ammunition issued to the troops in the field will be suitable for use, in fact very little of it is likely to come within the requirements as demanded by the sniper. Amongst my immediate associates [. . .] were any number of really good riflemen – experienced big-game hunters and guides who honestly knew good ammunition from bad. These men always selected their ammunition with the greatest of care, and when we happened to locate a case of some reliable, standard make they would promptly gather around and load up with it, often taking many times the amount actually required. They knew that the time would come when it would be impossible to obtain *any* good ammunition.[83]

Herbert McBride, a very experienced shooter, expressed very definite feelings on the subject of ammunition he preferred, much of which had been learned during his early time at the front as a Vickers-Maxim machine-gunner:

> During the earlier stages of the war the ammunition was made from the old, established factories and arsenals. Later [. . .] it became necessary to build and equip many other factories to keep up the supply [. . .] manned by new and unskilled workers. And their machines tools and gauges also hastily built and it was no wonder that much of this ammunition did not function properly. Dominion Cartridge Company and Kynock [*sic*] were generally dependable brands, Winchester was always dependable. UMC [84] and US[85] just about as good and all three of these latter we prized highly.[86]

Big Game Rifles

If decent ammunition was lacking for sniping use, so too were rifles able to defeat the German sniper plates. There were however, a very small number of sporting rifles that fell into a wholly different category to those used for deer and small game stalking, and these were big game rifles. They were normally of very large calibre – in excess of .450 inch and were built to kill the most dangerous of big game animals, such as elephant, rhino and buffalo. Manufactured on an individual basis, usually at considerable cost, they were not designed for use at long ranges but their projectiles possessed sufficient energy to kill instantly, for wounding and enraging such animals was often a hunter's passport to eternity. This energy translated into penetrative power way beyond that of any military cartridges in existence. The trouble was that, quite reasonably, the army didn't see fit to possess any. It is well documented that in 1915 the War Office purchased some sixty-two large-calibre hunting rifles for issue to front-line riflemen, but there is no evidence they were fitted with optical sights. They comprised forty-seven rifles in .450-calibre, four of .470, one of .475, four of 500-calibre, two in .577-calibre, and four massive .6-inch rifles. These rifles were designed for big-game hunting, and thus should be fired from a standing position, where a slight leaning-forward stance was necessary to enable the shoulder and back to absorb the heavy recoil. They were certainly not designed for prone shooting, as Lieutenant Cloete recalled:

> There were no armour-piercing bullets, so we used a heavy sporting rifle – a 600 Express [. . .] and when we hit a (loophole) plate we stove it right in, right into the German sniper's face. But it had to be fired from a standing or kneeling position to take up the recoil. The first man who fired it in the prone position had his collarbone broken.[87]

Most of these rifles were single-shot or double-barrel weapons, although a few of the smaller calibre examples did have magazines. For the destruction of the German loophole plates, however, they were ideal, as their big, slow bullets generated massive energy. But they were not designed with long-range accuracy in mind, for they were primarily big-game rifles with simple flip-up rearsights graduated to no more than 200 or 300 yards, as few hunters would attempt to shoot dangerous game animals from longer ranges. For trench sniping the smaller calibres were actually far more practical, and it is no coincidence that both Hesketh-Prichard and Crum opted to carry .333-calibre Nitro-Express rifles.

The Jeffery ammunition was actually .338-calibre (coincidentally identical with the calibre now preferred today by the British Army and Royal Marine snipers over the 7.62mm NATO round). Filled with smokeless nitro powder its 300 grain bullet was propelled at a modest 2,200 fps, which appears unexceptional until one appreciates that the bullet weight was double that of the issue .303 bullet. It was a superb calibre for sniping, as Hesketh-Prichard proved time and again, as he toured the trenches in early 1915, attempting to introduce the concept of sniping to a largely uninformed Army and apathetic staff. It was to prove an uphill struggle.

Chapter Four

The Tools for the Job

Despite lacking a single standardised system of scope and mounting, it seemed not to have prevented German snipers from working efficiently with their Mausers, which worked well for sniping use. Although Britain also lacked any standardised sniping system, there was little question that the Mk III Short, Magazine Lee-Enfield[88] would have to be adapted for sniping purposes, although by what method was conjectural, as was the suitability of the standard weapon.

Curiously, it was a Mauser action, not the Enfield that had very nearly become the choice of service rifle for the British Army in 1914. Despite the reliability of the Mk I Enfield rifle there had been trials conducted since 1910 by the Small Arms Committee to determine if the Enfield rifle could be improved. They were particularly keen to adopt a rimless cartridge for military use, as well as a better bolt locking system and one-piece stock design, all of which were common to the Mauser. To aid accuracy, aperture sights and a heavier barrel were also suggested. The thicker barrel would doubtless improve matters, for the comparatively thin-walled tube of the Mk III Enfields did not lend itself to consistent accuracy at long range. The problem was twofold: when fired, a barrel vibrates like a tuning fork and this property is part of the complex science of barrel harmonics. The problem was well understood by shooters and covered in some detail in sniping lectures, Major T. Fremantle outlining the problem succinctly in his 1916 lecture notes:

> a rifle barrel is not really rigid. It can be bent by the fingers to an extent perceptible to a skilled observer. If a blow is given to it, it vibrates like any other tube in accordance with its length, size and rigidity. Rifle barrels begin to vibrate under

the blow of the explosion, before the bullet has quit the muzzle.[89]

Increasing the thickness of the barrel reduced the vibration, leading to more consistent accuracy, but it also prevented the second problem from manifesting itself. It had been found that, if saturated, the all-encompassing fore-end woodwork of the service rifle would expand and put pressure on the barrel, fractionally bending it out of true and resulting in significant alterations in its accuracy (this was to prove an enduring problem for three generations of snipers and it was not until the late 1960s that sniping rifles devoid of covering woodwork and fitted with heavy target barrels were adopted into military service). Some idea of the effect this pressure had upon a rifle's accuracy can be gleaned from notes made by Major B. Penberthy, who calculated that a barrel one-hundredth of an inch out of line would shoot 9 inches off-centre at 100 yards and 54 inches at 600 yards.[90]

Unfortunately, the production of rifles solely for sniping use was not high on the list of War Office priorities, but the adoption of a new rifle that already had these shortcomings remedied was a possibility, and a thousand experimental Enfield Pattern 1913 rifles based on the Mauser action were issued for troop trials. As with any new weapon, they had teething problems, although many were associated with the new, high velocity cartridge that had been introduced, the .276 inch. Nevertheless, the P13 suffered from poor extraction, excessive muzzle blast and severe barrel erosion. And, where the SMLE barrel suffered from a noticeable drop-off in accuracy after about 1,000 rounds, the P13 barrel was badly affected after only 250 rounds. The outbreak of war gave Britain little chance for further experimentation, so the design was rapidly modified to chamber the issue Mk VI & VII .303-inch ammunition, and contracts were issued to Winchester and Remington in the USA for the supply of rifles, which were designated the Pattern 1914.

This was not to be the end of the road for the P14 though, for it was to surface again at the end of the war, rather fittingly as one of the best sniper rifles to emerge from the conflict.

British Sniping Rifles

Despite the dearth of suitable sniping equipment available early in the war, from early 1915, there was a small trickle of telescope-equipped rifles emerging from Britain and being issued to front-line snipers. With no instruction as to their care and use, and little in the way of sniper training, these rifles were largely wasted. Hesketh-Prichard reckoned that 40 per cent of all telescopic rifles issued were so badly adjusted as to be useless; and after two months, fully 80 per cent were in need of re-zeroing or repair.

In late 1914, in an attempt to provide some means of response to the German sniper domination, the Ministry of Munitions had sent contracts to all the major gunmakers in Great Britain and Ireland, asking if they were able to furnish and fit telescopic sights to the service Lee-Enfield No. 1 Mk III rifle. There were, at this time, over twenty gunmakers capable of undertaking this work, but there were no standard specifications, drawings, or even supplies of telescopic sights for them to work with. Still, it was a matter of some urgency that rifles were produced, so all available commercial telescopic sights were purchased and, ironically, these included a large number of German- and Austrian-manufactured sights. The exact numbers involved are documented as 1,470[91] up to July 1915, although the exact type of telescopes fitted by contractors are not detailed, and to confuse matters further, many gunmakers – such as Holland and Holland – bought in unmarked telescopic sights from outside contractors (normally in Germany) and then engraved them with their own names. Consequently, identifying the origin of these scopes is very difficult, but they certainly included: German-made Dr Gerard, Kahles 'Mignon', Voigtlander 'Scopar', Zeiss 'Jena' as well as Aldis, Certar, Fidgelands, Pernox, Periscopic Prism, Standley, Watts, and Winchester. A number of gunmakers fitted these scopes to SMLEs and the contracts show William Evans, Thomas Bland, E.J. Churchill, George Gibbs, W. Jeffrey, Holland and Holland, J. Rigby, Westley Richards, James Purdey and James Woodward all supplying and fitting scopes. Apart from the fact that the telescopic sights supplied were of varying types and quality, they also had differing power characteristics, varying from 2 x for the

Periscopic Prism or Certar, to 5 x for the quite rare Fidgelands, so finding any two identical rifles in service at the front was well-nigh impossible.

Despite the war, business was still business, and the scopes were sold to the Government at commercial prices. They were not cheap either, varying from £3, 2s, 6d for a Fidgelands to £6, 7s for a Voigtlander. In addition to this, brackets and mounts had to be designed and manufactured and each rifle had to be set up and collimated. This was painstaking work and followed the traditional path of custom gunsmithing, with every rifle being hand-fitted by a skilled gunsmith, in exactly the same manner as was undertaken by the German factories. Brackets and bases were manufactured in batches, blued and one set put aside for each rifle. Most would be numbered by the gunmaker to prevent their accidentally being taken for use on another gun. The work took an experienced man about a week and cost depended on the complexity of the mounts and bases and the price the company placed upon their own workmanship. Thus, to supply and fit a telescope to a rifle it was little surprise that Purdey charged £13, 13s, 6d, although others were not far behind: a Rigby cost £12, 12s; Holland and Holland £12, 18s (or £10, 10s depending on the type of scope and mount); Thos Bland £11, 11s; Periscopic Prism Co. £11, 10s; James Woodward £9, 16s and W. Jeffrey £7, 10s.

Some contractors also fitted but did not supply scopes: thus, Charles Lancaster & Co. charged the War Office £6, 15s simply for the work undertaken. All telescopic sights were supplied in a fitted leather case, designed to be carried over the shoulder, plus leather lens caps and a cleaning brush were provided. Of course, none of these prices include the initial cost of manufacture and supply of a service SMLE rifle of £3, 10s. This made sniping weapons extremely expensive. As supplied by Purdey, for example, the cost to the Government in total was an incredible £17, 3s, 6d per rifle. For comparison, in July 1917, the production cost of the very complex Vickers medium machine gun was calculated at £50 per unit.[92] The exact number of telescopic sighted rifles produced during the war is disputed but it was in the region of 10,000 rifles.[93]

Trouble with Scopes

There was little organisation regarding supply of these rifles in 1915, and their issue was arbitrary in the extreme. The method of issue for such weapons, supplied to line regiments, followed no set procedure and particular serial number blocks of rifles were not selected for issue to specific regiments (indeed, while employed at the Royal Armouries, one of my most frequent requests was for information as to what unit a particular rifle was issued to, and when).

During the war, all service arms were despatched by the crate-load to huge Royal Ordnance storage depots in France and requests for replacement or additional rifles were handled on an ad hoc basis: so, if, for example, fifty standard rifles had been indented for by the 2nd Battalion, Royal Fusiliers, then the nearest available rifles on the storage racks would be selected, the correct quantity marked as supplied, and the rifles delivered to the Army Service Corps to be sent along with any other required trench stores (uniforms, boots, rations) for delivery as near to the Front as possible. From there it was the regiment's responsibility to send carrying parties to collect stores. In reality, this meant that the batch of rifles received by a unit armourer may be from different factories of manufacture, with wildly varying serial numbers. This in itself was no problem to the Quartermasters, for once a rifle was allocated to an individual and the serial number noted, that was all the QM cared about. This process was the same for sniping rifles and while unit armourers could specifically ask for telescopic-sighted rifles, their supply was never guaranteed, and the conditions of issue were just as arbitrary. To confuse matters further, they were often supplied along with batches of ordinary SMLEs, so a bemused QM, having ordered fifty rifles, may find he had suddenly received forty-seven SMLEs, and three scoped rifles, which he may or may not have wanted.

Then there was always the thorny problem of who, exactly, to issue them to. In the early part of the war sniping rifles were often given to the first man who needed a rifle, as Hesketh-Prichard found when in early 1915 he happened across a young soldier holding a new scoped rifle:

I had gone down on duty to a certain stretch of trench and there found a puzzled looking private with a beautiful new rifle fitted with an Evans telescopic sight. I examined the elevating drum, and saw that it was set for one hundred yards. 'Look here,' I said, 'you have got that sight set for a hundred. The Hun trenches are four hundred yards away.' The private looked puzzled. 'Have you ever shot with that rifle?' I asked.

'No, sir.'

'Do you understand it?'

'No, sir.'

'How did you get it?'

'It was issued to me as trench stores, sir.'

'Who by?'

'The Quartermaster Sergeant, sir.'[94]

In the meantime, the War Office was looking more closely into the practicalities of standardising the manufacture of telescopic sights to keep down the spiralling manufacturing costs, simplify issues, and prevent problems of repair. Some of the systems employed were frankly of questionable practical use and no matter what system (or systems) were decided upon, it was clear that some regulation of the supply and fitting of scopes and mounts was urgently required. And so on 4 May 1915 specifications were drawn up by the Small Arms Committee and issued to contractors, spelling out exactly what was required when setting up a rifle with a scope and mounting combination. It is of some importance, for it is the first document that gave official sanction to the issue of specially modified rifles for sniping use in the British Army. In slightly précised form, it read as follows:

Specification No. S.A.390 to govern manufacture and inspection.[95]

Fitting of telescopic sights to Rifle, Short, Magazine, Lee-Enfield Mk III.

The work to conform to the conditions laid down in the specifications.

If one-fourth of any delivery to be found inferior to the Contractor's sample, or contrary to the terms of this Specification, the whole consignment will be liable to rejection.

Both material and workmanship to be of the very best description.

No advantage whatever to be taken of any omission of detail in this Specification.

The work to be finished in every respect in the most complete manner and to the entire satisfaction of the Chief Inspector of Small Arms, who shall be at liberty to inspect [. . .] the work during its progress, and to reject as unsuitable or defective any materiel or workmanship.

The fittings will be made to the Contractor's design, which must be approved by the Chief Inspector.

Rifles and telescopes will be supplied to the Contractor by the War Department, and the Contractor will be liable for all damage done to them by him.

Rifles and telescopes will be supplied to the Chief Inspector [. . .] The drums must not be engraved with the range scale, but the telescopes must be fitted in such a manner that there is no lateral error, while they must be browned, blued or blacked before submission, and must not be subsequently dismantled, except that the drum may be removed for engraving. The rifles and telescope will then be sent to Bisley for shooting and calibration, after which they will be returned to the Contractor, who will engrave the range scale on the drum and return the rifles [. . .] to Enfield Lock.

All charges for carriage will be paid by the Contractor.

These specifications did not in any way determine exactly *what* scope and mounts should be used on a sniping rifle, of course, save that the War Office insisted that all systems adopted must be suitable only for the Enfield rifle, allow it to remain free to be clip-loaded, and for the shooter to make use of the iron sights. The clip-loading codicil was a decision all snipers found puzzling in the extreme, as the magazine could easily be detached if ten rounds were required to be loaded:

Why the telescopic sights were set on the sides of the rifles was never [. . .] satisfactorily explained, but it was always said it was done so that rapid fire should be possible. I believe this decision was taken in the War Office and if this is true [. . .] then surely whoever was responsible can have had no knowledge of the use of telescopic sights.[96]

This decision was possibly the most inexplicable of any taken with regard to the use of sniping weapons during the conflict, for it placed British and Commonwealth snipers at a grave disadvantage over their German counterparts. The reason was straightforward, for most German rifles had their optical sights mounted overbore, in a direct line above the barrel (while a few were partially offset to the left, this did not materially affect their aiming). However, all the British rifles had scopes mounted heavily offset to the left, in most cases, to such a degree that obtaining a comfortable head position and cheek contact with the stock was difficult, if not impossible:

At the sniping school [. . .] the rifles we trained with were fitted with an Aldis optical sight which was attached to the left of the receiver by a sort of sliding bar. Having only shot with the standard sights on the rifles, these telescopes took some getting used to and while we were taught to shoot using the right eye, it was difficult to get a comfortable position for one's head. Later, in the lines I learned to shoot left-eyed but I used to wrap a field-dressing around the [rifle] stock to have a decent rest for my cheek.[97]

It was not just a matter of comfort, however, for the offset caused a more serious problem, which Hesketh-Prichard and many others railed against, and this was to do with the use of loophole plates. Most of those in use had a vertical keyhole shaped aperture, which meant that, if a rifle with offset scope was used, the firer simply could not see the target, his vision blocked by the left side of the plate:

It was impossible to see through the loophole of the steel plates [. . .] as these loopholes were naturally narrow; and looking into the telescopic sight [. . .] one got nothing but a fine view of the inside of the steel plate.[98]

There were protestations from every level of the sniping establishment but once fixed, it proved impossible for the clumsy and slow contracting system to be modified to enable any improved design to be manufactured. It was a decision that undoubtedly saved many German lives:

> It was early in the morning [. . .] when a working party of Germans appeared. They had but a few yards to go to regain their own trench. The sniper who was next to me got off a shot. Two of the snipers armed with the Government weapons [. . .] who were waiting at loopholes found that neither of them could bring their rifles to bear at the extreme angle at which the Germans were [. . .] both ran out from their posts to try and get a shot [. . .] but were, of course, too late.[99]

The only solution readily to hand was to enlarge the loopholes, which, while it made shooting easier, created the additional hazard of providing a larger aperture into which an enemy sniper could shoot. This nearly terminated Private Tom Durst's sniping career in the KRRC while searching for German snipers during the first week of the Somme campaign:

> I was in a hide forward of our trench, just a small tunnel really, with a steel loophole plate in front, camouflaged with sandbags and things. It had a wider aperture than normal, and didn't have a sliding cover plate on it like the others did, although visibility through it was excellent. I was lying flat on my belly looking through my telescopic sight, when 'crack' a bullet came through the loophole, creased down my left arm and across my bottom and hit my heel. I tell you, I got out as fast as I possibly could. I looked a real mess with blood everywhere, but really it was only flesh wounds, although my heel took some time to mend and I limped for months. Oh, it was as close as I wanted to get to dying.[100]

Although his wounds were not serious, Private Durst spent over five weeks in hospital near Bapaume, musing on his good fortune while his injuries healed. Undaunted, he returned to 'A' Company and resumed his sniping activities.

The Periscopic Prism, Winchester and Aldis Scopes

The issue of Specification 390, however, still left contractors free to use their own mounting systems and many patterns saw service. Also, a number of variants evolved that would see constant use through the course of the war. But three primary types were to emerge in the greatest numbers: the Periscopic Prism scope and mounts being the most prolific, with Aldis telescopes being widely used in a number of differing mounting combinations, and the Winchester A5 following close behind.

By far the most prolific was the SMLE/Periscopic Prism telescope combination, which had grown from a patent applied for on 24 February 1915 by Arthur Bernard Rolfe-Martin. A mechanical engineer from Surrey, he was employed by the PP Co., whose factory was based in Kentish Town, London. The telescopes they had been supplying to the War Office had actually been in production for some time prior to the war, used mainly for stalking and big-game hunting, and they were of a fairly standard type, based largely on the German scopes of the pre-war period with a large ocular lens in a bell-shaped housing and smaller objective lens. They were of relatively low power (2 x) and unlike earlier pattern tube scopes, such as the Winchester, were variable focus instruments, being adjustable by means of a metal plate secured by a lock-screw on the tube just behind the range drum. This was not ideal, as firing the rifle often caused problems with the adjustment:

> The Periscope [scopes] that we used were [. . .] low powered and often lost their focus when you fired, as the locking screw worked loose. They had a little leather washer on them, but it often rotted so we did them up with pliers to stop them coming undone.[101]

The mountings were simple, comprising a female dovetail screwed and soldered to the left side of the receiver, and a double ring, into which the scope was soldered, giving it a pronounced offset to the left. The ring mount had a corresponding male dovetail that slid into the base, being locked into place by a spring catch. Although designed to be interchangeable, few of these scopes could be fitted to other rifles, as they were hand-fitted and there were fractional dimensional differences in the bases.

If there was an operational weakness with the early PP scopes, it was in providing lateral (windage) adjustment, for this required two tiny capstan screws just in front of the range drum to be slackened off, the left one being tightened if the rifle was shooting to the right, and the right for left shooting. One complete turn of the screw provided 8 inches of windage at 100 yards, but zeroing was a slow procedure and one that snipers tried to do as little as possible, as Private Durst commented:

> Whenever possible, once our rifles were zeroed, we shot only using the range drum and we learned to aim off for longer ranges [. . .] you couldn't adjust your telescope for windage in the lines because it just wasn't practical. Anyway, most of our shooting was under about 300 yards and aiming off usually gave us the result we wanted, with practice you got very good at it.[102]

Range scales were marked on the drums after test firing at Bisley and usually rose in 100-yard increments up to 600 yards, although occasional scopes have been seen with 800 yards on their drums. However, Private Durst's comments about sniping ranges are borne out by Hesketh-Prichard, who wrote that:

> I used to have some firing practice at five and six hundred yards, and when I went to First Army School, I gave this up. The chances of hitting a German head at six hundred yards with a telescopic sight, if there is any wind blowing at all, are not great [. . .] I came to the conclusion that popping away with telescopic sighted rifles at six hundred yards simply wore out their barrels. We therefore, until warfare became more open, never went back more than four hundred yards.[103]

In general this was sound practice, but there were snipers whose ability enabled them to make successful long-range shots, as Herbert McBride recalled:

> It pays to have one set of sights on the rifle that you know are going to 'stay put' and it also pays to have them ready for an instant's notice. I remember one morning when my very first shot was made [. . .] at a soldier who was standing up behind the German lines at some six hundred yards from our position. There was no time whatsoever for sighting-in shots; I just cut loose and put him down cold.[104]

Although the PP was the lowest powered British telescope available during the war, this actually had some benefits, for the higher the magnification of a scope, the smaller the field of view became. The PP scope provided the shooter with a fairly broad field of view of 9.5 degrees, which made it ideal for the comparatively close ranges that many front-line snipers worked at, and the post and cross-hair reticle, standard on most British scopes, also worked tolerably well at close ranges, only being disadvantageous at longer distances, where the thickness of the post could actually obscure a target. It was particularly good at light gathering in lowlight conditions, and dawn and dusk were favourite times for catching the unwary:

> One morning at stand to (just before dawn) I was watching the German line and saw a pale face looking out between two sandbags. He was only a hundred yards away but I suppose he thought in the half-dark he was safe enough. It was the only shot I made through the whole war where I saw the bullet hit and he jerked back like someone had pulled a rug out from under his feet. There was no doubt [about the shot] but it didn't give me any satisfaction, it was too easy.[105]

It was also the physically largest of the Great War telescopes, being 12 inches long and very solidly constructed, weighing in at almost 1½ lbs with its mount, and some snipers wryly commented that if a German got too close, they could simply beat him to death with the scope. This weight raised some problems with regard to the mounting system, for the recoil of a .303 cartridge is fairly punishing and the slightest slop in the fit between the dovetails on the mount was magnified, causing the scope and mounts to slide fractionally within the dovetail. As well as manifesting itself in poor accuracy this could also result in the front mounting plate of the base eventually shearing its securing screws as it bore the entire weight of the recoiling scope. The solution was to screw and solder the plate in position, but this could only be done by a skilled armourer, necessitating the return of the rifle to one of the Army sniping schools for repair. Having any sort of accessible screws was also an open invitation for meddling by the soldiers, who then, as now, often believed that they could fine adjust their scopes by trial and error, although this was a practice that gradually died away as training improved:

> I never let any of my chums near my rifle though, I had it spot-on and I hated anyone handling it. They used to rag me about it and they called it my baby. I never, ever took the scope off the rifle in the line and I re-zeroed it each time we went back [. . .] Not all the snipers did that but I knew if I shot I had one chance and didn't intend to miss.[106]

Despite these shortcomings, the PP scope and its mount proved an enduring combination with some 4,836 being supplied, mostly, but not exclusively on Mk III SMLE rifles, identifiable by the lack of magazine cut-off latch and absence of long-range sights. This was by no means a hard-and-fast rule though, for numbers of earlier Mk III rifles with commercial pattern PP scopes fitted to them have also been noted. As with all such optical sights, they were issued with their fitted leather carrying case, with a lens cloth in the lid.

The next most widely encountered combination was the Aldis and PP mount, produced by the well-established and highly respected firm of Aldis Brothers, who had been producing high-quality camera lenses, signalling lamps and artillery sights for many years at their factory in Sarehole Lane, Hall Green, Birmingham. They were one of the earliest suppliers of telescopic sights to the War Office, fulfilling an order in June 1915 for 200 scopes, but they produced only the telescopes, and did not manufacture any mounts for the SMLE rifle.

There were to be four patterns of Aldis scopes, and these were logically referred to as Nos. 1, 2, 3 and 4. The first two were similar in appearance and function to the PP and its counterpart German scopes, but they had a more useful 2.5 x magnification (later raised to 3 x) and a field of view of 8½ degrees and were slightly smaller than the PP at 10.8 inches, although their weight was almost identical. They were fitted into a very wide range of mounts by makers such as Holland and Holland, Purdey, Periscopic Prism and two firms called 'Bartle' and 'Atkins', who, it is believed, also manufactured a mounting system for Aldis themselves, as records indicate some 1,400 rifles were supplied by Aldis with mounts and bases manufactured by Bartle and a dozen or so by Atkins. Alas, no genuine examples seem to have survived of these set-ups, so the methods of mounting must for the time being remain conjecture. The different models of scope can be fairly easily identified by the fact that Nos. 1 and 2 have a distinct stepped brass ocular housing and the range drum clamping screw is at the rear, facing the shooter. The Nos. 3 and 4 scopes have the screw projecting forward of the drum and the No. 4 is an identically bodied instrument with a smoothly tapered cone-shaped ocular housing.

The method of adjusting for range was typical enough, by means of a graduated drum, and some few Aldis scopes have been noted with ranges of 1,000 yards inscribed on them. The No. 1–3 scopes were not manufactured with a means of lateral adjustment, this being done by the mounting system. However, the prism cells were sometimes retrofitted to earlier model scopes; but the windage adjustment was, if anything, more complex than even the PP Scope. To alter the lateral plane, the brass housing on the objective end of the scope had to be unscrewed, and three minuscule set screws slackened off. The prism cell can then be altered by means of turning it in its housing using a coin or special tool that engaged in slots cut into the collar. It was important that this was done before final zeroing, as any change in windage adjustment also altered the elevation. Of course, attempting to do this in trench conditions was clearly impossible and snipers used impromptu ranges when out of the lines to re-zero their rifles:

Once we went back [. . .] we cleaned all our kit and had to turn into soldiers again. Boots, brasses and all that had to be spruced up and we had to do drill again which we hated as we snipers were given a lot of latitude in the lines. Our most important task really was to clean our rifles and scopes and restock with ammunition, which always meant re-zeroing them. I never understood why they just didn't keep a special supply of ammunition for us so we didn't have to do it each time, but that was the way it was. It wasn't bad though as we had a little range set up, I think it was 200 yards [. . .] we used to spend hours up there. Mostly while one of the platoon kept watch and popped off the occasional shot we would sleep and even Mr Bartlett, he was our officer, used to come up and join us.[107]

The final version of the Aldis, the No. 4, was generally regarded as the best British optical sight of the war until the introduction of the Pattern 1918 telescopic sight (the final development of this scope and its Pattern 1914 rifle will be covered fully a little later). There were 3,196 Aldis scopes produced and fitted to SMLEs from 1914 to 1918, although now they are markedly rarer than either the PP or Winchester: testimony perhaps to the numbers that were sold off to be used post-war on hunting and target rifles.

The third most prolific telescope in use was an American design, the Winchester A5, whose antecedents stretched back to the early tube sights of the pre-American Civil War era. The US optical industry had benefited greatly in the early nineteenth century from the arrival of a number of German and Swiss émigrés, who brought with them considerable expertise in lens making, and while the story of the emergence of this industry is outside the scope of this book, it is worth understanding just what a huge contribution to shooting science men such as Alvan Clarke[108] and William Malcolm[109] made. In a comparatively short period (about thirty years) they took optical science from the ancient to the modern, producing scope bodies of strong, light, steel instead of brass, developing achromatic lenses that were free of imperfections, to the delight of the target-shooting fraternity, as well as a method of mounting scopes that is still, in slightly modified form, in use today on long-range target rifles. There is a certain satisfaction in mentioning that this mounting system was invented by an ex-patriot Englishman, John Ratcliffe Chapman, using 'saddle' mounts that clamped to tapered bases attached to the receiver and barrel of the rifle. He realised that the traditional method of fitting scopes to rifles, using fixed mounts soldered to a front dovetail with a worm-screw elevating mechanism at the rear were both fragile and unreliable. His simple mounts allowed the scope body to be supported within two steel rings by sprung lugs that provided not only shock absorption but were fitted with micro-adjustable screws, providing fine elevation and windage adjustment. They were to become the benchmark for most scope mounting systems in the United States from around 1840 onwards and were adopted by Britain in 1915 and used in conjunction with the Winchester A5 and B4 scopes fitted to the ubiquitous SMLE.

The A5 scope was originally developed in 1907–08 by Professor E. Hastings, then Professor of Optical Science at Yale University.[110] He had been approached by the Winchester Company, who had heard of experiments he had been undertaking in advanced lens design, his genius being in devising a means of eliminating any imperfections in the objective lens by correcting them in the ocular lens. With his assistance three scopes – the A5, B5 and B3 – were produced by Bausch and Lomb in 1909 to the very highest quality. But it was the A5, with a 5 x lens that was to prove the most popular.

These telescopes actually look little different from the Davidson pattern scopes of the late nineteenth century, being simple steel tubes of three-quarters-of-an-inch diameter, with no range drum. Their lens arrangement actually did not normally require focal adjustment, but it could be altered by means of a locking ring at the ocular end of the scope. Elevation and windage were taken care of by means of the micrometer adjustment on the rear mount. One peculiarity was the fact that the scope body was free to move forwards and backwards in its mounts, so the rearward recoil of the rifle after each shot resulted in the scope appearing to have slid forwards in its mounts, from where it had to be manually pulled rearwards. This, in artillery terms, was known as being 'returned to battery'. Its greater magnification made it useful for longer range shooting but this was countered by the limited field of view, of a mere 3.2 degrees. Although long at 16 inches, its construction made it very light at six ounces, and after tests with nine rifles equipped with the A5, 200 were ordered by the War Office in early 1915 to be set up by Whitehead Brothers and Company of London, an established firm that had been in the firearms business since Thomas Whitehead founded a general gunsmithing business in London in the late 1850s (producing castings, barrels and other firearms items). The A5s were supplied to Whiteheads and fitted at the not inconsiderable cost of 4 guineas each. The scope used a fine cross-hair target reticle, which many snipers preferred to the broad post type, but its small lens diameter made it very difficult to use in lowlight conditions, for its light gathering properties were poor. It, too, was mounted to the left of the rifle on a pair of bases that were soldered and screwed to the receiver and front sight protector 'ear' of the rifle. In view of the ease with which the bases could be fitted to the top of the rifle, a small quantity (probably less than fifty) of the 907 produced were actually set up with overbore mounts and proved very successful.

The majority of snipers were issued with one or other of these three pattern scopes and if not outstanding, they certainly proved adequate for trench sniping:

> I had a Periscopic [Prism Co.] Scope on my rifle and I can still remember the number engraved on it, W36784. It came in a leather case with cleaning kit and instructions printed in the lid [. . .] my rifle was a BSA dated 1915 and brand new, it was a lovely thing. I went straight off and zeroed it and it shot very well, it was really accurate. I had that rifle until I was wounded in 1918 and I had to leave it behind, though I kept the telescope. They were not good at long range though, the magnification was not powerful enough and I shot mostly between one and four hundred yards and the offset to the left was always very awkward to use.[111]

Hesketh Vernon Hesketh-Prichard, photographed in 1910.

A fine example of a commercial 8mm German Mauser sporting rifle, fitted with a telescopic sight. Thousands of these weapons were taken into service as impromptu sniping rifles. *(Dr R. Maze collection)*

INSTRUCTIONS FOR USE OF S.m.K. CARTRIDGES
AND RIFLES WITH TELESCOPIC SIGHTS
1915

With the manufacturing of the K bullet being difficult and expensive, this cartridge must be used only for precision shooting when a great penetration is sought. The S.m.K. cartridge is distributed only to marksmen supplied with the Model 98 rifle and telescopic sight. These men must use these cartridges wisely and not give them away.

If necessary, these cartridges can be fired from a machine gun against a fortified implacement, armored shelter (pillbox) or armored aircraft.

The rifles with telescopic sight in the German Army are of two kinds:

a) The standard rifle Model 98 on which a telescope has been installed. The first order (late 1914) was for 15,000 rifles.

b) Hunting rifles with telescope. All of these in Germany have been requisitioned. These rifles have less strength than the rifle 98 and can fire the 88 cartridge only.

The weapons with telescopic sight are very accurate up to 300 meters. They must only be issued to qualified marksmen who can assure results when firing from trench to trench, and especially at dusk or during clear nights when ordinary weapons are not satisfactory.

The marksman must shoot with discretion and the rifles must not be fired for salute or suppressive fire. Marksmen are not limited to the location of their unit, and are free to move anywhere they can see a valuable target. Sentries have the duty to signal the marksman, such targets they themselves can determine.

The marksman will use his telescope to watch the enemy front, recording his observations on a note book, as well as his cartridge consumption and probable results of his shots.

Marksmen are exempted from additional duty.

1915 instructions for the use of the newly issued 7.92mm German armour-piercing bullet. *(Via P. Senich)*

Snipers of the 20th Battalion Canadian Expeditionary Force. The man on the left has a cut-down Ross, the others have SMLEs with PP or Aldis scopes. Most wear the scout/sniper's Fleur de Lys badge on their left shoulder. *(Canadian official photo)*

An original WWI Issue US Marine M1903 Springfield sniping rifle, fitted with a Winchester A5 scope. Very few of these rifles ever arrived at the front. *(Springfield Armory collection)*

ONE OF THE BUFFALO BOYS
SPINNING A ROPE

BELL Photo

A pre-war photo of Canadian sniper Henry North-West Wind ('Norwest') during his cowboy days. *(Glenbow Museum photo)*

Norwest's original grave in Warvillers churchyard cemetery, on the Somme, *circa* 1920.

The Ross showing the degree of offset of its Warner scope, the prominent eye-cup and its straight-pull bolt mechanism. *(Simon Deakin photo)*

SNIPER
435684 L/C H NORWEST
M·M
50TH BN CANADIANS
OFFICIAL RECORD
115 HITS

One of a series of photos taken by sniping officer, Capt. C.W.R. Knight of the Honourable Artillery Company, in Ypres, late 1915. It shows two of his sniper team in their barn. The rifle at centre is an SMLE with a PP scope. The sniper (left) holds binoculars and watches as his partner cleans his rifle. *(IWM photo)*

A British sniper poses for the camera, wearing full camouflage clothing. The only clue to his presence is the muzzle of his rifle, just visible above and slightly to the centre right of the photo. *(IWM photo)*

The German lines as seen from the loophole in the barn wall, visible in the top picture. Once the barn was identified as a sniper's position, it would rapidly have become a very unhealthy place to be. *(IWM photo)*

Billy Sing, the scourge of Gallipoli. (*Australian War Memorial*)

Gallipoli. An Australian sniper team using a periscope rifle. The observer looks through a simple two-mirror periscope while the rifleman searches for targets. It was not a particularly effective means of sniping, but served its purpose. (*Australian War Memorial*)

The lack of sniper plates was a serious problem on Gallipoli. Here an Australian sniper waits to take a snapshot behind a sandbag screen, while his mate (out of camera shot) spots for targets. (*Australian War Memorial*)

A captured and well camouflaged Turkish sniper. He was a lucky man, as most snipers were killed on the spot. *(Taylor Library)*

A sniper of the King's Own Regiment on Salonika, June 1916 holds his PP Co. equipped SMLE. Of greater interest however, are the rifles lying on the wall. The first and third have Galilean sights fitted, possibly of Lattey and Barnett types. These are the only evidence so far found of the combat use of these magnifying sights. *(Taylor Library)*

A French sniper with Lebel rifle and A.PX Mle. 1916 scope, with its long leather eye-cup. Tracy le Val, Oise, February 1917. *(Musée Historial, Péronne)*

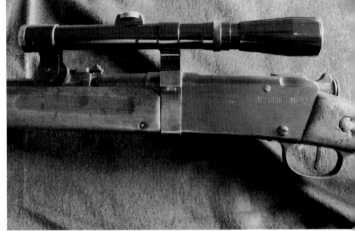

A Lebel rifle with A.PX Mle. 1917 scope. The front mount utilises a rotating lug, and the quick-release thumb-latch is just visible underneath the rear scope mounting block. *(Author's collection)*

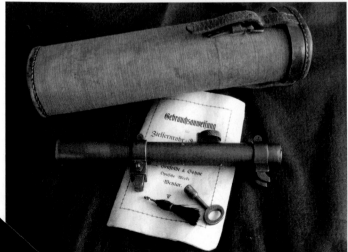

The short Hensoldt scope that provided the basis for the successful No. 4 Aldis scope. It is shown with its carry case, lens brush and windage adjustment key. The adjuster worm is visible on the rear claw mount. *(T. Meyer collection)*

Other Telescopic Sights

For those not issued with the PP, Aldis or Winchester, then the most likely alternatives to find their way to the front line were scopes manufactured by Messrs Evans or Watts. Of these, the larger concern was the business of William Evans, who had served his gunmaker's apprenticeship in London with both Purdey and Sons and Holland & Holland. As a registered member of the gunmakers' company, he opened his own business in 1883 in Buckingham Palace Road, and soon expanded to larger premises in 1896 at 63 Pall Mall. This was the area much frequented by the upper echelons of British society and pre-war Evans' guns became very popular among wealthy Guards officers, as well as Members of Parliament, whose clubs in St James's were just around the corner.

There was also some demand for telescopic sights for big-game hunting, so Evans began importing scopes from Germany and fitting them to sporting rifles. Contrary to popular belief, no telescopes were manufactured by William Evans: all were externally sourced and the majority in existence today on First World War sniping rifles are commercial scopes retailed by Otto Bock and Carl Paul Goerz, the Bock having a very distinctive knurled focusing ring just forward of the ocular bell-housing. In view of the extremely high finish and quality of the work normally produced by Watts, the mount for this scope was rather ugly and used a ribbed, light alloy casting (itself unique for the period) and somewhat fiddly double mortise slot, although this was undoubtedly due to the patent held on the single dovetail fitting by the PP Company. The explanation of this unusual pairing according to Messrs Evans was that these mounts were not produced in-house but were supplied on contract from another manufacturer, although exactly who this was remains unknown. This explains the utilitarian appearance of the rings and mounts, but in fairness, it was light and worked as well as any other contemporary mount. How many were supplied is also unknown but bearing in mind the scopes had originally come from Germany, once stocks were used up, it was unlikely more could be procured. Thus the number was probably quite low, the figure of 120 units being based on surviving War Office contracts, although the true number may well be slightly higher.

The Watts scope, however, was manufactured in-house by E.R. Watts and Son,[112] Camberwell Road, London, who, pre-war, had concentrated on production of very high-quality alidades, theodolites, rangefinders and clinometers.[113] They had the capability for producing very high-quality lenses required for telescopic sights but did not manufacture their own mounting system, supplying their scopes to other manufacturers for setting-up, predominantly Frazer, Rigby and Woodward, and from surviving War Office contracts it would appear that, at most, no more than 200 telescopic rifles were fitted with the Watts.

Of the other patterns of mounts in use there are insufficient surviving examples to determine how all of them were constructed, but it is safe to assume that all used a variation on a theme of side-mounting. For those examples that do survive, the type of mount used seems to be fairly similar, not unnaturally, bearing in mind the patent that the PP Company held on its sliding bar mounting system. The Purdey has a beautifully made vertical front locking post, which was retained by a swivel catch, and a distinctive hooked rear latch; whereas the Holland and Holland used a rather ungainly hooked front and rear mounting system, which used a rear mortise slot and locking catch. No genuine example of a Rigby mount has survived that the author is aware of, but a rare drawing of one (reproduced in this book) is held in the National Firearms Collection at the Royal Armouries in Leeds. The reason for the lack of any surviving information, in particular drawings, was that, in most instances, the mounts and rings were developed in-house by the resident gunsmiths and adapted to suit the SMLE. At a time when fine craftsmanship was still regarded as the norm in gunmaking, a working pattern would be produced, and from it others would be made and hand-fitted to their rifles. As a result these mounting systems were produced only by gunsmiths who knew exactly what they were doing, and as such there was no need for the production of drawings. Certainly some drawings must have been done, but were probably destroyed at the end of the war, when there would have been no conceivable further use for them, so the survival of any drawing, as in the case of Rigby, is very rare indeed. There no longer seem to be any surviving examples of the many other types supplied, such as

Jeffrey, Churchill and Lang, from which it is possible to draw any conclusions.

There were also a number of German telescopic sights adopted into British use, the author having owned a Kahles scope fitted to Purdey mounts and seen three other examples: a Goerz, and two Fuess scopes, alas, without mounts, but marked with British rifle serial numbers and WD broad arrows. How many were used and how they were acquired is difficult to assess. Certainly the gun trade held some stocks of commercial scopes, although they cannot have been large, and even in 1915 there was a modest trade in optical sights being conducted via Switzerland with telescopes and optical glass being brought into Britain. Until well into 1916 Hesketh-Prichard, Colonel Fremantle, and others, were constantly asking for any commercial scopes that could be procured to be sent to them: 'How splendid to get Molly's [telescopic] sight. Am sending the rifle to Rigby's for it. Every telescope is so valuable.'[114] Prichard's demands for optical sights even reached the ears of some more elevated figures, and in January 1916 his wife received a letter from Mr St Loe Strachey, the influential editor of the *Spectator*, with an unusual offer:

My Dear Mrs Prichard, A high-spirited lady in America has entrusted me with £200, which I am to dispose of as I like. I cannot think of a better use than helping our snipers to keep down the fire in the German trenches. If therefore, the Government has not given your husband what he wants in the way of telescopic sights I should be very glad to make a gift out of this money to the fund.[115]

The numbers involved cannot have been great but many certainly found their way to the front lines, as Prichard mentions in passing a rifle fitted with a German scope that was clearly used with some effect. It seems Britain was gradually beginning to equip its snipers to a level where, in material terms at least, they could actually meet the Germans on a fairly equal footing.

Chapter Five

A Gradual Response

The situation with regard to training was not entirely without hope either, for there had existed from the earliest days of the war a small but vociferous group of competitive shooters based at Bisley Camp, in Surrey, who believed, with some justification, that the situation in France could be greatly improved if consideration were given to the proper training of snipers. There were many experienced and dedicated pre-war shooters who had, between them, won virtually every shooting prize available, and they included Arthur Fulton, George Grey, Langford Lloyd, Harcourt Ommundsen,[116] Philip Richardson and Thomas Fremantle, who had captained both the 1908 and 1912 Olympic Games shooting teams. Many of these names will crop up again, but it is probably Thomas Fremantle who is of most interest at this point. He was fifty-two years old in 1914, too aged by far to be accepted into front-line service, but he had behind him a lifetime of shooting knowledge, as well as very rare and valuable experience with all forms of optical sights. Indeed, in 1901 he had written a book (widely read by shooters but sadly ignored by the military) in which he expounded theories on the use of optics for shooting that were both highly advanced and prophetic. He believed that the use of telescopic sights should be encouraged by both target shooters and soldiers and the recent experience of the British Army at the hands of the Boer sharpshooters during the Boer War elicited his interesting comment that:

> In fighting a civilised enemy, every device of concealment and
> of taking cover has to be resorted to, which makes it difficult
> for the enemy to be seen, and an effective reply given to his
> fire. In the hands of a properly trained soldier it is quite
> possible that the results which could be obtained in increasing

the effectiveness of fire at all distances might make the telescopic sight well worthy of adoption [. . .] for some small proportion of men.' [117]

If this was regarded as heresy by the Army establishment in 1901, then it was not quite so easily dismissed in the face of evidence from France regarding the effectiveness of German riflemen in 1914. Indeed, Lord Cheylesmore, the chairman of the National Rifle Association, had gone so far as to suggest to the Secretary of War, Lord Kitchener, the possibility of raising a battalion of marksmen from within the ranks of Bisley shooters. Although this was rejected, probably quite wisely, the concept of using these experienced riflemen to provide a cadre of instructors for the Army was a sound one, and it was deemed a prudent move.

Thus, in September 1914, a new School of Musketry was formed at Bisley and foremost among the instructors were Staff Sergeant Henry Lattey, inventor of the optical sight that bore his name, and Captain Philip Richardson, who was not only a dedicated long-range target shooter but also one of the foremost authorities on the use of optical sights – fortunate appointments for all concerned. Of course, the Army was concerned with more pressing matters than Bisley, so the school began its life without budget, training facilities, instructors or equipment. But such minor inconveniences did not deter the officers and men who were to comprise the operating staff, so they borrowed Boy Scouts to act as range staff and accepted help from absolutely anyone, military or civilian, who could assist in any way. Ammunition was not provided by the Army and was purchased at much reduced prices from Fultons Ltd., the Bisley gunsmiths, or 'borrowed' from any Army units in the area. Indeed, complaints about missing boxes of ammunition were frequently made to Major Fremantle, but despite many exhaustive investigations, no traces of misappropriated ammunition were ever found. The long-established School of Musketry at Hythe also helped materially, providing staff, weapons and ammunition, as well as tables, chairs and even blankets. The Bisley staff worked miracles and by the end of November of that year, it was reported that seventy-seven officers and 261 men had passed through the course. These men were of course, spread very thinly along the front lines but their knowledge and enthusiasm were to prove invaluable.

The fledgling industry producing telescopic sights in England was also much aided by the staff at Bisley, for at the time there was no practical method for the newly built rifles and telescopic sights to be properly collimated or zeroed (indeed, the scopes' range drums were unmarked when fitted to their donor rifles and needed to be range tested and calibrated prior to being issued), so Captain Richardson and his staff were made responsible for this undertaking. The Enfields were zeroed at 200 yards and test-fired at 100, 300 and 600 yards (although a few telescopic sights were graduated up to 1,000 yards). The huge numbers of men required for the war effort meant that, from its modest staff of eighteen officers and eighty-two instructors, the school expanded rapidly to sixty-six officers and over 300 NCOs. It took some time to work out a suitable syllabus but by the end of 1915 over one and a half million men had passed through its gates, one of whom was Fremantle's own son, Thomas.[118]

While it was not in any way a sniper school *per se*, it did instil the elements of shooting discipline. It also provided soldiers with some of the skills required to successfully pass through one of the several sniper schools that were soon to be established in France. The experience gained by Fremantle in running the school was to prove of significant benefit to the future of sniping, for it led to his promotion to Lieutenant Colonel with a brief, in the spring of 1916, to establish and run the Northern Command School of Scouting and Sniping at Rugely in Leicestershire. But of all these early disciples of sniping, there was perhaps one man whose name was to become synonymous with forcing the Army to comprehend the nature of the problem they faced, and that was Vernon Hesketh-Prichard.

The Prichard Effect

From March 1915 Hesketh-Prichard had been serving in France as an intelligence officer in charge of War Correspondents, a public relations position that he neither sought nor wanted. He had tried to enlist in both the Guards and Black Watch but his relatively advanced age (he was thirty-eight) had precluded him from obtaining a commission.

Desperate to join up, he had resorted to pulling strings to enable him to get to France in some military capacity or other, and had finally been accepted into the Intelligence Corps. Ever hopeful of being able to utilise his prodigious shooting talents, he took with him several scoped commercial rifles, some borrowed from friends, with which he waged a one-man campaign against the enemy. While escorting the newspapermen around the lines he was horrified by the extraordinary amount of sniping from the German lines and the lack of effective response from the British:

> May 29, 1915. All along the hill you dare not show your head, as the whole German line is in full sight.[119]

This one-sided war frustrated him hugely, so whenever he had the chance he used one of his rifles to indulge in his own personal sniping war: 'after crossing the hill we got above the German position [. . .] I sniped at Germans, but did not get any definite results I could see.'[120]

His experience of big game hunting, and his understanding of the technicalities of shooting with an optical sight, made him one of the few line officers able to exert any influence: but it was an uphill struggle. Questioning regimental officers, NCOs, and the few available snipers, made him realise that their knowledge of the subject was almost non-existent and that there was an urgent need for some form of organised training to be introduced: 'It seemed to me that here was something definite to go upon towards the organisation of sniping in which I so much desired to have a hand.'[121]

While he was appalled at the lack of will on the part of the Army high command to do anything positive to tackle the sniper shortage problem, he was, nevertheless, heartened by the number of individuals who were trying, albeit with limited success, to take on the might of the German *Scharfschützen*. The method of snap shooting over the sandbag parapet, so often used on Gallipoli, did not work on the Western Front against a skilled enemy armed with optically equipped rifles. The three seconds' exposure required for a German sniper to aim and fire, and their effective system of crossfire from their sniper posts, meant that any possible target was very quickly identified and eliminated:

as every German sniper seemed to be supported on either flank by other German snipers, looking for him with one's head over the top of the parapet was [. . .] simply a form of suicide.'[122]

Hesketh-Prichard observed that there was nothing in the way of trench material to help British snipers: 'I rarely found a (steel) loophole from which I could reconnoitre, and camouflage of any kind was conspicuous only for its complete absence.'[123]

And he despaired of the obsessive neatness of the British trenches:

The parapets were made of sandbags beaten down with spades, and it is not too much to say [. . .] a mouse could not move without being spotted by the most moderate sighted German sniper.[124]

Convinced that the Army could and should do better, Hesketh-Prichard began a personal crusade in mid-1915 to inform and educate units about how to deal with the enemy, mostly by appearing in the front lines and engaging the Germans in sniping duels that, fortunately for the future of British sniping, he won. His ability and enthusiasm impressed the officers and men, and it became obvious in the sectors where he was working that effective counter-sniping had a deleterious effect on the Germans, who became far more cautious. Indeed, he commented gleefully that after taking on German snipers who had plagued a Highland battalion, that they subsequently had no further trouble at all from sniping. At the same time, he began using his skills to try to convert senior officers to his way of thinking. Early on, he had found one staunch ally in the shape of an interested and sympathetic officer, Lieutenant Colonel A.G. Stuart, under whose command Hesketh-Prichard had worked. He sought out an interview with the Colonel, in which he explained the shortcomings of the existing system to him:

'You say,' said he, 'that nearly all the telescope sighted rifles you have seen are so incorrect as to be worse than useless?' – 'Quite sure,' said I. 'And that is only one side of it. The men have no idea of concealment, and many of them are easy targets to the Hun snipers.'

'The proper authorities should move on the matter,' said Colonel Stuart.

'There don't seem to be any proper authorities, sir. The officers know no more than the men [. . .] and what I want to do is this; if it is possible I should like to be appointed as sniping expert to some unit. I believe I could save hundreds of lives.'

I went on. 'Will you help me get a job of this kind, sir? I am asking because it seems absurd for a fellow like me who has spent years after big game to let men go on being killed when I know perfectly well I can stop it.'

'Are you sure of that?'

'I am willing to go on a fortnight's trial and if I do not make good, there is no harm done.'

'Well,' said Colonel Stuart, 'we will talk to people about it and see what they say.'

Stuart was as good as his word and his support materially assisted Hesketh-Prichard.

Also helpful was the commander of the Third Army, General Lynden-Bell, and his Senior Intelligence officer, General Sir George Macdonagh who readily accepted that something had to be done and gave permission for Hesketh-Prichard to begin visiting some of the units of the Third Army in September 1915 to instruct on the care and use of scoped rifles and try to find a means of organising sniper units on some sort of local basis. He was eventually released from his employment at GHQ and attached as sniping officer for the Third Army. The magnitude of his task could not be underestimated and his brief was a very tall order indeed as there were within the Third Army, fifteen infantry divisions, each with three brigades. Each of these brigades normally held four combat battalions so this gave Prichard the potential responsibility for trying to educate the officers and NCOs of some 180 line battalions into the mysteries of sniping. Apart from the rifles he had with him (he was constantly requesting that his wife find and send any available scoped rifles to him in France) and his batman, a marksman from the Somerset Light Infantry named Private Plummer, he had no staff, no training aids or classrooms. Undaunted, he began the demanding process of travelling from unit to unit to try to improve their sniping skills but at times he nearly despaired. He wrote home at the end of September:

> Patience, I must preach, and patience again! I am determined that no risks are taken that are avoidable; it is the only way. And of course, it is not my job to shoot, but to teach others.[125]

This of course, seldom stopped him for he fully understood that only by example could he make the officers understand that properly organised opposition would reap its own rewards. When in the trenches of the 12th Infantry brigade, he dealt with a persistent sniper in the only way he knew how:

> I killed the sniper at 11.25 today – very exciting. He had a telescopic sight I am sure. He very nearly killed a sergeant who was looking through [a loophole] and when Fritz shot [. . .] I shot also. The shot went right into his loophole, and after it no more reflections could be seen, nor did he shoot again. The men were fearfully pleased. I am afraid you will think this rather grisly, but Fritz and his like are taking a very heavy toll of our best.[126]

It was a slow and exhausting process, one of Hesketh-Prichard's continual themes in his letters was his continual tiredness, but he was utterly determined to prove his point. So he travelled from brigade to brigade, lecturing, sniping and examining rifles and scopes, but he was still woefully short of resources. He found a mentor in the unlikely form of John Buchan, then a reporter for *The Times* newspaper in France, who had himself been aghast at the losses inflicted on the British soldiers and who believed some sort of response was urgently required. It is, perhaps, of incidental interest that it was Buchan who, with his frequent use of the word 'sniper' in his columns, may well have been responsible for its introduction into everyday language. Certainly, from being a term little known outside game-shooting circles in the pre-war Indian Army, the word had become commonplace by late 1915, although doubtless that was also due to its use by regular soldiers in the BEF. Through his influence, Buchan was able to interest others of greater influence in Hesketh-Prichard's work, and a fund for the supply of rifles was begun, sponsored by Lord Haldane, Lord Glencomer and Lord Finlay, as well as the editor of the influential *Spectator* newspaper, Mr St Lo Strachey. Prichard had finally started the ball rolling.

Periscope Rifles

If a heightened awareness regarding sniping had begun to seize the upper echelons of the British Army, the rank and file needed no reminding. The soldiers were nothing if not inventive and solutions were constantly being found to the many problems trench life raised. In late 1914 an increasing number of comments in contemporary memoirs and diaries appeared, regarding the introduction of a simple, yet life-saving item of trench equipment – the trench periscope:

> About February [1915] periscopes were introduced in the trenches; they were little mirrors stuck up on the back of the bayonet, and day-sentries could sit on the fire-step of the trench and view No Man's Land in front. Before they were introduced, day-sentries would have to get up on the fire-step [. . .] many a day-sentry has been drilled through the head before periscopes had been introduced.[127]

They were both simple and effective, and varied from the most basic form of a small mirror attached to the bayonet with a spring clip, which the viewer then held up to enable him to see over the parapet, to the more complex forms of box periscope, using two mirrors enclosed in a tin or wooden casing. A tubular brass pattern, with a wooden handle and adjustable eyepiece was often privately purchased by officers from retailers, such as the Army and Navy store, but they were officially issued from early 1916. The introduction of these devices saved hundreds of lives but also provided the German snipers with a splendid new form of amusement:

> We liked breaking the lenses of the periscopes of the British. At 100 metres they were not difficult to hit but [the British] became much better at camouflaging them and soon it was hard to see any along the lines.[128]

The German snipers' enjoyment at shooting them could prove to be their downfall however, for the British using them were developing their own cunning and beginning to play the Germans at their own game:

> There were no loopholes in our parapet and a little watching showed that there was a Bosche sniper quite close. I think they expected me to shoot over the parapet, but this I refused to do. They put a loophole in, and when I arrived the sniper Fritz had found it and had blown it about. He very nearly killed a sergeant who was looking through, another two inches would have done it. So I directed them to show a periscope near our loophole. Meanwhile Fritz had shot twice more [. . .] and when Fritz shot, I shot also. The shot went right into his loophole, and after it no more reflections could be seen, nor did he shoot again.[129]

Neither was the use of periscopes limited to observation, for a number of inventors immediately appreciated their possible use for mounting to a rifle, to enable it to be fired remotely. Battery rifles were a common sight in the trenches, mounted on frames in a fixed position to fire at a predetermined spot, but the new periscope rifles were something different. Introduced into the trenches in the early months of 1915, the actual inventor is disputed, although improvised periscope rifles had first appeared during the Boer War, inexplicably called 'infascopes'. These were mentioned in detail in T.F. Fremantle's book of 1901, and he devoted quite a large chapter to them:

A little device may here be mentioned which is the outcome of the Boer War [. . .] called the 'infascope'. The Boers found the storm of shot and shell directed against them so overwhelming that they held up their rifles over the edge of the entrenchment and discharged them in the general direction of the enemy, without attempting to take aim. At Mafeking [. . .] where the trenches got to be very uncomfortable close quarters indeed [. . .] an impromptu device was arranged to enable effective fire to be brought to bear under such circumstances. Two small pieces of mirror were attached so that one could be clipped on behind the backsight, while the other hung down below [. . .] and in the latter could be seen the reflection of the line of aim [. . .] this enabled shots to be truly directed while the whole head of the firer was below the sheltering level of the sandbags. The application of this arrangement could hardly be very extensive since it admits of no large field of view, but under special circumstances it has proved its utility.[130]

Despite this account, the introduction of these useful tools has often been erroneously attributed to an idea proposed by a director of the BSA Company, T.S. Walker, in mid-1915, in response to complaints about German snipers from his son, serving in the Warwickshire Regiment. He constructed a simple wooden framework that was strapped to the butt of an SMLE rifle, with a wire rod passing through it to act as a remote trigger mechanism. Sighting was by means of a box periscope screwed to the rear of the false stock, and it enabled the firer to take shots without exposing any part of his body above the trench. In fact, William Youltens – a prolific inventor in the field of optics and sights – had already placed a similar patent with the London Patent Office back in December 1914,[131] for a simple periscope attachment that clamped to the rifle butt, enabling the rifle to be aimed and fired while resting on the sandbags of a parapet, with little danger to the firer. It was called the Hyposcope and was made by the London Hyposcope Company, which produced variants for both service rifles and Vickers/Maxim machine guns. Other, equally crude, trench-variants had appeared in early 1915, it not requiring a genius to put the concept of a mirror and wooden framework together to create a remote firing device. The Royal Engineers invariably had supplies of wood and wire and unit armourers could usually get what they wanted in exchange for a packet of cigarettes. A simple lattice wooden framework, wire trigger and two mirrors would suffice. Although the result was rarely pretty, it was workable, if not necessarily up to true sniping standards. One problem, in particular, was the long, creepy pull of the improvised trigger, making shooting difficult, with a resultant lack of accuracy. Contemporary accounts seem to show that they were of little use beyond 150 yards, although they must have been reasonably efficient at forcing enemy riflemen to keep their heads down, and doubtless some casualties were caused by lucky shots. But it was hardly the apogee of sniping. They could be very effective, however, where opposing trenches were close.

Optics and Glassmen

Lens manufacture was well established in Europe by the thirteenth century, Roger Bacon having been described on several occasions as possessing an early form of telescope, and in Britain, in the sixteenth century, published works by John Dee and Thomas Digges in 1570 and 1571 talk of both reflecting and refracting telescopes. However, the large-scale production of telescopes did not begin until the first decade of the seventeenth century, primarily in the Netherlands, and within twenty years they had become commonplace over Europe, greatly aided by the work of a Dutch scientist named Jan Lippershey. Using already established technology, Galileo Galilei made his first telescope in late March 1609. It was a 3 x item, but within a year he had produced a 33 x device, with which he discovered the satellites of Jupiter, as well as the existence of sunspots. Whatever the truth of its actual invention, the modern telescope as we know it was certainly firmly established as an indispensable part of the naval and military arsenal by the early eighteenth century.

In many respects, the British Army was very fortunate in having at its disposal a small but excellent home-based optical industry, being well supplied by manufacturers such as Negretti and Zambra, Davidson, the Periscopic Prism Company, Aldis, and a number of lens makers who provided glass for sporting scopes used on rifles built by makers such as Holland and Holland, Rigby etc. There were also imported optics by manufacturers such as Winchester, Ross, Bausch and Lomb, Zeiss and many other German companies, who supplied off-the-shelf telescopic sights for large-bore sporting rifles. Pre-war British optical makers had been supplying both the sports shooting market and the armed services with a broad range of optical equipment such as binoculars, observation telescopes, Galilean optical and telescopic sights, rangefinders and artillery sights.

The increasing power and range of artillery in the early twentieth century made telescopes a particularly vital item for spotting targets and calling range changes, and by the outbreak of war in 1914 the British Army and Royal Navy were using large numbers of very high-quality spotting and observation telescopes. Many hundreds had also been purchased by target shooters for use on the rifle ranges of Britain and Europe and these telescopes were to provide the Commonwealth snipers and observers with one of their greatest advantages on the battlefield: the three-draw 20 x observation tele-scope. Observers – known pre-war as 'glassmen' – could view targets at ranges in excess of 1,000 yards, and skilled observers could see movements in detail at several miles on a clear day. It took consider-able training to use one effectively, and without a doubt, the best glassmen were the Ghillies who came from the highlands of Scotland. During the Boer War a small number had been formed into a regi-ment of scouts/soldiers called the Lovat Scouts, having taken their name from their clan chief, Lord Simon Lovat (1871–1933). Their tracking and observation skills in the veldt, during the Boer campaign, had proved second to none and upon the outbreak of war in August 1914 some 1,200 men had mobilised, forming two regi-ments of mounted yeomanry. It was not long before they lost their horses and picturesque uniforms, to be replaced with 'Shanks's pony', khaki and webbing, and the majority soon found themselves en route to Gallipoli. Their time there was spent in honing both obser-vation and sniping skills, which were shortly to become of great importance in the training of snipers.

In early 1915, a very few had been seconded to units serving in France and Flanders to pass on their skills. One, 62-year-old Lieutenant C.B. Macpherson, had not been sent to Gallipoli on account of his mature years, and was attached to Major Hesketh-Prichard's neophyte sniper training school as an instructor. It would not be long before more men of the Lovats would emerge as an important factor in the Commonwealth's sniper training programme.

Galilean Sights

While, pre-war, little use was made of the true telescopic sight for target use, what did exist, in considerable numbers, were the simple optical devices known as 'Galilean sights'. The properties of these lenses had reputedly been discovered by the scientist and astronomer Galileo Galilei (1564–1642), although the science of optical lenses pre-dated him to Roman times and possibly even prior to that. There is some evidence that Emperor Nero (reigned AD 54–68) used what was referred to as a *smaragdus* to view games and this may have been either a correcting lens (similar to spectacles) or a form of early telescope. What is more certain is that the science of lens making was well known by the twelfth century, for archaeological finds at a Viking site in Gotland, Sweden, have uncovered near perfect flat and ellipsoid lenses, comparable in quality to commercially produced aspheric lenses made in the 1950s.[132] Galilean sights required little in the way of technology, as they provided a simple magnified image that enhanced the shooter's ability to make long-range shots. If few telescopic sights were available, then at least these simple magnifying type sights were, having been accepted by the target shooting community as one of the best optical instruments to be introduced to the sport since the observation telescope. They were manufactured by several companies: Barnett, Gibbs, Lattey, Martin and Neill, and they were the simplest form of optics available, comprising little more than two lenses, a largish convex objective of 1 to 1½ inches in diameter, normally placed on or near the foresight of the rifle, and a smaller, concave objective lens, placed close to the shooter's eye by being fitted to the aperture sight or backsight. They used a number of methods to provide the shooter with an aiming mark: either a dot on the objective lens (as with the Martin or Neill sights), by using the foresight itself (as with the Lattey), or having a pointer and cross-hair (as found on the Gibbs).

For the Army – desperately searching for something that would enable them to fight the German sniper menace on more advantageous terms – they were a godsend. Of all of the types adopted, only the Lattey was not available commercially, being manufactured solely for military use, and it was supplied in the largest numbers – unsurprising in view of the fact it was the cheapest. Both the Lattey and Neill were approved for use on 28 September 1915 and the totals of types of Magnifying Sights supplied were: 9,000 Lattey, 4,250 Neill, 755 Martin and 100 Gibbs. Costs per unit varied widely, the Lattey was 7/6d (37.5 pence) the Barnett (or Ulster) sight as it was often known, was £1, 10s (£1.50), the Martin £3 and the Gibbs an astronomic £5, but crucially, they were all available off the shelf in reasonably large numbers. In theory, one could be attached in minutes to the service SMLE rifle, although in practice, fitment was not quite as simple as it appeared, for tiny manufacturing differences meant that the supplied mounts did not always mate properly and the clamping screws used were not designed for sustained military service use, often shearing or working loose. Colonel Fremantle was clearly aware of these deficiencies, commenting that:

Many rifles however, differ from one to another in measurement sufficiently for it to be impossible for these sights to fit with any real accuracy on all alike.[133]

From personal experience, the author can agree with this, for only rarely do these sights fit straight onto a standard rifle: at the very least a certain amount of filing is necessary to obtain a good fit, and this would have been impossible for an infantryman in a fire trench, unless access was available to an armourer. Once in place, there were certain limitations on their use, for not being enclosed, they used ambient light, and as a result did not have the ability of a telescope to magnify light. Neither were the lenses protected in any way, so they were vulnerable to poor handling as well as dust and dirt.

A major problem for snipers was that their field of view was very narrow – commonly 1 degree to 1½ degrees – which equates to between 5 and 7 feet at 100 yards. In practical terms, this was fine for shooting at a static bullseye, and in all fairness, it was for this purpose that they were designed, but for use on a moving target it meant that any lateral movement would quickly cause the target to vanish from the sight picture. On the credit side, as they were open lenses, it meant that it was marginally easier to following a fleeting target than with a scope.

There were other benefits, of course, for there was little need for instruction as to their use, no adjustment was required for windage or elevation, both being achieved by using the standard iron sights, and they required no special care aside from cleaning. In his instructional booklet, Fremantle devoted several pages to the use and care of these sights, indicating their widespread use and commenting: 'Many thousands of magnifying sights have been used for sniping in the present war.'[134] However, their effectiveness (or otherwise) in combat remains largely unknown, the only reference I have ever come across being a comment made by a veteran sniper of the Durham Light Infantry, who said he had a Lattey sight that he had used with some success in France, and with which he shot several German soldiers and a couple of officers. There also exists a photograph, reproduced in this book, of a sniper section in Salonika in mid-1916, in which two such sights are visible on rifles, so there is more than anecdotal evidence for their use in combat.

Aperture Sights

There was one other common form of optical device in use, frequently overlooked where sniping is concerned, and that is the aperture sight. These were the most commonly used form of target sight pre-war and are also known by a wealth of other names, the most common of which is the 'peephole', 'globe' or 'pinhole' sight. They had long been in use and examples can be seen fitted to wheel lock target rifles manufactured in the seventeenth century.[135] A variation of this sight, in the form of the Long Range Dial Sight, was fitted to the original Mk I Enfield, on the left side of the stock, and its purpose was to provide a sharp image at long range by using a very small hole through which the shooter viewed the target. Commercial patterns were made by BSA and Parker-Hale and these screwed to the left side of the stock, usually by utilising the retaining screw of the safety catch. They used the simple science of reducing the aperture through which the eye sees to the size of a pinhole, providing a sharper image of the target. There is, of course, no magnification, and this works both for and against them, for the target must be clearly visible to the shooter for a sight picture to be obtained. Very distant or moving targets can be difficult to see, as the aperture was designed primarily with target shooting in mind, but the lack of glass lenses meant that the sight was not unduly affected by dust or dirt, and once mounted on the rifle, they were very firmly fixed and not easily dislodged. The aperture provided a very sharp definition of the foresight blade as well as a broader field of view than the standard rearsight, typically 50 per cent greater. Herbert McBride was a great lover of the aperture sight, commenting:

> One thing I have been harping on, ever since the war; this matter of sights. I cannot for the life of me, understand why, in a country that has developed some of the finest types of aperture sights for use on sporting rifles, we cannot have an equally good one on the military rifle [. . .] If the light was right, I would use the 'scope sight; if not, the iron ones. The service sights on the Ross rifle were so good that, by using the large aperture, one could see plenty of the territory in the vicinity of the target – a very important point [. . .] the telescope sight is not always better than the iron ones [. . .] never as good in fog, and some-times even on bright days when there is a heavy mirage. The 'scope exaggerates everything, including the ground haze [. . .] but in the average light, and especially early on some mornings and late evenings the telescope is all to the good.[136]

To what extent these sights were employed on the Western Front is unknown, but there are strong indications they were put to very good use on a battlefront a long way from France: for the Dardanelles campaign signalled the start of a series of battles unlike anything Commonwealth forces had previously experienced, and it was to be one in which sniping would play a fundamental role.

Gallipoli, the Sniper's War

The military rationale behind the landings on the Gallipoli peninsula were sound enough: if the straits of the Dardanelles could be taken, then the Allies would be able to command the Black Sea, and Greece, Bulgaria, Romania and Italy could be persuaded to join a Balkan coalition against Germany's ally, Turkey. Moreover, vital military supplies could be delivered to Russia, and sorely needed Russian grain could be imported to the Allies in Europe. But the landings on the beaches of Gallipoli, on 25 April 1915, did not bode well for the future of the campaign, for stiff resistance was meted out by the Turkish Army, which at that time was held in little regard by the Allies. Australian and New Zealand (ANZAC) troops suffered particularly badly during the landings and it took considerable determination for a foothold to be established on the bare, rocky hillsides that characterised the peninsula.

As was to be so often the case on the Western Front, the defenders held all the cards, having defensive positions that were placed higher than those of attacking troops, providing the Turks with better observation and fields of fire. In most cases, the British and ANZAC forces had little option but to dig in wherever they could, and inevitably this spawned a war of stalemate, with the Turks unable to dislodge the invaders and the Allies unable to advance in sufficient strength to push back the enemy. Trench warfare began in earnest, for the Commonwealth troops found to their surprise that 'Johnny Turk' was neither inept, cowardly or stupid.

One of the earliest lessons learned was that casual exposure from the protection of a trench instantly brought forth a shot from Turkish snipers, who seemed to exist in large numbers. Like their German *Jäger* counterparts, many Turkish soldiers had hunted from their youth and were excellent shots, and the Army provided a training course for sharpshooters well in advance of those that eventually came into being for the Commonwealth soldiers on the Western Front. The Turks used ordinary service issue Mauser rifles but with no optical sights, and there is no evidence that any were supplied during the entire course of the Gallipoli campaign. Training was provided using German methods, often with instruction by German NCOs[137] seconded to assist their Turkish allies. Selected men were formed into sniping squads and given basic but effective training in range estimation, shooting and camouflage. Snipers were not generally employed as intelligence gatherers or observers, the hierarchical

Turkish Army leaving such matters to NCOs and officers. The number of men in a sniping section is not known for certain but seems to have been between sixteen and twenty. All were expert marksmen and they were trained to shoot accurately to about 400 metres, using open sights.

There was no limitation placed on what an individual soldier could do with regard to sniping and a private who was a good shot was just as likely to find a vantage point to shoot from, as a picked sniper, which may have been why the Allies believed that, at times, the entire Turkish Army consisted solely of snipers. Their job was made easier, initially at least, because most of the Commonwealth troops who landed on the peninsula were green, had no previous experience of the war, and they made the same, often fatal mistakes that their counterparts in France did. Their arrival in the firing lines was always made to the accompaniment of viciously accurate rifle fire, which the men could seemingly never escape from:

> The cracking of the rifles is still menacing [. . .] mainly from snipers. The rifles never cease; every minute they crack! crack! crack! The beach is strewn with discarded equipment [. . .] and now and again a trampled-on felt hat, the little hole and black blood patch.[138]

With trenches dug and lookout posts established, the men kept a wary watch on the Turkish lines, but as the ANZAC and British soldiers tried their best to find some way of fighting back, the body count grew inexorably:

> Snipers shot fifteen Aussies this morning [. . .] no matter what peaceful errand we go on, death goes too. A man was just shot dead in front of me. He was a little infantry lad, quite a boy with snowy hair that looked comical above his clean white singlet. Just as we were crossing Shrapnel Gulley he suddenly flung up his water bottles, wheeled around, and stared for one startled second, even as he crumpled to my feet. In seconds his hair was scarlet, his clean white singlet all crimson.[139]

Some men tried to find enemy snipers by using the tried and tested 'hat on a stick' method, marking the angle from which the bullet entered and exited, pinpointing the sniper's position, then dealing with the sniper by snap-shooting over the parapet. This was at best a chancy and at worst a suicidal method of sniping. Although the Turks had no optical sights, their keen eyes were materially helped by having an enemy whose trenches faced the sun during the day and were silhouetted against the evening sky. This meant that day and night there was little safety. A British officer, A.P. Herbert, recalled:

> We lost twelve men each day [. . .] as they stood up from their cooking [. . .] or carelessly raised their heads [. . .] and in the night there were sudden screams where a sentry had moved his head too often against the moon.[140]

As in France and Flanders, it soon became clear that the practice of peering over the parapet to try to spot snipers was simply a form of suicide, and so a large number of trench periscopes began to appear, some commercial but most home-manufactured in engineers' work-shops, using plywood made from packing cases, with two angled mirrors. Even then they were not safe from the snipers:

> I had two periscopes shot from me in ten minutes, and got a bloody nose for my pains. Johnny loved them and we must have lost hundreds. Eventually we had to camouflage them to look like sandbags or wooden stakes [. . .] those snipers were a menace.[141]

While initially dismissive of the abilities of the Turkish soldier, the Commonwealth troops who held a meagre toehold on the peninsula soon began to take them very seriously indeed. The Allies held one material advantage over the Turks, though, which was the use of the powerful observation telescopes, although these were solely issued to Army signallers and artillery observers. But it was not long before the Aussie snipers took to them with a passion, resulting in many artillery units in the locality mysteriously finding themselves suddenly bereft of their telescopes.

In order to meet the Turks head on, it was clearly necessary to ensure the trenches had suitable sniping posts set up, which was something of a problem in a place where absolutely everything – wood, sandbags and wire – was in short supply. Proper steel loophole plates were unavailable, so naval artificers were ordered to use spare ships' boiler plate to fabricate makeshift plates, which were inserted into the parapets at strategic points. Unlike the obsessively neat trenches in France, those at Gallipoli tended to be rough and ready, the parapets reinforced with whatever was to hand, often including the dead, so camouflage of observation posts was considerably easier. It is not an exaggeration to say that access to these loophole plates transformed the lives of the neophyte snipers, giving them the edge they desperately needed. Ion Idriess, commenting on the casual manner in which Turks exposed themselves, having little to fear from distant Australian riflemen, wrote that:

> If the Turks facing the old 5th [Light Horse Regiment] where we have steel loopholes and our own good rifles were only a quarter as game [. . .] or foolhardy, we would put up some record sniping tallies.[142]

The Turkish trenches were already well supplied with loophole plates so the increasing availability of these simple pieces of iron to the Allied troops enabled sniping to be undertaken on a far more equal footing. It often became a personal duel, in which not only good shooting, but good nerves, were required:

> I've just been indulging in a duel with a Turk, shot for shot. I'd fire and the dust would fly up against his loophole. Then slowly and cautiously the tiny circle of light on the trench parapet that was Johnny's loophole would fill up with half his square, grim face. Watching like a cat [. . .] I'd see his rifle-muzzle slowly poke through the loophole then a spurt of smoke with the crack-ping! and his bullet would plonk into the sandbag above my loophole. Then my turn. I'd wait with my rifle-sights levelled evenly at the distant tell-tale gleam of light [. . .] I'd fire. And vice versa. It was thrilling. I waited for each

of my turns with every sense keyed to concert pitch, thrilled through and through. I tried to kill him, he tried to kill me. Yet we have never seen one another and never will.[143]

In fact, Idriess's account is interesting on several levels, for it gives a rare insight into the mentality of men who would voluntarily expose themselves to an enemy sniper – men who were hunters at heart and who hated to see their quarry escape, regardless of the danger they themselves were in. It also illustrates the comparatively amateur level of sniping, for an equivalent scenario on the Western Front against Germans armed with telescopic sights would have been the equivalent of playing Russian roulette. It also showed the shortcomings of the issue rifle, with its open iron sights, when shooting against very small targets. In order to try to deal with the menace of the Turkish marksmen, officers started the selection of the best British and Commonwealth riflemen and formed them into loose anti-sniper teams. Their organisation was casual to the point of being almost non-existent, as one Royal Naval Division man recalled:

I was a marksman, and our officer told me and another chap off to try and deal with the Turk snipers. We had our rifles, a big naval telescope and four bottles of water but we had no clue at all about what we were supposed to do.[144]

Billy Sing

While the British Army had some very good shots within their ranks, it was the Australians and New Zealanders who had the greatest advantage, possessing many men who had been professional kangaroo or deer hunters back home, and who regarded the ability to make snap shots at 400 yards as perfectly normal. In addition, their knowledge of stalking, camouflage and observation was invaluable. Naturally, it was not long before a few individuals began to emerge as true exponents of the new sniping game at Gallipoli, one of the most famous being a small, quiet man of mixed European-Chinese parentage, named Billy Sing.

Born in 1886 in Clermont, Queensland, Billy was both a competitive rifle shooter and kangaroo hunter. His expertise with the rifle was not lost on his officers and he was requested to do something about the local Turkish snipers – a task he took to with a passion. His normal day was spent in the area of Chatham's Post, and he would occupy his lair (or 'possie') before dawn. He seemed to possess extraordinarily sharp eyesight, as he could see and hit a target visible to his observer only through a telescope. Exactly what rifle he used is a matter of debate, although it seems to have been a service SMLE fitted with an aperture sight. These were quite common, for many Australian target shooters who enlisted had used Lee-Enfields back home and took their Parker Hale or BSA aperture sights with them. Sing and Ion Idriess served together in the 5th Light Horse Regiment and Idriess spotted for him on several occasions, but none of his accounts specifically mention the type of rifle Sing used. What was certain was that he had soon notched up a score of over 100 Turks and his fame had spread across the entire battlefield. In a place where any good news was scarce and death was a constant lurking companion, Sing's ability to inflict fatal retribution on the enemy was regarded with glee and his presence provided a major psychological boost to the beleaguered ANZACs. Idriess provided a rare glimpse of Sing at work:

> I spotted for Billy Sing this morning. He is a little chap, very dark, with a jet-black moustache and a goatee beard. A picturesque looking mankiller. His tiny possie is perched on a commanding position high up in the trench. He does nothing but sniping. He has already shot one hundred and five Turks. He has a splendid telescope and through it I peered across at a distant loophole, just in time to see a Turkish face [. . .] he disappeared. At last further along the line, I spotted a man's face framed enquiringly in a loophole. He stayed there. Billy fired. The Turk vanished instantly, but with the telescope I could partly see motion of men inside the trench picking him up. So it was one more man to Billy's tally.[145]

Such was his notoriety (he was universally referred to as 'The Assassin' by ANZAC soldiers) that in a scenario reminiscent of a Hollywood film, the Turks ordered that every effort be made to eliminate him. His position was well known to the Turkish riflemen and one morning his observer, Tom Sheehan, had his telescope struck by a bullet that shattered both lenses, entered his mouth and exited through his cheek, also bruising Sing badly on the shoulder en route before it dropped to the ground. Sing was quite shaken by this and it was a week before he returned to duty. Another attempt was made by a highly skilled Turkish soldier known only as 'Abdul the Terrible' and this too almost succeeded, Abdul having carefully plotted Sing's movements and his favourite firing position. But the powerful observer's telescope once again proved to be the sniper's best friend and Sing's unnamed spotter saw the Turk first, enabling Sing to fire before his opponent, the bullet striking him in the forehead. There are few clues to Billy's mentality, other than comments that he took his sniping very seriously. When once asked by General Birdwood how he felt about shooting men in cold blood (itself an interesting insight as to how High Command viewed sniping) Sing replied that shooting the bastards never caused him to lose any sleep. His final official tally was 205 and he left Gallipoli with a richly deserved Distinguished Conduct Medal.

Not all of the snipers were up to Sing's standard, however, and many suffered accordingly:

> One morning moving into Lone Pine trenches one soldier just ahead of me turned to his mate and said 'Come on Dick, you and I will go on together this time.' One used a periscope to see what Johnnie Turk was doing. The other was ready for any quick sniping at anything that moved. The next minute 'bang' Dick got a bullet right through the head, and he fell at our feet. We think an enemy sniper must have been just out in front using slight ground cover waiting for our relief to come on.[146]

The British and ANZAC snipers soon realised that their foe was way ahead of them in the application of sniping knowledge and considerably cleverer than they initially gave him credit for:

> Sometimes Johnny is daring and dangerously cunning. Out of our loopholes and through artillery telescopes two of us are

now watching No Man's Land. Telescopes are deadly aids. Behind that oh-so-natural looking little bush is a 'foxhole' which Johnny has dug in the night and painstakingly carried the tell-tale earth away. There are quite a number of these inconspicuous holes, artfully hidden by the bushes that cover the ground in front of his trench. Lying snug in the hole we are now watching, is Johnny, his rifle poked through the bush. Thus, when he does fire, the momentary puff of smoke will be hidden. Ah, but we have patience – and our powerful telescopes show us even the wee black hole of his rifle-muzzle. I am putting my diary down now, for I am going to let the light in through my loophole and slowly and slowly pass a piece of bag behind it. Then, when Johnny fires at the supposed face, my mate will . . .

Later, he recorded tersely in his diary: 'We have got Johnny.'[147]

The Turks excelled in the use of camouflage and were one of the earliest armies to appreciate the value of proper concealment both for observation and sniping. One unnamed journalist wrote in wonderment in *The Times* newspaper of the Turkish use of camouflage:

> Some most remarkable devices seem to have been adopted by the Turkish marksmen. Thus one man had his face painted green so that it would be indistinguishable among the leaves of the tree in which he hid. He was dressed in green clothes. Another sharpshooter, who worked from a trench, had erected a bush in front of him; his presence was betrayed by the disappearance of the bush into the trench during a period of inactivity.[148]

Many Turkish snipers worked their way behind isolated outposts during the night, and would fire into the soldiers' backs, but their fate was sealed if caught:

> Some of our chaps found a Turk hidden in a grove of trees up behind our line. They hauled him down and finished him on the spot with bayonets. I didn't see it and I was glad, because

he was a brave man and I should not like to have had that on my conscience.[149]

From this stage of the war, it was becoming clear that snipers were both feared and admired in equal amounts, and their death, if captured, became increasingly likely – an attitude that continues to the present day. The ANZACs learned quickly, and two-man sniper teams patrolling the lines became a common sight, on the lookout for hot spots from where they could exercise their skills. Within three or four months of landing the dominance that the Turkish snipers had initially enjoyed had been eroded and they, too, were forced to exercise far greater care. This was in part because of the improved siting of sniping posts and the growing skill of the Commonwealth snipers, but it also owed something to the introduction of periscope rifles. While not much use for long-range shooting, at Gallipoli, where trenches were very close or targets in plain view, they certainly had their uses. Idriess's diary mentions using periscope rifles several times against targets in open view, albeit with variable results:

> I'm blest if a Turk didn't unconcernedly walk down a ravine five hundred yards away [. . .] another Johnny sauntering behind him. How unconventional! I quickly trained the periscope rifle towards them; the dashed thing felt very wobbly and I had to crouch right back to the extreme edge of the firing possie. Then, reflected in the wee mirror I watched two Turks walk leisurely out of a sap. I was so staggered at their cheek that I gazed for a while, then crack! – the bullet spurted into the dust directly between them. But the blasted periscope frame had kicked me on the jaw and nearly knocked me back down the trench.[150]

There were even persistent rumours of the Turks employing women snipers on the front, one published report stating that:

> An Australian patrol had caught a Turkish woman sniper who had the identity discs of several British soldiers hanging round her neck.[151]

This tale was apparently confirmed by a number of other observers, but mostly seem to stem from one incident at Suvla, where a female villager was found with British dogtags, personal effects and money taken from the dead. The fact a rifle was also in her cottage would not have made her a sniper by any stretch of the imagination, merely a poor farmer's wife who regarded looting the dead a reasonable method of reducing the family's abject poverty.

For many of the inexperienced Commonwealth snipers on the peninsula who survived the primitive living conditions, disease, shelling and snipers, the experience gained in fighting the Turks was to prove invaluable. For one unit in particular, it was to be a particularly rewarding proving ground. The trenches recently vacated by the Fife and Forfar Yeomanry and Scottish Horse had been totally dominated by enemy snipers, in particular 'Percy', a persistent Turkish sniper who had killed many of the former occupants. In early October 1915, they were taken over by the Lovat Scouts, who at once organised sniping teams, constructed posts and set about teaching the Turks a lesson in marksmanship. Careful observation by the glassmen and good shooting soon began to unnerve the opposition and the pinnacle of their success came in killing Percy. Lance Corporal Angus Mackay had made Percy his personal crusade and spent several days patiently tracking his movements, finally stalking and shooting him. When they were moved to a new front in late September, in appalling weather conditions, despite having flooded trenches and sub-zero temperatures, the Lovats were not about to relax their grip. One wrote:

> They [the Turks] were to be seen, all over the place walking about, trying to keep warm and, in the early morning, there were a lot sitting, like scaups [birds] on a rock, along the top of their parapet. We accounted for about thirty by midday. One of the men told me it was better fun than hind shooting.[152]

One cannot but have some sympathy for the hapless, frozen Turkish soldiers.

There was little future for the campaign at Gallipoli, for once the initial impetus of the landings had been lost, the trench stalemate could not be broken. The decision to abandon the peninsula in late

December 1915 was a sound one, and it was fitting that the Lovats were selected to be the last men to leave, having kept up their sniping until the last minute. The loss of half a million Allied and Turkish casualties had achieved nothing, and it would not be long before such monstrous numbers became commonplace. But for most of the veterans of the campaign, the sniping that they had experienced was merely a foretaste of what was to come.

Chapter Six

Selection and Training

For the semi-official British and Commonwealth sniper sections that had been formed among the regiments on the Western Front in the early months of 1915, the first priority was to create an environment in which they could respond to enemy sniping without putting their own lives in unnecessary danger. As almost every type of war *matériel* was in short supply, the practical means to do this was initially unavailable. As far as snipers were concerned there was virtually nothing they could ask for, as there were almost no scoped rifles, and whatever else that was needed was usually hastily improvised *in situ*. The men who occupied the trenches in France and Belgium in this period were learning much the same lessons as their comrades at Gallipoli: that being inventive was no substitute for training, or having the tools for the job.

It was not simply the mechanics of sniping that were proving difficult though, for the officers and NCOs tasked with recruiting and training snipers had an even greater problem in finding the men with the right qualities for the job. As Major Neville Armstrong, himself a sniping officer, was to write:

> Unorganised sniping has proved to be more or less useless. There is no one to guide them, to instruct them, to see that they snipe and not sleep, that they keep the Hun sniper in hand and that they take an intelligent interest in their work.[153]

Initially, the answer had apparently been to select men who were marksmen and assign them as snipers. At a time when no alternative means of selection existed, this was probably the only method by which a man could be found for a job for which, outwardly at least, he appeared suited. But many officers began to realise that some men detailed for sniping duties simply did not meet the demands of the task, although they were at a loss to know what to do about it. Even men who were keen to volunteer often did not have the necessary mental or physical abilities, despite being good shots. The selection of the right men for the job was vital, not only because of the time, cost and effort required to train them, but also because subsequent failure on their part could lead to unnecessary deaths and reflected badly on the sniping schools. While an instructor at Bisley Camp, Major F. Penberthy, a Canadian who became commander of the 3rd School of Scouting and Sniping, wrote of his concerns at the methodology used to select men for sniper training:

> a good 'competition' shot of, say a high Bisley standard, did not necessarily make a good sniper. There is the width of the world between the leisurely peacetime business of firing at a distant target at a known, calculated range [. . .] and getting one quick and accurate shot at such almost invisible and momentary targets as the Bosches present in trench warfare.[154]

This sentiment was echoed by others who had mused over the personal qualities needed to ensure snipers were the right men for the job. Major Crum, whose experience with riflemen in the Boer War and subsequent founding of the sniper school at Acq in France, had thought long and hard about what was required. He succinctly summed up his beliefs in a sniping manual, which was privately printed during the war:

> Men selected should be reliable, intelligent, good shots, fit, educated. We are not likely to find the ideal man. The qualifications of the perfect sniper are unlimited. Moreover, the Company Officer naturally does not want to part with all his best men, and there are other equally important branches to be considered such as bombing, signalling or the Lewis guns. On the arrival of drafts the sniping officer should see if there are any likely men [. . .] men who have done well with the snipers have been sent for training at the NCOs school and promoted

into various companies. In the past year several of the snipers have been recommended for commissions and most of them have become NCOs.[155]

At the most basic level, men selected needed the ability to read and write, and in 1914–15 this was not necessarily something that could be taken for granted. It became clear that men of above average intelligence were required, preferably with the hunter's instinct. Major Armstrong (later to help found and organise the hugely successful Canadian Corps sniping school) has been famously and frequently quoted for his observations about the best type of men, who were 'game hunters, trappers, prospectors, surveyors, lumberjacks and poachers', and while he was primarily referring to those who proved successful in the Canadian Army, his comments are a generally accurate indicator of the self-reliant types best suited to sniping. Of course, there were relatively few trappers or lumberjacks in the British Army but there were substantial numbers of men who possessed the right attitude:

> I was selected for sniper training partly because I was always a good shot, shooting was easy for me, but I was never really happy unless I was at a loophole [. . .] I was always watching the Germans' lines, and would spend hours in one of our hides waiting for a chance to pot a Hun. I suppose I was a bit of a loner really but I liked the element of hunting so when the sergeant told me I was going to be sent on sniper training, I felt it was what I should have been doing all along. I was very pleased.[156]

Getting enough of the right men was to prove a fundamental problem and many of the early instruction manuals devoted considerable space to the subject. The theory of selection was succinctly spelt out by Major Armstrong, who specifically stated:

> [Men] should be carefully selected by their officers and NCOs and in no case should they be detailed to attend a specialist course or any other course for that matter.[157]

This may have been well and good in theory but in practice it was not always the case. Private Thomas Durst, of the King's Royal Rifle Corps, had qualified as a marksman on the ranges, and on his arrival in France was 'volunteered' by his Sergeant for sniper training:

> I was told off to report behind the lines to a new training school where I should be taught to become a sniper. I was unsure about exactly what that entailed, but there was no arguing with the sergeant. If he said 'go', you went. I had to hop lorries to get there and met up with a few other fellows from the regiment who had all been volunteered for sniper training. We wondered what it was all about but it was good to get away from the front lines for a while as well as the prospect of receiving an extra two bob a day specialist's pay.[158]

Despite the penchant that some NCOs had for selecting men for sniper training regardless of ability or personality, by 1915 it was becoming widely accepted throughout the Army that these specialists should be carefully chosen, and those who volunteered were far more likely to prove successful than those ordered to become snipers.

Prior to the publication of official manuals, some early advocates of sniping – such as Armstrong and Crum – had privately published (at their own expense) sniper training pamphlets, which were distributed to sniping and intelligence officers in line regiments. Most covered what was required with regard to the selection of men and it was recognised that a good sniper needed a complex mix of abilities that not every man possessed. Neville Armstrong listed the following as necessary:

1. Good eyesight – if possible quick sight. The eyes should always be restless when in the field.
2. Should not be colour-blind or deaf.
3. Should be keen and intelligent.
4. Persistent, patient and plucky.
5. Not of an excitable nature.
6. Truthful.
7. Good day and night sight. Not everyone possesses both.

Too often, troublemakers, slackers, or the utterly inept were sent for sniper training as a means of getting them out of the hair of their regiments:

> Company commanders dislike parting with really good and efficient men [. . .] and in the past have detailed men to attend schools because they may be undisciplined [. . .] have bad eyesight, be deaf or lazy, and for many other causes. This practice is unfair to the men and to those detailed to train them, and the battalion which repeatedly sends a poor type [. . .] very quickly ensures a bad name for itself.[159]

Those who were sent to sniping school but did not meet these criteria were immediately returned to their units, and word soon spread along the line about which regiments were sending sub-standard men for training. Commanding officers did not wish to be labelled as hostile or uncaring towards sniper training, so it became a matter of pride for regiments to have men who excelled on the training courses, and of course this paid dividends. The training schools often organised competitions for their snipers. Hesketh-Prichard, among others, offered prizes for the best sniper on each course: 'I had a competition with the prize of a telescope, which was finely won by a small corporal.'[160] There soon evolved intense competition between the men, which not only fostered a fine team spirit but encouraged them to try harder:

> Our course had some very good instructors, I recall a Scots Captain who lectured us in map-reading and compasses. I had great trouble with this so in the evenings he coached me and another chap, I recall he often gave us a tot of whisky from his flask to encourage us [. . .] in my exam I got nine out of ten on map-reading thanks to his patience.[161]

It was, in many ways, an attractive proposition for an ordinary infantryman, for there was the lure of two weeks out of the line, as well as added proficiency pay, and like their German counterparts, once qualified, they were excused normal trench duties. They were also free to come and go without too much interference, but it was a dangerous game and snipers soon earned the soubriquet 'suicide sections'. If there was, by now, a modest wave of enthusiasm at command level in favour of training men to become snipers, the big questions were: who could organise it, how, and where?

The Sniping Schools

By virtue of his sheer determination and incredibly hard physical work, Hesketh-Prichard was gradually persuading many senior officers that they must take the German sniper menace seriously, and on 6 September 1915 he was finally given the job he longed for: sniping instructor to the Third Army:

> General Lynden-Bell [. . .] has given me a wonderful job – practically to go wither I will in the lines. For a start I am to be attached to the 4th Division. When the General rang up the 4th Division I heard him say 'I am going to attach the King of Snipers to you. Mind you are good to him.'

By the end of the month he had established a school, of sorts, behind the lines at Amiens, where he gained the services of 2nd Lieutenant G. Gathorne-Hardy as assistant instructor. It was also at this time that he met with Colonel Langford Lloyd, who, despite being a doctor in the Royal Army Medical Corps, had lost little of his lust for killing as many Germans as possible:

> October 26th, 1915. I am here with Colonel Langford Lloyd doing our brochure on telescopic sights. He knows an awful lot. He shot for Ireland year after year. I am getting very good with telescopic sights, and can alter and correct them reasonably well. I had to shoot today. Curious how nervous I am of shooting before audiences. I hit a matchbox three times running at 300 yards.[162]

Prichard's knowledge of telescopic sights was fairly basic, but working with Lloyd soon changed that:

I had the opportunity at Colonel Lloyd's school of learning a great deal I did not know about telescopic sights and many other matters. He listened with great interest to the various ruses [. . .] that we had employed in the trenches.[163]

Lloyd was, at the time, in the middle of writing a much-needed instructional pamphlet on the use of telescopic sights, so it was inevitable the two would combine their considerable expertise to produce what *should* have been the first practical manual for issue to snipers. Unfortunately, this seems never to have been published: thus the Army lost a vital chance to improve the knowledge and performance of its snipers.

By November, Prichard and Gathorne-Hardy had personally trained some forty-six officers and 300 men of VII Corps, on a sniper course that was split between the front-line trenches and a school behind the lines, with an eclectic mix of dangerous practical observation and classroom theory.

The front line was not the ideal environment for teaching, the two men having to split groups of officers and men into three-man teams, this being the greatest number of pupils they could effectively manage in the line. If this were not trial enough, Prichard was still in heavy demand in the trenches, to find and deal with troublesome German snipers. His work was still regarded by many as merely an interesting novelty act, but it was a double-edged sword, for as he commented:

Our arrival in the trenches became rather trying, as we were looked upon as something in the light of performing animals who would give some kind of a show.[164]

But it was important, for while it was risky for the trainees, it provided the two instructors with priceless experience and information:

It would be difficult to describe the various days spent in the trenches, or the duels that took place there; but each one threw fresh light upon sniping and showed the enormous extent to which it might be developed.[165]

After a young officer was sniped, Hesketh-Prichard was sent in search of the culprit:

> I had difficulty, as the range was of 600 [yards] in seeing the heads through my telescopic sight though I could see quite plainly through my [observation] telescope. You will see I had my rifle laid on the exact spot [. . .] it was a good shot, as the bullet hit the earth about three inches under the head of the German, and on the earth of the parapet [. . .] as I could see afterwards the score of the bullet clearly on the top of the parapet. It must have taken him in the head. Anyhow, they showed no more, and the shot was a mortal certainty.[166]

The importance of this pioneering work, which he was undertaking in late 1915, cannot be underestimated. His knowledge was gained by the best possible method – personal experience – as he and Gathorne-Hardy undertook their instructional tours of the lines. But it was proving too demanding an environment in which to instruct, so in January 1916 he was given permission to establish a *pro-tem* sniping school at Béthune. He had a small range constructed on the outskirts of the town, as well as a replica of the trenches, complete with a small cottage equipped with loopholes and sniper posts. Of possibly more significance was the coincidental meeting between himself and a young Scottish officer, George Grey, of the Black Watch, who had sought out the little range and was watching with great interest the work going on:

> January 15, 1916. Yesterday I found an officer in a kilt watching me on the range. As he seemed keen I went and spoke to him. It was George Grey, winner of the King's Prize and Scottish Rifle Shooting Championships. They were using him to teach six Tommies to shoot! I am writing to the General suggesting that he should teach thirty thousand men! When 40 per cent of the telescopic rifles won't hit a German at 200 yards, and Grey is on the spot, one would think the idea of employing Grey would occur. Isn't it marvellous?[167]

His plea for Grey's assistance was granted and he was transferred to the new sniping school in the nick of time, for overwork was causing Prichard health problems and he was invalided home in early February, ostensibly for two weeks, but fever, jaundice and eye strain caused him to be away for three months, during which time Lieutenant Grey performed admirably as second-in-command.

Hesketh-Prichard's time was not wasted, though, for he spent much of his leave contacting everyone he knew who might be able to supply the much-needed telescopic sights. On his return in mid-May he continued gathering a team of good men around him, recording with satisfaction in his diary that he now had 'an expert telescope armourer (Sergeant L. Carr) and two Sergeant instructors (Blaikley and Fensome) [. . .] also markers, workmen etc., and a good staff'.[168]

News of his work had spread beyond the British lines and he began to receive visits from French officers, including five generals, who, to his amusement, referred to him as 'Le Capitaine qui a tue les Boches' (The Captain who kills Germans).

On a trip to Amiens, he was intrigued by his visit to the French Camouflage Workshops, where they were manufacturing papier mâché heads for use by their snipers. He managed to persuade them to make very realistic British heads, which he carried back in triumph.

Although the French lagged behind in terms of production of sniping rifles and scopes, they were far ahead of the British in their effective use of camouflage and inventive use of paint, as well as natural and man-made materials, and much of their pioneering work was soon to be copied by the Commonwealth armies. There were 'Sections de Camouflage' established in Paris and on the Aisne, Marne and Chemin des Dames during late 1914 and early 1915, using many talented stage painters under the command of a well-known artist, Guirand de Scevola.[169] Initially, they were turning out painted canvas and mesh to cover guns, but gradually turned their attention to producing fake battlefield debris and camouflage posts for machine guns, observers and snipers, as well as painting all manner of artillery and tanks in dazzle and other disruptive colours. Indeed, the chaotic (and to British eyes, filthy) trenches that the French had occupied since late 1914 were perfect for sniping, being constructed of any materials available, with clever sniper loopholes placed in the most innocuous places.

It was the French, not the Germans, who first used fake trees, manufactured of wood and steel, in which to hide observers and snipers, and who constructed 'dead' soldiers from straw, papier mâché and old uniforms, behind which snipers worked in comparative safety. Impressed, the British soon followed suit, placing their first metal tree in the Ypres sector in early March 1916. It was so realistic that it could not be detected as a fake unless struck with something, upon which it emitted a loud 'clang'.

For the rest of his tenure at sniping schools, Hesketh-Prichard would call upon his French allies for supplies of materials and completed heads with which to train his men. Happy with the progress the Béthune school was making, it was not long before he had worked out a basic but effective training syllabus, based on a mix of theory and practice, which covered most of the requirements for snipers, reproduced here:

HQ 11th Infantry Brigade, 48th Division, October 11 1915

8.45 to 9.45.	Talk on methods. Bosches and ours.
9.45 to 10.15.	Spying a series of objects raised by me at 450 yards; men in trench. Frenchmen, Indian, rifle barrel, lighting pipe, opening loophole, and many other things.
10.15 to 11.15.	Steady telescope work in an area of 150 yards by fifty in which objects are hid.
11.15 to 12.	Sighting of a rifle of which the shooting is out some inches.
12 to 1.	Laying sniping battery.
1 to 2.15.	Lunch.

2.15 to 2.45.	The right and wrong way to open loopholes with telescope work as to the part exposed.
2.45 to 3.15.	I stalk the class, and see if they can spot me. Today I got the lot as dead as ninepins!
3.45 to 4.15.	Shooting with a paper head at 300, 400 and 500 yards, with instruction at finding enemy snipers.
4.15 to 4.45.	Talk on all kinds of points, and there is a lot more at the end.

Understandably this was very demanding work even for a man who was physically strong and exhaustion again began to plague him. He wrote:

> I am very weary [. . .] I do not shoot much, as the strain on my eyes is great. Always shooting, always spying.

The unceasing pressure of work was to be a common theme through his letters, and eventually his punishing schedule irreparably damaged his health, but he was utterly determined to ensure that as many men as possible were trained.

In late December the Army, working at its most typically incomprehensible, informed him that he was promoted to General Staff Officer in charge of sniping in the Third Army, while at the same time making it quite clear that the post could only be retained if he accepted reduced pay and the lower rank of Captain! However, he was philosophical:

> I have had [. . .] a letter from GHQ saying that my position must be explained and that I must accept a lower rate of pay! Isn't that like them? My pay will be £207 – but I am saving many lives.[170]

The Linghem School

Despite his 'promotion' Hesketh-Prichard's new position was not actually formalised in the Army's hierarchy, for neither he nor the School of Observation and Sniping he was to run had yet been placed on the Army's official establishment. However, his elevation, if it can be termed that, was at least some tacit acknowledgement that his work was bearing fruit, something he himself was delighted at. Prichard estimated that by the end of the year he would have had over one-third of the BEF's snipers through his course, with the consequence that his theories on sniping would be disseminated to thousands of others. It was not to last, though, for in late July of 1916 Prichard was ordered to leave XI Corps, as his work with them was now self-supporting through the use of officers and NCOs who had undertaken the course and were themselves capable of teaching snipers.

The news was not all bad, though, for he was instructed to proceed to First Army HQ and find a suitable place in which to establish a new sniping school for them. This was to be a small village called Linghem, near the town of Aire, usefully sited at the foot of a large plateau, which enabled a range of 1,000 yards to be established – the first of its type in France. It was a remote and rather barren place, Lieutenant Grey dryly describing it as 'trying to be Scotland'. Hesketh-Prichard took over the village Mairie (Town Hall) and set up workshops there with an initial staff of six NCOs. Army Service Corps personnel were seconded to him, to provide labour for making butts, backstop and trenches. Not being 'establishment' meant that the little group were, effectively, nobody's children, unable to apply for additional stores, equipment or personnel, so naturally there was no accommodation provided and no workshops. All they had – targets, rifles, optical equipment and personal kit – was carried with them by lorry. Fortuitously, en route, they saw a prefabricated Armstrong hut, fool-ishly left empty by its occupants, and the men quickly dismantled it and loaded it into the lorry. Upon arrival at Linghem it became their first permanent structure.

Alas, Grey, along with his division, was almost at once transferred to the Somme front, thus his expertise was lost to the school. Despite this blow, work continued apace, and Grey was replaced by the talented and hard-working Second Lieutenant J. Underhill of the King's Shropshire Light Infantry.

The school was finally given official sanction and placed on establishment, with Captain Kendall of the Royal Warwickshire Regiment joining as intelligence officer, and a Canadian, Lieutenant W.B. Curtis, as scouting officer, aided by Major Betts of the Army Physical Training School. Their work was constantly interrupted by visits from senior officers, curious to know exactly what was going on, and it exasperated all concerned:

> In two months I have had three ACs (Army Commanders) visits of inspections and four Corps Commanders, and perhaps fifty COs and staff.[171]

Salonika – The Forgotten Campaign

Since they departed from Gallipoli the Lovat Scouts had not been idle, having been sent to Salonika, to fight in the little-known war against the Turkish and Bulgar Armies. The front extended 200 miles from Albania, south-east along the Struma valley of Bulgaria, where it eventually stopped at an inlet of the Aegean Sea, the Gulf of Redina. It was this southernmost sector that was held by British troops and it was as static as the Western Front, neither side having the manpower to wrest victory from the other. The terrain was appalling, consisting of mosquito-infested marshes, heavy scrub that was all but impenetrable, and large tracts of open farmland with no cover. The summers were blistering and the winters freezing, with rain and snow making the ground impassable at times. It was, in many respects, Gallipoli writ large all over again, and the fighting was much the same, with limited objective attacks being made, usually without results, except, perhaps, to add forty or fifty men to the casualty list. However, evacuation due to sickness was far more likely than being wounded. Private Harvey recalled that:

> The conditions were awful and the mosquitoes were terrible, you couldn't get away from them. We hated them far more

than Johnny Turks and they caused far more casualties too I reckon.[172]

It was also a sniper's paradise and amazingly, some telescopic sighted rifles did find their way to the Salonika front by the summer of 1916. The Lovats had soon begun using their telescopes and rifles to good effect. Although not a sniper, Private Harvey also had some pertinent comments relating to the British use of snipers:

> They [Turkish snipers] were deadly, you only had to forget and stick your head up too high and crack, you had a bullet through it. We lost a lot of men and often the Turks' lines were so far away we couldn't tell where they were firing from [. . .] we had our own snipers I know because sometimes we were warned they were out in front and they had to give a password before we could let them back. I wouldn't have done that for all the tea in China.[173]

While there is no evidence of the Turkish using scope-equipped rifles at this period, there is the possibility that some German-built rifles could have found their way there, particularly in the wake of Harvey's comments that the Turks were shooting at extreme ranges. Certainly, the British (and Lovats) ability to use their rifles for sniping was put to considerable test, and the scopes enabled them to fire from ranges beyond which the Turks were easily capable of retaliating. Private Huxford, of the Royal Berkshire Regiment, who saw service in Salonika, had been through the Northern Command Sniping School at Rugeley prior to being sent to Salonika:

> I went on a sniping course, I think it was two weeks, up in Staffordshire and got back just in time to be sent to Salonika. I had no idea where that was, someone said it was Greece but it seemed a blooming sight better than the Somme or Ypres. We didn't mind [. . .] it was Greece as it turned out and the Turks there were all Gallipoli veterans, and a bloody tough bunch they were too. We worked in pairs and had big observers' telescopes and telescope sighted rifles. It wasn't

easy as Johnny [Turk] was very experienced, particularly in camouflage and we had a lot of casualties, but we set up sniping posts on the hillsides. A lot of our shooting was done at longer ranges than later in the war, sometimes five or six hundred yards and it was very difficult to know if we had really hit someone. We spent a lot of time just watching them [. . .] soon they couldn't move a muscle without one of the sniping section reporting it.[174]

Like Gallipoli, the Salonika campaign was to prove costly and largely inconclusive, and while it was regarded as a sideshow compared to events in France, it proved useful in enabling a significant number of British snipers to obtain experience without the level of risk faced by their comrades in France and Flanders. This was to become exceedingly useful when units were returned to France or Flanders later in the war, and one of those were the Lovat Scouts.

The Lovats in France

Some Lovats who had served in Salonika or the Middle East had been returned home (due to wounds or illness) and been sent to the 3rd Reserve Regiment in August 1916, ostensibly to form a new force called the 'Lovat Scouts, Sharpshooters'. The original intention was that they be fielded as snipers, but in practice this was never to happen, as a result of a casual visit to the First Army School at Linghem by Simon Joseph, the 16th Lord Lovat, in the autumn of 1916. This visit was to change the game-plan quite drastically, for he had been greatly impressed by the work being undertaken there. Moreover, he listened with interest to Prichard's plea for help in training his men in the use of the observation telescope.

This vital tool had long been issued to artillery observers and signallers, and was quickly approbated by the snipers. There were by this time three primary types in use: the Scout Regiment Telescope, Mks I and II (a 22 x three-draw brass-bodied telescope); the General Service or Signallers' Telescope (in 20 x used by signallers and artillery observers); and the Canadian Ross (also a 20 x, three-draw instrument, which was issued for general observation use). All weighed in the region of 2 pounds (1kg) and were leather covered, with a sliding sunshade to prevent glare giving away the position of the observer.

The major problem with them was that they were difficult to learn to use properly, and Prichard needed help in finding more experienced glassmen. Salvation was at hand in the guise of the new Lovat Sharpshooters, which had been formed by October of that year. The unit consisted of ten platoons, comprising one officer and twenty-one NCOs and other ranks. Alas, the 200 available men were clearly insufficient to provide an effective sniping force. Lord Lovat appreciated very quickly that attempting to train his men to become snipers was ignoring their primary ability – that of highly skilled stalkers and observers. He discussed the problem with Hesketh-Prichard during his visit to Linghem and changed the focus of training so that Lovats would become instructors, observers and 'glassmen', rather than snipers. Moreover, they would be seconded to the sniping schools that were being established, although both men agreed that far more men were needed. As a result, an unusual advertisement was placed in the Scottish highland newspapers. It read:

> **Wanted – 100 Stalkers and Glassmen**
> Between the ages of 41 and 45
> For stalking – Bosches!
> Apply Colonel Macdonald of Blarour, Spean Bridge.

Highland regiments were also combed for ex-Ghillies and stalkers, and the first Lovat attached to the 1st SOS was Corporal Donald Cameron, sent personally by Lord Lovat. On arrival, he was asked how old he was. 'Officially forty-one' was the quick reply, although it was reckoned he was nearer sixty. His observation skills were to prove phenomenal. Hesketh-Prichard recalled asking him what the nationality of some soldiers were that had been observing through a telescope some 6,000 yards away. All Prichard could determine was that they wore blue uniforms, but peering through his own telescope, Cameron replied: 'they must be either Portuguese or French [. . .] and as they are wearing British helmets they must be Portuguese.' [175]

It was generally accepted that a Lovat Scout could observe troop movements in detail at distances of 10 miles in clear weather and report on activity at distances of up to 15 miles. The first of the Lovat groups arrived in France in November 1916. Hesketh-Prichard was delighted, as he wrote:

> Since 1916 [. . .] nine Groups, each about twenty strong and each under an officer, were attached to certain Army Corps. Every man [. . .] was a picked stalker and glassman and they were used largely for observation [. . .] Keener men never lived, nor more dependable. For long distance work and the higher art of observation, the Germans had nothing to touch our Lovat Scouts. It sounds a bold statement to make, but the Lovat Scouts never let one down. If they reported a thing, the thing was as they reported it.[176]

The employment of Lovat Scouts had further introduced into the world of sniping arguably the most important article of camouflage ever adopted, the Ghillie suit. Named after the Scottish Ghillies, who stalked the moors, and carried by the Lovat instructors, the suit was a loose robe or poncho (no two were the same) of dark-coloured material. Sewn onto it were lengths of green, brown or black cloth, as well as loops, into which local flora could be tucked, suitably blurring the outline of the human body. It had a hood that could be pulled up to cover the forehead, and properly used could make a man invisible to a skilled observer at 10 yards. Hesketh-Prichard recounted how he had fun with a cynical officer who was visiting the sniper school and whom he asked to spot a sniper:

> Had a fellow up here who was rather 'Ha Ha!' over backgrounds and hiding of men. Put out a man he was to look for, and he went walking up and down the parapet of sandbags looking [. . .] as he did so parapet put out its hand and pulled his leg! You see, the man had been provided with a suit of sandbags, and was sitting against the parapet. One up, I think![177]

Sniping School Curriculum

Using experience gleaned from teaching in the trenches, at Béthune and at Linghem (and also the schools formed by others), Hesketh-Prichard and his instructors quickly worked up a curriculum they believed covered everything necessary for the effective training of a sniper. The course lasted seventeen days and was so comprehensive that, in its basic form, it was to remain the foundation for most subsequent sniper training taught throughout the world.

Prichard felt that sniping, in its most basic form, consisted of three main elements:

1.   Finding your mark

2.   Defining your mark

3.   Hitting your mark.

He further sought, once and for all, to define the role of a sniper, which he felt had never satisfactorily been done before. Snipers, most commanding officers believed, were there to deal with troublesome Germans, but very early on Prichard realised that the value of a sniper was not simply in what he could shoot, but what he could see. In the small training pamphlet written in 1916 for instructors at the First Army School, he had spelt out the duties he believed a sniper should be employed for. These were:

1.   To dominate the enemy snipers, thereby saving the lives of British soldiers and causing casualties to the enemy.

2.   To hit a small mark at an unknown range, but without the advantage of a sighting shot.

3.   To keep the enemy's line under continual observation and to assist the Intelligence of his unit by accurate and correct reports with map references.

4.   To build and keep in repair his loopholes and major and minor sniping posts.

The curriculum was therefore based around these requirements, but was expanded to cover the necessary skills needed to enable snipers to act as observers and intelligence gatherers. The syllabus was as follows:[178]

Day 1

AM. General lecture on the objects of the course and discipline. Examination of all rifles brought by students. (Many were seriously defective.)

PM. Lecture: The care of arms, shooting to obtain groups, and observation on a German trench.

Day 2

AM. Lecture: The stalking telescope. Repetition of grouping practice at 200–300 yards. Observation of bullet strikes on target.

PM. Practical observation on German trenches and in open country.

Day 3

AM. Lecture: The Enfield P1914 rifle. Judging distance up to 600 yards. Snapshooting at 100–200 yards, 4 seconds exposure. Application at 200 yards. Shooting positions.

PM. Map-reading and long-distance observation with reports.

Day 4

AM. Lecture on map-reading. Shooting at 400–500 yards and shooting at unknown ranges, up to 400 yards.

PM. Use of ground and cover. Selecting and constructing hasty observation posts for open warfare. Selection of cover from view rather than cover from fire.

Day 5

> AM.   Lecture on patrolling and scouting. Shooting at 300 yards, snapshooting at 100 and 200 yards, 3 seconds exposure.

> PM.   Demonstration of camouflage and its uses. Snipers are given an area in which to disguise themselves using local material. Observers will watch while snipers fire blanks at them from their concealed positions. Observers will locate and provide map references for snipers they see.

Day 6

> AM.   Lecture: Elevation and windage, spotting enemy snipers. Snapshooting and movement. Students to advance unseen from 500 to 100 yards. Targets to be hit are enemy heads appearing at intervals in the butts.

> PM.   Building and use of night firing boxes. Observation of enemy trenches, the appearance of which is altered by moving materials around.

Day 7

> *Sunday.*   Open range for voluntary shooting under an instructor. (Students could choose to have a day off. In practice almost all used the day to improve their shooting skills.)

Day 8

> AM.   Lecture: The construction of forward and sniping posts. Patrolling using night goggles. Use of cover and keeping in touch. Shooting practice at unknown ranges.

> PM.   Marching using compass bearings with and without box respirator.

Day 9

AM. Lecture: The use of telescopic sighted rifles. Practice on the zeroing of same.

PM. Continue practice on zeroing of telescopic rifles. Long-distance observation.

Day 10

AM. Lecture: Duties of scouts, observers and snipers in attack and defence. Grouping at 100 yards with telescope sighted rifles. Practice in scouting in open country and reporting.

PM. Practical in securing woods and open country using scouts and snipers.

Day 11

AM. Lecture: Front-line observation and reporting. Shooting at 200 yards with telescopic sighted rifles. Snapshooting at 100–200 yards, 3 seconds exposure.

PM. Directional march. Students will be put into four platoons and given map co-ordinates at which they must concentrate at a given time. Gas alarms will be given and box respirators worn.

Day 12

AM. Lecture: Duties of a Battalion Intelligence officer. Shooting at 300–400 yards. German trench observation.

PM. Demonstration of the use of scouts and snipers as a protective screen for the infantry in open warfare.

Day 13

> AM.   Lecture: Understanding aeroplane photos, with lantern
>   slides. Practical study of aeroplane photos on the actual
>   ground depicted on the photographs.
>
> PM.   Examinations in long-distance and front-line observation.

Day 14

> Open range day.

Days 15 and 16

> Examination of students' notebooks, oral and written examinations,
> shooting proficiency competition.

Day 17

> End of course, passing out and award of certificates.

This syllabus is interesting for several reasons, for it contains almost
none of the drill and discipline of the earlier course at the Northern
Command in England. Men who attended these SOS courses were
already experienced and did not require their duties as soldiers to be
laboured upon:

> It was refreshing to be treated like a human being, not just a
> uniform. Many of my fellow students were educated men and
> I suppose some could have been officers if they had wanted.
> The instructors treated us with respect and a lot of patience
> and no one I can recall abused that. The course was hard work
> but we all enjoyed it and no one wanted to flunk it.[179]

Hesketh-Prichard, Crum, Armstrong, and other school commanders
realised that the men attending the classes were often worn-out from

previous service, many never having had leave since their arrival in France:

> I soon found the officers and men [. . .] were in need of a mental change, and this we attempted by giving long hours to games.[180]

So all sniping schools adopted an enthusiastic regime of games for the men – football and cricket being the most popular (the First Army School had three ex-Football Association players on its staff and they were encouraged to raise teams). But early forms of close-combat, such as ju-jitsu, were also taught, as much to help the men work off tension as for their own protection, and it seemed to work well.

Use of Snipers

While it was all very well training the men to be snipers, there existed some great challenges in effectively utilising their skills. Officially – and perhaps indicating exactly what Army Command thought of the importance of sniping in general – the strength of a battalion sniping section was fixed at a mere eight men, plus an officer, sergeant and corporal in charge. The Second Lieutenant commanding was originally dubbed the 'Sniping Officer', but later became the 'Intelligence Officer', as it became more vital for the officer to correctly interpret the men's observations and send clear reports to Brigade Intelligence HQ. In practice, the number of men selected for sniping would vary greatly, depending on the attitude of the lieutenant colonel commanding the battalion:

> When we got back from the [sniping] course, we were told we were on fatigues and we worked like bloody navvies for the next week carrying wire and all sorts up to the lines at night. We got back and were put straight on stand-to in the mornings but we were also supposed to occupy our sniping posts during the day. It wasn't possible, and it came to a head when our Major found two snipers asleep in their post [. . .] they were put on charges but Lieutenant Gibbs, our sniping officer stuck

up for us and told the divisional Commander about all the work that we had to do. There was a real hue and cry about it and our Colonel got a rocket about misuse of trained men. We were left alone after that, but until the Colonel left the battalion, we were always out of favour.[181]

Fortunately, there were a great many senior officers very keen on the effective use of snipers and they often trebled or quadrupled their official allocation. The make-up of sniper sections was rarely recorded, but the war diary of the 1st Civil Service Rifles (the 15th London Regiment) contains a breakdown of the men selected, noting that, in June 1916, the sniping section was:

> 30 strong, being 3 per cent of the strength [of the battalion] drawn evenly from the battalion. Three men including the Sergeant Instructor were pre-war regulars, the rest post-1914.

Interestingly, the report goes on to give a breakdown of the men employed:

> Average age was twenty-two years, eight men were married. Half were Civil Servants, the rest clerks, merchants, commercial travellers, engineers, a tailor's cutter, gardener, waiter and student. By 1918 50 per cent were still employed [as snipers]; of the rest, five were dead, eleven wounded.[182]

According to Crum, a sniping establishment should comprise at least sixteen men plus officer, sergeant and corporal. But he added:

> On the other hand, twenty-four or even more might be required. A list of suitable spare men should be kept by the Sniping sergeant and arrangements made to train them as occasion arises. These men may be used as company snipers.[183]

The numbers of snipers employed would also vary greatly from unit to unit, depending on the serving strength of the battalion at the time.

Although most battalions were nominally made up of 1,000 officers and men, in the line this was often reduced to 700 or less, and after combat could be as low as 200–300: so the numbers of men available could vary widely, depending on circumstances.

The battalion sniper was free to move anywhere along the regimental front, working wherever he believed best, or at the specific request of a company or platoon officer, who might be experiencing problems in his sector. However, when more open warfare began in 1917 this changed, as snipers began working with the advancing fire platoons, dealing with enemy resistance as necessary. From late 1915 the increasing acceptance that the sniper was part of the regular establishment of a front-line battalion was to have a profound effect on the German sniper's dominance of No Man's Land. In areas where British snipers were actively working the level of British casualties began to drop dramatically, and some indication of the effect this had can be gleaned from a letter sent to Hesketh-Prichard by an officer in the 70th Infantry Brigade in February 1916: 'We have only been in the line eight days and have got more Germans (certainties) than in the month before we came out.'[184] In places, the Germans were so stunned at the retribution being reaped upon them, that they all but ceased sniping:

> On the Somme, we had no problems with British sniping until perhaps May of 1916 when we were faced by a new regiment of Welshmen [probably the Royal Welsh Fusiliers] who had some very excellent shots. We began to suffer very greatly from their shooting and it was here I was wounded by a bullet that went through my cap as I was looking through my binoculars. It was good for me though for I was in hospital through the Somme battles of July and August so I was also very lucky I think.[185] [German soldiers on the Somme were not issued with steel helmets until late July of 1916.]

In some places, the level of German sniping dropped to the comical. When a Scottish sniper was seen walking down the trench with a brace of pheasants in each hand, he was challenged as to where they had come from. He explained he had been in No Man's Land stalking, but there was no danger, as the Germans dare not show themselves in daylight any more.

The Royal Engineers and the Special Works Park

While the use of camouflage was pioneered by the French it was rapidly embraced by Britain through the war. Much of the developmental work on new types of camouflage was due to the formation of the Royal Engineers' Special Works Park, although its work in assisting the various schools of sniping has largely gone unmentioned. The raising of this unit was initially due to the requirement, early in the war, to provide some method of camouflage for artillery units, particularly from the prying eyes of German reconnaissance aircraft.

A British portrait painter named Solomon J. Solomon[186] had, for some time, been interested in the art of visual deception and had begun experimenting with primitive camouflage prior to the outbreak of war. He had contacted the War Office in mid-1914 with an idea for using painted cloth hung on poles to screen roads and trenches from observation, but with typical official sloth, the War Office did nothing for almost another year. Eventually, Solomon was asked (one suspects rather reluctantly) to become the technical adviser to a new Royal Engineers section dedicated to camouflage, with a Regular Army Engineer, Captain F. Wyatt, as its commander. Based in Wimereux, where all metal items (such as sniper plates) were produced, they also had workshops at Amiens, and, fortunately for the 1st SOS, at Aire. Working in close co-operation with the French Sections de Camouflage, the initial brief was to provide cover for artillery in the form of netting, but Solomon's idea of painted screens stretched alongside the roads was soon adopted and they became a familiar sight along the Western Front. Painted cloth (either of muslin, burlap or hessian) was produced, as well as a close-woven netting covered with knots of green and brown cloth, now commonly known as 'scrim'. These were widely used to cover artillery, ammunition or ration dumps, and as a by-product, proved of considerable practical benefit to snipers.

The trainee snipers were expected to make their own Ghillie suits, but the 1st SOS often profited from its close association with the

Royal Engineers in having acquired lengths of pre-painted material that could be quickly cut up, the men then sewing on the loops of cloth into which they could put foliage. Not all had the use of such a handy supply though, and Major Crum, commanding the 43rd Brigade School at Acq, taught his men to improvise and make their own Ghillie suits using whatever was to hand:

> Muslin, wire gauze, coats, gloves, veils, bandages for rifles, periscopes etc. [. . .] masks [. . .] may be useful. An ordinary sandbag over the head, with the strands pulled apart [. . .] for the eyes is often the simplest and best disguise.[187]

However, the inventiveness of the Special Works sections did not end with simple camouflage, for the civilian experience of many engineers with theatrical stage sets, gave them the ability to produce uncannily realistic backdrops, and Crum mentions that, when sniping from buildings, his men were supplied with face masks painted to look like foliage, brick or stone. For the three tiny Special Works workshops – staffed by only twenty or so men – the increasing demand for material proved impossible to meet, so a radical approach was taken. Against all official advice, Wyatt employed some 400 French female workers and this vastly increased output, freeing up the Engineers to manufacture the more complex items required.

For the sniper schools and front-line snipers the most immediate result was undoubtedly the rapid increase in the number and quality of sniper plates being produced. While a standard pattern was produced, there were also several special types custom-made for specific locations. Around this period there appeared a double-plate shield, as German use of armour-piercing bullets was becoming far more prevalent, but their weight made them impractical, except in particularly exposed sections of the line. More useful was a design thought up by the Engineers, consisting of a loophole plate that had chicken wire attached to its outer surface. This enabled almost anything to be attached to it, from foliage to plaster or pieces of sandbag, and they proved very effective indeed.

The demand for dummy heads continued to expand for training purposes and also for drawing fire from hidden enemy snipers. They became very realistic indeed and some even had burning cigarettes placed in their mouths.

By early 1917 the Special Works Park had even printed a small catalogue of items it offered as standard trench equipment. This list was naturally regarded as top secret and it was forbidden to take it into the front line, as the consequences of it falling into enemy hands were considered too dire to contemplate. Neither did the Royal Engineers limit themselves to smaller items, for they produced a very realistic man-portable farm building for use by the sniping school at Acq!

By the end of the war camouflage was accepted as a vital part of military culture and its use materially aided the war effort, and the pioneering work done by the engineers of the SWP was to lay the foundations for much of the specialist camouflage produced during World War II.

Chapter Seven

The Commonwealth Snipers

From the outset of the war, the Commonwealth countries had been champing at the bit to help Britain fight the Germans. To the majority of Canadians, Australians, New Zealanders, South Africans and ex-patriots living in South America and the United States, Britain was still their Mother Country. Many of those young men living abroad were first generation emigrants, who had left Britain looking for a better life during the preceding decade, and who still had close ties with families and friends who were suffering as a result of the war. Some had simply gone looking for adventure, and the prospect of being several thousand miles away when there was a war in Europe was too much to bear, so they undertook long and arduous journeys in order to enlist.

Canadian Sniping

The Canadians were the first Commonwealth troops to see action, having arrived in France in December 1914. Many suffered badly in the first gas attack of April of 1915, and others took part in the disastrous Battle of Loos in September. A large proportion of these men were already inured to an outdoors life, for Canada was a vast untapped wilderness, and many were, as Fremantle recorded, the 'trappers, lumberjacks, hunters and poachers' that the sniping schools desperately needed. They provided the perfect raw material, and unlike their British counterparts, the Canadian Army commanders saw the need for training and fielding their own snipers as quickly as possible.

Foremost in the pursuit of this goal were Princess Patricia's Light Infantry, whose ranks contained such an abnormally large proportion of British ex-soldiers that Kitchener once dryly remarked that the Princess Pat's was clearly where all his old soldiers had gone. Other units were soon raised, men flocking to remote towns to sign up for the duration, and many were of interesting racial backgrounds. A large number were of Scottish parentage, but a significant number were Native Indians who also heeded the call, although not necessarily for reasons of jingoistic loyalty. Men from the Algonkin, Cree, Ojibwe and Metis tribes enlisted, bringing with them their unique tracking and hunting skills. One Ojibwe trapper and future sniper, Bill Semice (who was unable to speak any language other than his native tongue), walked the 500 miles to his recruiting office and refused to let the fact that no one could understand a single word he said deter him from joining up. Alongside these recruits were many French Canadians, among whom were trappers whose lineage extended back to the Anglo-French-Indian wars of the eighteenth century. There was also a polyglot mix of other nationalities, including many Americans, who crossed the border in order to enlist in the Canadian Army.

On arrival at the Canadian Training Establishment at Shorncliffe in Kent, all troops were given musketry training under the very competent command of the senior musketry officer, Captain Peter Anderson. This officer was a pre-war militia volunteer and competitive shooter who, having managed to escape from German captivity in October 1915, had returned to England, where he was placed in charge of the newly established Divisional Sniping Instruction wing at Shorncliffe. He later helped form the 3rd Canadian Expeditionary Force's first School of Sniping and Scouting at La Clytte. Major Neville Armstrong, although British by birth, had emigrated to Canada pre-war as a mining engineer, but became a professional guide and hunter. His subsequent transfer to the Canadian Expeditionary Force was of considerable significance to the future of their sniper training, as he was later appointed Chief Reconnaissance Instructor to the Canadian Army. With the assistance of his instructors the instructional pamphlet he had written for the use of the NCOs at the School of Instruction in late 1915[188] was to be gradually expanded to become the basic training manual for use of all CEF scouts and snipers. Some of his instructors, such as Capt. F.I. Ford of the 1st Leicestershire Regiment, had already passed through Hesketh-Prichard's hands at the First Army School of Sniping before being attached to the CEF. Quite reasonably, they made much use of training and information already gleaned from the British Schools, but the tone and format of the Canadian work was slightly different to the British. This was doubtless due, in no small part, to dealing with Canadian snipers, whose individual natures and independence of spirit ensured they had a rather looser concept of regulation and discipline than their British counterparts.

The Canadians regarded the eight-per-battalion number for snipers merely as a guideline and most battalions contained considerably more. It was also recommended that Canadian snipers were used in groups of three, unlike the pairing of the British. Armstrong remarked that the reason was to prevent fatigue, as it was felt, with some truth, that it was unnecessarily tiring for two men to spend all day observing and two observers were better than one. Consequently, as Armstrong noted: '"A" was the firer, "B" the spotter and "C" the odd-man used for helping "B".'[189] However, while admirable in theory, it was seldom possible in practice. For, as with their British counterparts, Canadian snipers were relieved of all trench duties and it was believed that, like the Germans, every sniper should be free to roam along their entire Battalion frontage.

Some of the Canadian sniping instruction material is worth reproducing, as it differs somewhat in methodology and contains some sage advice. The purpose of a sniper, the Canadians believed, was fourfold:

> To shake the enemy's morale
> To cause him casualties
> To stop him working
> To retaliate against his snipers.

The syllabus was also different in content to that of the British, being fourteen days long and limited to forty officers and men, split equally. Officer students were given a different course reflecting the increasing importance with which scouting and sniping was regarded in terms of intelligence gathering: 'with a view to them becoming Battalion or Brigade Intelligence Officers'. This comprised eight modules:

Duties of a battalion and Brigade Intelligence officer.

Map-reading, enlarging maps, filling in maps, making plans of trenches, making range charts.

Study of aeroplane photographs.

Reports, general, artillery, identification and patrol.

Indirect fire.

Siting of Ops.

Training observers and snipers.

Adjustment of telescopic sights and special musketry training for snipers.

For the other ranks the syllabus was listed in order of importance:

Practice in scouting and patrolling by night and day.

Demonstration in using cover.

The use of a prismatic compass with practice in marching on a bearing by day and night.

Practice on construction of OPs and snipers' posts at night.

Practice in observation in the open and in trenches, with reports.

Musketry. Examination of rifles and sights for defects. Practice in adjusting sights; group test; application at ranges from 30 to 500 yards; snap shooting; shooting at unknown ranges.

Practice with sniper scopes and fixed rifle rests.

In addition lectures were given on:

Scouting and patrolling.

Duties of snipers in attack and in defence.

Front-line intelligence.

Use and care of telescopic sights.

Causes of inaccurate shooting.

History of sniping in warfare.

The course lacked no shortage of volunteers, one of the earliest being Herbert McBride, a champion Camp Perry shot (the American equivalent of Bisley), whose commanding officer was, rather fortuitously, Colonel G.B. Hughes, himself a keen exponent of sniping and later to become the commander of the 2nd Canadian Infantry Division. In November 1915 McBride went on a training course with another neophyte sniper, George Paudash, who was to become one of the highest-scoring snipers of the war:

> If any of us felt any particular emotion on that day when we first went into the line, it was very successfully concealed under the usual grousing and joshing. 'Bet I get the first shot,' was George Paudash's last word to me. 'Like hell you will,' says I.[190]

There was considerable keenness on the part of the Canadians in using their snipers as quickly and aggressively as possible, and the Army began to supply Ross sniping rifles to the front-line snipers from autumn 1915. But, as with the British Army, a shortage of suitably scoped rifles initially proved a problem and instructions were issued that:

> These rifles when received will be handed over to the two battalions in the trenches [seven to each battalion]. They will not be taken out of the trenches, but will be handed over on relief to the incoming battalion as trench stores.

This was a poor method of guaranteeing that proper care be given to the weapons and few snipers liked the idea of handing their rifle to another man, regardless of how competent he was. McBride ensured he retained his own Ross rifle throughout his front-line tour, but the situation gradually improved as more weapons became available. The 'Rosses' were often supplemented by scoped SMLEs, a report to the officer commanding the Canadian 31st Battalion on 4 September 1915 noting that:

> One Lee-Enfield Telescopic rifle will be delivered to you today and it is expected that thirteen Ross telescopic rifles will be issued shortly, making fourteen per brigade. It is suggested that you place these in proper use as soon as possible, arranging that the selection of firing points is properly

supervised. Telescopic rifles should always be in action. That is, the rifle should not go into reserve, but should be operated by a pair.[191]

While the number of Warner/Rosses is well documented, there were also issued somewhere between 75 and 100 Rosses equipped with Winchester A5 scopes and an unrecorded number of SMLEs, mostly fitted with PP or Aldis scopes.

As men were selected for sniping school on the basis of past hunting and stalking experience, and not simply because of their ability with a rifle, there was little doubt the Canadians would prove more than a match for their opponents. Many of the snipers had a great deal of expertise hunting dangerous game in the Canadian forests and they soon began to rack up large scores against the Germans. Probably the most successful was Francis Peghamagabow,[192] an Ojibwa from the Parry Island tribe,[193] where he had worked as a fireman for the Department of Marine and Fisheries. Known to his comrades as 'Peggy', he was one of the first snipers to go into action in March 1915 with the 23rd Northern Regiment, and he quickly built up his kills during the Second Battle of Ypres in April/May 1915. He was to be awarded the Military Medal no less than three times: at Ypres in 1916, Passchendaele in 1917, and during the Battle of Amiens in 1918. His confirmed score was 378 and he was responsible for the capture of no less than 300 German soldiers.

Researching the personal lives of these men is usually difficult – particularly as few talked or wrote of what they had done subsequently – but occasionally, more than the bare military details survive, as in the case of a colourful character called Henry Louis North West Wind (also referred to as 'Norwest', 'North West', and 'North-West Wind' in contemporary sources). He was a Metis or French-Cree from Saskatchewan, a tough, silent man with dark leathered face and black, piercing eyes, which observers commented appeared to bore straight through one. He had started his working life on a farm and had been a cowboy and occasional rodeo performer, where he was noted for his skills as a trick-roper. He initially enlisted as Henry Louis, stating his occupation was 'cow puncher', but his fondness for hard liquor led to his being discharged from the Army for drunkenness, although he

An observation section of the Lovat Scouts, with a couple of men of the Fife and Forfar Yeomanry also in the ranks. Two big scout regiment observation telescopes on their tripod mounts are visible in the foreground. *(Pete Smith collection)*

A rare picture of an Italian sniper with a scope mounted Carcano rifle. The scope could be a French A.PX model. *(Col. G. Mele photo)*

Sniper's lair. A British front-line sniper post with the sniper observing, albeit rather casually, indicating that there may not perhaps be much enemy sniper activity. *(Taylor Library)*

'III (3) HUNS' reads the tally in cartridges. The timing of this photo is exact, 3 June 1915 and the scratched initials on the trench read 'QWRR CPB' possibly the Queen's Westminster Rifle Regiment and the snipers initials? The rifle is an SMLE with Purdey mounted PP Scope. *(Taylor Library)*

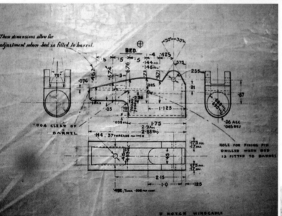

A rare drawing showing the manufacturing dimensions for Rigby mounts for the SMLE rifle. *(Royal Armouries Leeds/Simon Deakin photo)*

Austrian snipers using a rare carbine variant of the M1895 Mannlicher rifle. It might be a commercial rifle pressed into service, but it would nevertheless have been quite useful for sniping at moderate ranges. *(Simon Deakin photo)*

American snipers undergoing training with a British officer of the King's Royal rifles. They have made their own sniper hoods and one wears a partial Ghillie suit. *(US Army photo)*

US Army snipers in full Ghillie suits advance across typical chalk Somme terrain. Their Springfield M1903 rifles are wrapped in Hessian and camouflage painted, but the scopes have been dismounted, probably to prevent damage while training. *(US Army photo)*

November 1918, the first US Marines snipers to graduate from the training school at Quantico, alas just too late for combat. The officer at extreme left is Captain M.M. Marsden, a Canadian instructor seconded from the 1st Canadian Army. *(US Marine Corps photo)*

SNIPER & TRENCH O.Ps.

Order by Numbers only from <u>Special Works Park R.E.</u>

SECRET. SNIPER & TRENCH O.Ps. Order by Numbers only from – Special Works Park <u>R.E.</u>

No.1	No.2	No 6	No 8
CONCEALED PLATE	FITZGERALD PLATE	PARAPET COVER – SNIPERS POST.	DUMMY STRETCHER BAG. Direct View.

No.3	No.4	No 9	No 10
HEADER LOOPHOLE	LOOPHOLE LID (treated with Grass, Earth, Etc)	DUMMY HEADER BAG. Direct View.	SNIPERS HOOD

No.5	No.7	No 11	No 12
(Side Section)			

Some of the sniper OP camouflage offered by the Royal Engineers' Special Works Department. Taken from a Canadian 1st Army instructional pamphlet dated March 1917.

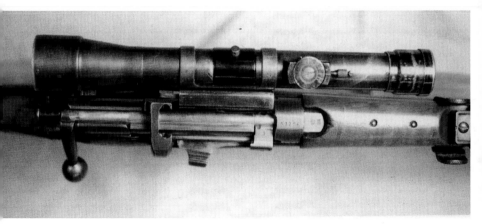

An SMLE with PP scope and mounts. Although not as offset as the Ross/Warner combination, it was still awkward to use in conjunction with a loophole plate. (*Author's collection*)

Two of the most common forms of Gew 98 bases, offset and partially offset. The mounts were curved to counteract this, and to ensure the scope remained in line with the barrel of the rifle. (*Geoff Sturgess collection*)

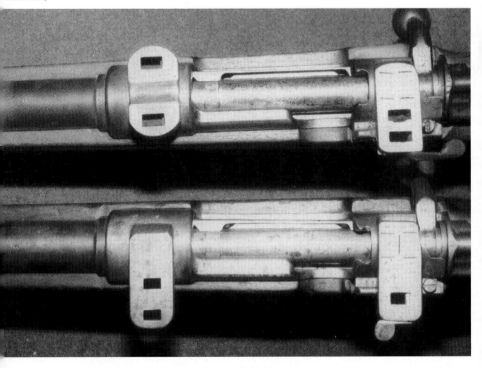

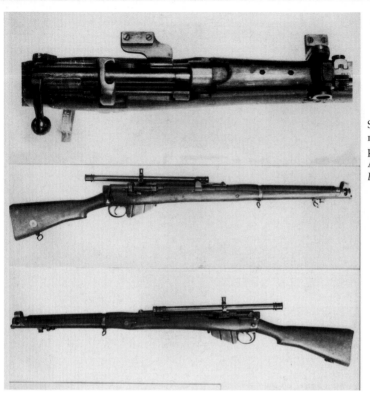

SMLE with Whitehead mounts and the popular Winchester A5 scope. *(Simon Deakin photo)*

An SMLE with the ugly but functional Evans mount and base. *(Pattern Room collection/Simon Deakin photo)*

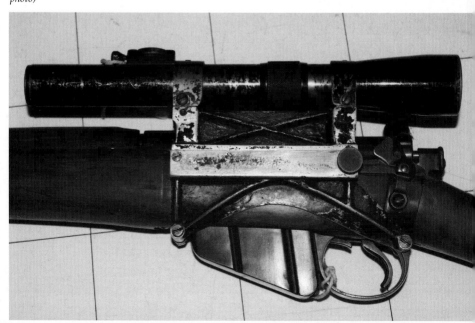

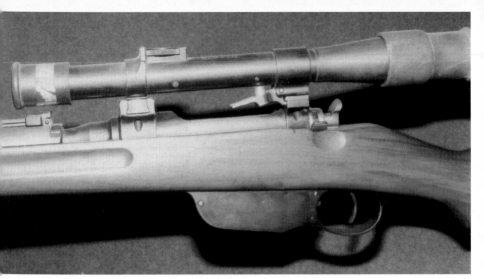

The Austrian Mannlicher M1895 with Kahles scope. The distinctive and rather vulnerable locking latch is clearly visible forward of the rear mount. *(Geoff Sturgess collection)*

During the retreat of 1918, a German machine-gunner with light Maxim 08/15 works in conjunction with a sniper, who is using his scope to observe. The soldier at left is wearing the heavy body armour issued from spring 1917. *(Private collection)*

The sniper sniped. This German sniper caused much disruption at the crossroads near Bray in August 1918 but was subsequently shot through the neck by an Australian marksman. *(Australian War Memorial)*

A typical British observation post with camouflaged box periscope. Snipers would sit and observe the enemy lines for hours, frequently not firing a shot. Unusual levels of activity would be noted and times and locations relating to map references carefully recorded. *(Taylor Library)*

The Pattern 1914 sniping rifle with Aldis scope and carry case. Probably the best sniping rifle to emerge from the war, it would see considerable use during World War II. *(Simon Deakin photo)*

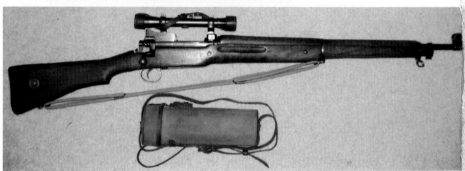

Ninety years on, this relic Mauser Gew 98 sniping rifle was found in a quarry near Miramont on the Somme, still in the possession of its original owner. Although the sniper could not be identified his ID disc showed he was from the 185th Infantry Regiment and it is believed he was killed by shellfire on Nov. 16th 1916. New woodwork has replaced the rotted original. *(Photo Mme. Pique/Jean Verdel)*

quickly re-enlisted under the name Henry Norwest in the 50th Canadian Infantry Battalion. He arrived in France in 1916, where his swarthy good looks attracted many girls, and he explained to his friends that on several occasions, as a married man, he had to duck out of their clutches – almost inevitably he was soon christened 'Ducky'. He was quickly singled out for sniper training and took to his task with a near obsessive dedication:

> Our famous sniper no doubt understood better than most of us the cost of life and the price of death. Henry Norwest carried out his terrible duty superbly because he believed his special status gave him no choice but to fulfil his indispensable mission. Our [. . .] sniper went about his work with passionate dedication and showed complete detachment from everything while he was in the line.[194]

He mostly worked with an observer named Oliver Payne, to whom he once confided that he knew he would not see the end of the war, as he believed that he would be shot through the head. Norwest's skills as a scout meant he would often work behind enemy lines – a very dangerous occupation indeed – but his cool daring soon led to his being awarded the MM and Bar. In early March 1917 he arrived at Hesketh-Prichard's First Army SOS, an event notable enough for Prichard to comment on:

> at a [Canadian] brigade I was told that their best sniper's rifle was wrong, so I said 'Fetch him along, and I will take him back to the school.' When I went out I found a fine Indian, who had half an oiled sheet hung round him; but of all curious things his name – Private North West Wind! Well, I have got him here. He has got fifty-eight Huns to date. North-West was in great form today. Only spoke twice! Each time he said 'Huh. Fine shooting.' At two or three loopholes we had a little match. I got eight out of ten in, he was not so lucky, but did well. Poor Walton,[195] who was here a fortnight ago, has been killed by a Hun sniper. Private North-West thinks it is a bad business. 'Huh. Me kill 'em Huns!' The class goes tomorrow

and North-West goes too. He is a real *quick* shot. Mostly Indians are poor shots, but I had to be all out to get off my shots in less time than he. I was quicker because I shoot on the upward swing, while he waits to steady, but there is not much in it. He shoots more like me than any man I have ever met.

Class gone, and North-West with them. He hardly spoke when he was here, but just now came up and solemnly shook hands, then retreated a little, grunted, came back and shook hands again.[196]

On 18 August 1918, as the German Army was gradually pushed back, Norwest was tasked with locating a troublesome German sniper's position near Warvillers. As he searched for a target through his telescopic sight, he was instantly killed by a sniper's bullet through his head, thus fulfilling his own prophecy.[197] Such was the anger of the Canadians at their loss that an unprecedented artillery barrage was ordered along the whole German front in retribution. His official total was 115 Germans.

The Canadian Corps continued to pursue sniping aggressively as a means of waging both material and psychological warfare on the enemy. That this policy was effective is beyond doubt, and German units intensely disliked being in the lines opposite the Canadians, as Mannfried Gossen later recalled:

I returned to the front near Vimy Ridge, in early 1917, and we had the Canadians in front of us, who were the very devil. Our snipers could not shoot without retribution and we lost many good men there. Many of my comrades were returned wounded like myself and we were very careful to keep our skins intact so [. . .] we did little sniping there as even for us old trench veterans it was too dangerous.[198]

The Canadians also made extensive use of pre-manufactured camouflage, provided both by the Royal Engineers' Special Works Park and their own engineers, and their ingenuity was breathtaking. Portable observation posts, some armoured, sniping posts supported on legs that could be quickly erected in any trench, hollowed out dummy sandbags, ranges of Ghillie suits that were adapted for different terrain (including, later in the war, brickwork camouflage), all aided the Canadians in their purpose of breaking German dominance of No Man's Land, and eventually they fielded the largest and most successful sniper teams of any Commonwealth country.

ANZAC Sniping

Canada was not alone in working hard at training its snipers, for other Commonwealth armies had followed suit. Australia and New Zealand, having extracted themselves from the debacle at Gallipoli, found a large proportion of their men shipped to Palestine to help fight the Turks, in a long and hard campaign much overlooked by historians. Many of the Turkish snipers were also Gallipoli veterans and, ironically, faced the same men in Palestine that they had done while on the peninsula. For their part, the ANZACs were, by now, both experienced and wary of the Turks: no longer did they regard them merely as ill-trained conscripts, as Ion Idriess dryly commented: 'The respect you gain for a (Turkish) sniper when a bullet smacks within half an inch of your jaw is thrilling.'[199]

While long desert columns of sweating men trudged endlessly across the largely featureless landscape, mounted ANZAC scouting units moved quickly across the open desert to observe enemy troop positions, often closing in quick for bloody skirmishes with en- trenched Turkish troops:

> Ours was a risky job. The Turkish Army was retreating pell- mell but we expected the bullets of their rearguard every moment. If so any of us that were left would gallop back and tell the regiment that we had 'found' the Turks.[200]

Although by mid-1916 the Turkish Army was being forced into retreat, it was anything but a rout, and they adopted a policy of leaving scattered groups of snipers as rearguards to cover their troops – a very effective method of slowing up the Allied advance. Stopping the Australian and British reconnaissance horsemen was a priority for the

Turkish snipers and the ANZACs could never drop their guard. Even a moment's relaxation could prove fatal:

> Suddenly Bert shouted, 'A well boys, here's water!' We clustered like bees around the lip of the well. A bullet smashed a man's temple and the blood sprayed across the clear water surface. Soon we got into quite a hot spot – a series of stumpy sand mounds each with its clumps of shrubby bush. Turks waited behind every mound [. . .] We rode in among hills of rolling sand, bare of bushes which lessened our fear of snipers. Three chaps jumped off their horses and peered among the gloomy trees, when 'crack!' Corporal Logie slung up his rifle and 'crack! crack! crack!' sang through the palms. One (Turkish) chap was kneeling behind a palm frantically waving a tunic [. . .] the other was down [. . .] the poor fellow was shot through the arm and clean through the body, fatally. They were snipers, their ammunition belts were half empty [. . .] we breathed freer when we climbed to the circle top of grim hills enclosing that nameless oasis. To have been caught down there would have meant a death trap.[201]

For the Turkish snipers left behind, there was little chance of salvation, but determined shooting by them could, quite literally, halt an Army in its tracks. Hunting down these brave, lone sharpshooters became the task of other snipers, and Idriess later recalled – in possibly the most graphic account written – an event that was to typify these lonely duels, when two snipers of equal skill were pitted against each other. Although the event happened during the fighting for Gaza-Beersheba in late 1916, it could equally apply anywhere along the Western Front, and it graphically illustrates the care, patience and heightened state of awareness that a sniper needed if he were to live to see another day. As the advancing Australian column suddenly came under fire:

> a man immediately collapsed with a bullet through his lung. There was a rush to pull the panting horses as close under the sheltering rise as possible, for the dread thought 'sniper'

flashed though every mind. A mate rushed out from cover and jerked the man's arm; even as he did so, a vicious, crackling whistle had come and gone. The emu feathers on the trooper's hat fell to his shoulder, sheared clean off to the hat rim. Very gingerly I looked from the side of the rise through a pair of splendid field glasses 'souvenired' from an Austrian officer of artillery. I had the reputation of being a sniper myself, so I nonchalantly examined the field of barley on our right flank, whence apparently the shots had come. It was a beautiful, sun-kissed field. Emerald-green, the crop was just about a foot high and as level as a billiard table. High in the clear air [. . .] a brown lark trilled as only larks can, but of life in the field there was not a sign. I knew there would not be. Over every yard, then every foot of its greenness I searchingly played those high-powered glasses. But I well knew that a trained man can lie perfectly still facing you not a hundred yards away on hard brown earth without even a blade of grass on it, and you can stare at the muzzle of his rifle for ten minutes without seeing him. And now, somewhere within that field of barley, a highly trained sniper lay easily concealed. Pulling back the barley from the edge of the bank [. . .] then arranging the foot long stalks in a row around my hatband, and carefully spreading barley in flat sheaves over my back under and over the bandolier and bayonet belt. Each stalk had to be done so very carefully, for if a barley stalk drooped where every stalk should be standing [. . .] Then came the stealthy climb up the *wadi* bank and into the barley field. First the length of the rifle poked gently on the earth, palms of the hand cupped protectingly round the firing mechanism. Just one foot advance for each drag, just one inch at a time; chin, chest, belly and toes pressed tight against the earth while the heart thumped. Then one long waiting breath and very slowly, on again. Somewhere in that field lay the waiting sniper. Where I knew not. He would not move. But his eyes would be seeing, his ears hearing. And he would shoot. So on I crawled, if possible slower and more cautious than before. The further in the barley I was when his rifle cracked, the better chance of locating him [. . .] he would simply wait, every instinct, every nerve, every sense tuned to the uttermost with the thrill of longing to put a bullet through my brain. He was waiting for me. High in the cloudless sky, a lark still carolled. Without lifting chin from the ground, my eyes would naturally rise slightly to the sky on each pause for breath. Each time they would alight on the carolling lark as it hovered so wonderfully balanced in the air, only to rise almost out of sight in an apparent attempt to sing its way into heaven – and it seemed as I wormed farther and further into the field, to hover constantly over one spot! I watched the lark for what seemed like a long time; then a breathless realisation gripped the mind. I felt my mouth open a little and eyes suddenly widen as I pressed back the rifle safety catch. Then twisting very slightly to the left so as to be in line with the hovering lark, I crawled off again. Sound! What a medley of sound there was! Each stalk harboured life that constantly hummed or hissed or chirped. And things to see! There were countless live things in that barley, some of them swarming over the stalks, things so minute I never dreamed anything but a microscope could have seen them. Wonderful too, how far a still man, chin pressed to the ground, could see through that dim green maze of stalks. Some had wee tufts of grass growing [. . .] and an odd wild flower or two. One scarlet poppy pushed up its crimson cup for sunlight and life. And over all was the song of the lark. Slow tense minutes passed in withdrawing the field glasses and carefully raising them just above the ground. How the barley stalks leapt into prominence! How much further a man could see! Then something moved. It was only the turn of his cheekbone, but it allowed me to focus right into the eyes of my man. Blazing black eyes that had gazed into the haze of the desert [. . .] only partly could I see the big brown nose, hawk shaped, for two twisted barley stalks camouflaged his black *burnous*. The perfectly shaped, tiny black dot of his rifle muzzle I could see, and below the telescopic sight the bony brown knuckles that gripped around the weapon. A Bedouin, with the eyes of a hawk. How my heart thumped. His eyes were continually roving in a motionless face, from left to right from right to left.

And I could almost hear him listening. Very patiently, between
the many barley stalks I concentrated on those two stalks which
still crossed his nose [. . .] then put the field glasses down while
never for the faintest breath of time letting my eyes miss his
eyes. Then the calculation on which one life would depend.
Dearly I would have loved to level the rifle foresight fair
between those two black eyes [. . .] but many barley stalks [. . .]
were in the way. Such a tiny thing might deflect a bullet – and
a man would be allowed only one shot. Aim right at the butt of
the stalks [. . .] the bullet should strike the little hollow below
the throat at the base of the neck [. . .] and go right down
through his body. He should never move after that. Then the
in-drawing of a deep breath, the raising of the rifle, the easing
of racing nerves as the familiar weapon settled its iron-shod
butt reassuringly into the hollow of the shoulder, the absolute
steadiness as the trigger finger took the 'first-pull' and the foresight lowered onto the barley stalk down past the eyes, past the
mouth, slowly past the chin, until engaging in the rear sight,
stopped dead [. . .] 'Crack!' I bounded out of the barley and was
on the spot even as he rolled over. He was dying. His flashing
black eyes fastened on mine in a gaze of instant realisation and
deathless hate. He attempted to raise his arm [. . .] as he tried
vainly to clench his fist. Looking down at him, like a great fallen
hawk in the crushed barley, I felt no remorse, only hot pride
that in fair warfare I had taken the life of [. . .] this man, older
and stronger physically than me [. . .] reared from babyhood to
regard warfare as the life of a man and splendid sport, this
desert irregular knowing every inch of the country, had fallen
to a stranger from a peaceful land who knew only three years of
war! Strung on a camel sinew around his neck were thirty-eight
identification discs, mostly those of British troops, but with a
sprinkling of Australian and one Maoriland badge. There was
a special silver medal also, and a parchment deed of recognition
from the Sultan. Within a foot of the Bedouin's body, cun-
ningly interwoven between four stalks of barley, was a little
nest, and in it one solitary fledgling, its eyes still shut but

hungry mouth wide open. Such an insignificant thing to cause the death of a man.[202]

The New Zealanders also fielded excellent snipers, similarly armed with the ubiquitous SMLE and PP or Aldis scope. Many had been farmers and hunters in the wild country that comprised much of New Zealand, expert at tracking and snap-shooting at fleeting targets:

> I was sent on a course after I returned [from Gallipoli] and we learned how to use telescopic sights. I had never used one before, always iron sights for my sniping and I must say I never took to them. They misted up and never seemed to keep their zero, but they did prove useful in the trenches as you could see Jerry's loopholes much better. I still preferred to shoot with open sights, as I found snap-shooting was much quicker with them.[203]

The South Africans

As was the case with the rest of the Commonwealth, the South African armed forces contained a far larger proportion of skilled shots than their British counterparts, many being of Boer extraction, whose fathers had fought in the two previous wars. However, South Africa was unique in being the only country to raise and field a specially trained Corps of Sharpshooters, known as 'Sir Abe Bailey's Sharpshooters'. This was due to the intervention of millionaire Sir Abe Bailey, whose friends serving on the Western Front during 1915 had complained of the terrible losses inflicted by German snipers. Not being a man to sit around, Bailey immediately offered to raise and equip a unit for sniping duties. As a result, the following advert was placed in all South African newspapers:

> A Corps of specially selected rifle shots is required for services in the western battlefront in Europe. By kind permission of the Union authorities, recruits will be attested, tested in rifle efficiency and also medically examined by the District Staff Officers at Johannesburg, Cape Town and Durban.

Ordinary pay will be at British infantry rates, but members will receive 1/- per diem extra pay for the whole period of their service in the Corps and 2/- per diem as well, if they have dependants entitled to receive separation allowance, at Imperial rates.

Absolute proficiency at snap-shooting is essential. The Corps will assemble at Wynberg under direction of the General Officer Commanding, South African Military Command. Good eyesight is essential. Age from 20 to 45 years.[204]

Finding prospective sharpshooters was not to prove quite so easy in practice, for the rush to join the colours in 1914 had left South Africa denuded of men, and in the end, only twenty-four were selected and trained, being sent to France under the command of a very experienced hunter named Neville Methven in early 1916. The Sharpshooters were armed with SMLE rifles, but not for Abe Bailey was there to be an issue of common-or-garden PP Co. equipped rifles: all of their weapons were fitted up by Purdey and mounted with the excellent No. 3 Aldis scope. What is of particular interest, is that much of the training schedule and personal information of the men who enlisted has survived. On volunteering, to be considered for selection to the unit, men had to place ten rounds into a bullseye at 100 yards, then snapshoot at a moving target at 200 and 300 yards, firing five rounds with each target exposure being of five seconds duration. Five rounds had to then be fired from cover at 200 yards, after running thirty paces. Finally five rounds had to be fired at 500 yards from any position. The maximum points that could be gained were sixty-five and to pass, men must score above forty-three. Those twenty-four chosen were listed by profession as:

Administrator/clerk (4)	Bank Employee (2)
Bricklayer (2)	Carpenter
Farmer (6)	Labour contractor
Machinist	Mine Fitter
Policeman	Railwayman
Shopworker (4)	

This was not South Africa's sole contribution to the sniping war of course, for many men had already been selected for sniper training from the three divisions of South African Army troops already in France, and they had formed sniper sections in the front lines, as well as serving in East and South West Africa and Egypt. However, the record of kills of the Sharpshooters is of considerable note, for by Methven's own recollections, taken from an interview in 1973,[205] his personal tally was over 100, which was unusual for a commanding officer, who normally would have little time for shooting. The unit, which mainly served on attachment with British Infantry units such as King's Royal Rifle Corps, Northamptonshire Regiment and the Sussex Regiment, exacted a toll of over 3,000 Germans during its 2½ year tour of duty. This meant that on average, each man killed about 250 enemy soldiers – a quite extraordinary feat of arms. But this was not achieved without heavy price, for Methven stated that only six of the original men returned home, and the unit suffered a 35 per cent casualty rate: six times that of the South African infantry.

French Sniping

By mid-1916 there was certainly no shortage of sniping rifles being supplied to the British and Allied front lines, indeed, Hesketh-Prichard commented that it was 'raining telescopic rifles', which may have been something of an overstatement, but did at least reflect the fact that Britain had finally managed to combine a proper training system with the issue of sufficient weapons, and that the Commonwealth snipers were giving as good as they got in the sniping war. For the French, the situation was less rosy.

In the face of the casualties inflicted on its troops by German snipers during 1914–15 the French had somewhat belatedly realised that telescopic sights were going to be required in quantities hitherto never dreamed of, and they began looking at the production of their own telescopic sights and mounts. The existing Mle. 1896 A.PX was available in small numbers only, but the scope was modified and improved with the introduction of the A.PX Mle. 1907/15. This was shorter bodied, and it was of 3 x with a reticule, which comprised a fine cross-hair with a field of view of about 7 degrees. A focusing ring was placed just forward of the ocular lens. Unusually, for this period, the entire body was made from heavy drawn brass tube, the only steel fittings being the mounts: in fact, it closely resembled the German Gerard telescope, which was not entirely accidental. A number of these scopes were selected for fitment to the Lebel Mle. 1886/93 so in late 1915 it was decided to expand production, although there is now little available material covering the quantities manufactured or their issue.

The new scope appears to have been issued in mid-1915. It was calibrated up to 800 metres. Windage was altered by means of a grub-screw at the front of the scope, enabling the objective lens to be rotated in the manner of the later Aldis scopes, but it was a fiddly process and not one to be undertaken in a hurry. There were three primary methods of fitting, all relatively strong and soldier-proof:

1. A rotating stud soldered and screwed to the left side of the breech next to the rear sight and a soldered mount on the left of the receiver just behind the hand-guard. The front mount of the scope is placed in the lug and rotated 90 degrees and the rear mount locks by means of a spring catch.

2. The second pattern comprises a front mounting block with a dovetail, offset to the left, screwed and soldered onto the breech next to the rearsight. The rear mount is a bar, soldered and retained by two large screws, fitted to the left of the receiver behind the hand-guard and this too has a dovetail fitting.

3. The third type was for the fitment of the Winchester A5 scope and uses an angled mounting plate that is clamped to the front of the receiver, unusually using a hinged bracket, and a rear bracket that is retained by means of a screw through the left side receiver just above the trigger-guard. Commercial dovetailed blocks are fitted, onto which the saddle mounts of the scope fit.

An improved telescope, the A.PX Mle. 1917, was introduced, which was slightly longer in the body, improving the quality of vision for the shooter, but appears otherwise identical, although some models appear to have an inverted 'V' reticle in place of the cross-hair. Exactly why this later model was produced remains unclear but there appears to have been little standardisation and variations of scopes and their mounts occur. As was the normal practice, each scope was hand fitted to its rifle by skilled gunsmiths or armourers, and every scope was stamped on its bell-housing with the number of its rifle. Interestingly, unlike British examples, French scopes generally seem to be interchangeable, the author possessing a Lebel with a mismatched scope that fits perfectly well.

Sources from the Historial Museum at Péronne indicate that sniper training was organised at schools based close to the rear lines and selected men – designated *Tirailleurs d'Élite* (TEs) – were selected for training, normally (but not exclusively) from regiments of *Tirailleurs*, who were roughly akin to the British rifle regiments.

Sniping was prevalent along the whole French front line, but rifles were never available in sufficient numbers, most being issued to the TEs on the basis of eight per Battalion. However, designated marksmen in infantry regiments were also given sniper training, which seemed to have been organised on an ad hoc basis behind the lines. In view of the co-operation that existed between British and French armies, particularly later in the war, it seems unlikely that French snipers would not have benefited from the accumulated knowledge built up by the Allied Schools of Sniping and Scouting. Certainly, some French-speaking Canadian units appear to have had French snipers on their courses, although this was possibly done on an unofficial local basis, but finding any concrete information on specific French sniper training has been difficult.

French snipers certainly gave a good account of themselves at Verdun. During the brutal fighting between February and July 1916 the carnage reached such proportions that, in some parts of the line, it was calculated that 100 men had died for every square metre of ground. Both sides used snipers, firing from every conceivable position: loopholes in the walls of concrete bunkers strung across the battlefield, and specially sited snipers' posts, which, as the fighting intensified, became virtually impossible to use as the enormous weight of shellfire rendered even deep dugouts useless. More often, sniping was simply done from impromptu positions where snipers occupied convenient shell-holes and waited, as localised attacks could occur at any time and targets were often no further than a few metres away. Snipers on both sides adopted defensive tactics that would be mirrored in the fighting that occurred on the Eastern Front in the Second World War:

> We sharpshooters occupied the line of craters behind the main body of our men and as soon as the French advanced, we would shoot the officers and leading ranks, our riflemen and machine guns dealing with the rest. These attacks were often over in minutes and hundreds were killed, it was a terrible, terrible warfare.[206]

The close fighting often rendered telescopic uses redundant and this meant that much sniping was done with open sights:

> Dust from the explosions and smoke as well as the use of gas meant that often we would be shooting with our (gas) masks on and this was impossible with an optical sight. Besides, the French troops advanced at a run, in short rushes, which made them difficult targets in normal conditions. At Verdun we often could see only yards so sharpshooting (snap-shooting) was necessary and the metal sights on our rifles were more practical.[207]

Under such conditions perhaps the term 'sniping' is a misnomer, for any rifleman with a sharp eye and quick reflexes could hit his target.

The French had many skilled hunters among their ranks and, like the German *Jägers*, they were perfectly at home in the dark, gloomy forests of the Meuse and Argonne. With difficult terrain, the defenders always had the advantage and attacking troops often suffered badly from the effects of the sniper fire that poured into them. The historian of the German 70th Infantry Regiment, writing after the war, observed that, in attacking the French positions, their snipers proved the greatest obstacle to advancing:

For, at each step, death would knock. The French tireurs [*sic*]
were solidly attached to the trees. Even if one or two were hit,
we still could not get past. In this situation the enemy positions
could not be found [. . .] it was like fighting phantoms.[208]

In desperation the Germans took to raking the treetops with machine-
gun fire, but this proved of little effect, as many snipers were concealed
in foxholes at the roots of the trees and simply shot the machine-
gunners. One French infantryman commented later of his snipers
that:

Their rifles [. . .] soon became too hot to handle such were the
number of enemy targets that presented themselves. Their
[telescopic] sights became fogged but they did not cease fire
until there were no more Boches to be seen. In places they
were piled three or four deep but they could not get past our
Tirailleurs.[209]

Where the French and Germans were concerned, the bitter fighting on
the Western Front had caused some reassessment with regard to their
rifles. The problem was that the French Lebel and German Gewehr 98
were relatively old designs, which were physically too long for the close
trench fighting that had become the norm. They were also unwieldy
and heavy, and both armies were concerned at finding suitable replace-
ments that could be manufactured using existing machinery.

Germany had, in fact, adopted a short carbine, the Kar98a, in 1899,
but ceased production in 1903. However, with some modifications it
was reintroduced in 1904 and began to be supplied to line regiments
in 1908, gradually replacing the old Gew. 98 as the issue service rifle;
although, by the end of the war, it had not entirely supplanted the old
model, tens of thousands still being in service. Its introduction was
significant for it proved that a short-barrelled rifle (6 inches less than
the Gew) was still an effective sniping weapon. There are now few
complete examples in unmodified First World War form, as many of
these First World War rifles were reissued during the early days of the
Second World War to SS units and fitted with a Short Side-rail
mount. However, it appears that some of these Kar sniping rifles were

adopted into service quite early in the war. Ernst Jünger, a fiery *Sturmtruppen* leader and occasional sniper, wrote of using one such rifle in the fighting for Rossignol Wood on the Somme in July 1916. Having been troubled by a British sniper post, he decided to retaliate and had made his way cautiously to a point that overlooked the British line:

> The weather could not be better so at twelve o'clock I went along to the right wing where I was to leave the trench. 'H' [his spotter] came with me to carry my rifle, a short carbine with a telescopic sight attached. The carbine is a short rifle and its barrel is almost entirely cased in wood so there is very little of it to reflect the sun.[210]

Although the French, too, had adopted a carbine pre-war (the Carabine de Cavalerie Modèle 1890), in that manner peculiar to them, they subsequently reverse-engineered it to produce a full-length infantry rifle, the 8mm Fusil d'Infanterie Modèle 1907 (Mle. 07/15), better known as the Berthier. Although it still had a long, 31-inch barrel, and was initially limited by its three-round magazine capacity (increased in 1916 to five), the Berthier was, in most respects, a superior rifle to the Lebel, the Mle. 16 having a turned down bolt handle, which eased the reloading action, and it was marginally more accurate than the Lebel. Mounting of a scope on the Berthier was done by the fitting of a soldered block on the left side of the breech, by the rearsight, in which there was a threaded hole. A second block was screwed and soldered to the rear of the receiver in the same manner as on the Lebel. This was slotted for a latch on the rear mount of the scope. With the front locking screw lightly threaded in place, the rear latch was engaged, then the locking screw tightened. The scopes were normally marked 'Mod. 1907/15 A.PX' but the numbers converted for sniper use appear to have been comparatively small.

Mountain Sniping

Elsewhere along the 450-odd miles of front line, other countries were also using snipers with varying degrees of success. Some of the least well-recorded fighting took place in the harsh mountain conditions of the Italian Tyrol and Macedonia. These were possibly the most inhospitable areas for any form of combat seen during the war, and the use of ordinary troops in such an environment proved disastrous for whoever attempted it. The solution was to raise special mountain troop units, such as the Italian *Reggimento di Alpinis* and Austrian *Tiroler Jägerregiment*, comprising men picked for their ability to ski, climb, and survive in harsh winter conditions. Some of these Alpine soldiers were hunters, specialising in that most elusive of quarry, the Chamois, and they were able to stalk prey in conditions that would defeat most other hunters. Large numbers of troops were not needed to fight in such inaccessible places, for the narrow mountain tracks and crags could be held by small numbers, but the opportunities for sniping, while more limited than on the French battlefront, certainly existed. Anyone who held the high ground had an almost uninterrupted view into enemy positions, but sniping under such conditions was difficult in the extreme. The thin air altered the ballistic characteristics of the bullets, estimating ranges was difficult, while the lack of earth or sand meant that trenches were constructed from layers of piled rock, which were almost completely bulletproof but caused lethal ricochets.

Nevertheless, both Austria and Italy had adopted sniping rifles, the Austro-Hungarian forces using their 8mm Model 1895 Repetier-Gewer Modell 95 Mannlicher straight-pull, upon which much of the action of the Canadian Ross rifles was based. Like most others of the period, it was a solid long-barrelled pre-war design, that lent itself readily to conversion for sniping use. As Austria had access to the Schott glassworks and the finest optical glass in Europe, there was no shortage of telescopic sights, although demand invariably outstripped supply. As a result, the few existing examples of scoped M95 rifles can be found with a wide number of different optical sights fitted, some of Austrian make, such as Kahles, others German, such as Oigee, Goerz and Busch. These are of 3 x or 4 x, and while the telescopes are of the same patterns found on the Gew. 98 rifles, the mounting system devised for the M95 is different, and appears to have been used almost exclusively for these models. It is a partially offset system, using a round post at the rear and single (occasionally double) claw at the front. It further differed from the Gew in having a front mounting dovetail that could be moved left or right to enable the windage to be altered. It was then locked in place with a small grubscrew. It is instantly identifiable by the long release catch that projects forwards from the rear scope mount under the body of the telescope. It is easy to use if wearing gloved hands, but quite vulnerable to accidental dismounting, particularly if the rifle was picked up by its scope – a poor practice but inevitable in the hands of soldiers. The design would then allow the scope to release itself instantly, causing the rifle to drop free, which was not the result one wanted if balancing precariously halfway up a slippery mountain track.

In parallel with the M95 rifle a carbine variant, the Repetier-Kavallerie Modell 1895, had been adopted for artillery troops, mounted troops and alpine units. This handy carbine had a 19-inch barrel and fired a lighter charge, propelling its bullet at a much lower velocity of 1,750 fps (as opposed to the 2,100 fps of the rifle). As a short rifle it was quite practical for mountain snipers, being easy to carry and capable of around 600-yard shooting. For the winter months, fighting was impossible in the high passes, and the only sign of warfare was the occasional 'crack' of these sniper's rifles, echoing across the deep valleys and mountains.

The Italians, often derided for their reluctance to wage war on a serious level, in fact fielded some of the best mountain snipers of the whole conflict, although they were somewhat let down by their Army's choice of weapon: for Italy had adopted the Fucile Modello 1891 rifle (more commonly known as the Carcano). Although mechanically similar to other rifles, it fired a small, somewhat underpowered 6.5mm bullet. Despite generating a moderately high 2,400 fps, its 123 grain bullet lacked both weight and penetrative power. Sniping variants were produced, although the number was probably fairly small, and examples exist with French A.PX telescopic sights, as well as some Austrian-made Kahles. None have so far been found with Italian-manufactured optics. The one minor benefit of the small calibre of the Carcano was its lack of smoke or muzzle flash, making it very difficult to detect. One of the most successful Italian snipers was Ottavio Bottecchia,[211] who was reputed to have amassed a total of over 100 kills while fighting the Austro-Hungarian Army.

Of course, fighting in harsh weather conditions was not solely the preserve of the mountain troops, for the war on the Eastern Front provided German snipers with a great deal of expertise against their Russian adversaries. From the first weeks of the conflict, the Germans realised that, in terms of sniping, they were waging an entirely one-sided war. The Russian Army, despite having the Mosin Nagant Model 1891 – a rifle as good as any other in use at that period – chose to ignore the need for either training or equipping snipers and it suffered accordingly. Thus, German units serving on the Eastern Front found themselves with a wealth of targets and almost no opposition:

> They [the Russians] occupied trenches only two hundred metres from us but they took little precautions against our sharpshooters. Often parties of Russian soldiers would be sent to gather wood from the forests behind them and our men would shoot them down. It seemed not to matter and more men would be sent [. . .] eventually they began collecting wood at night but our snipers could often find targets against the snow for the light was good. During this time we had no opposition at all from the Russians.[212]

Many of the German snipers scored considerable numbers of kills and were able to put their experience into practice when transferred to the Western Front, after the capitulation of the Russians in early 1917. Exactly why the Russian Army ignored the terrible cost of German sniping is difficult to comprehend. Possibly the answer lay in the acute shortage of *matériel* and rifles in particular. Often, attacking waves of Russian troops had only sufficient weapons for the leading men to be armed, those following simply picking up rifles from the fallen. Under such circumstances, diverting production for a specialist rifle would have been low on the list of the Army's priorities. In addition, Russia had virtually no home-based optical industry. It was to be a lesson the Soviets took to heart, for in the years preceding the Second World War, the Red Army fielded the greatest number of trained and equipped snipers of any force in the world.

A New Phase

As the desperate fighting of 1916 dragged itself inexorably towards 1917 the deadly game that was being waged by the snipers in the trenches had gradually become a more evenly matched battle. The weapons used were more or less equal in terms of accuracy, and any advantages were to be found more in the training and quality of men selected.

Up to a point, determining how useful sniping was is easy if looked at in purely military terms as the numbers of kills made. But its value was less easily quantified in terms of intelligence gathered by snipers who did not shoot, but merely observed. Prichard recalled how a sniper team kept reporting a cat sitting on the German parapet. Further investigation showed a new artillery dugout being prepared, which was subsequently destroyed by shelling. Increasingly, this observation function was proving of vital importance to intelligence officers, who were normally many miles behind the lines and whose knowledge of the terrain they commanded was limited to maps, aerial photographs, and the normally unskilled observations of the line infantry. In addition, and utterly incalculable to anyone was, the moral and psychological effect that the sniping had on the enemy:

> It should be borne in mind [. . .] how great a plague were the skilled German snipers to us. One of them might easily cause thirty or forty casualties. Besides, as I have pointed out, in these early days of trench warfare the continual attrition caused by German snipers was bad for morale. Nothing got more quickly on the nerves of the troops than a sniper [. . .] as had been proven time and again a thousand men within the range of one solitary sniper were often powerless to hit back. Each man simply had to crouch low wherever he was while the hidden menace systematically picked his targets one by one. That sort of thing on the nerves is ghastly; compared with it, shellfire is merely in the day's routine.[213]

In both the British and German armies, there was also a change in the type of men who were being trained as snipers, and an increasing chasm in experience. During the Somme battles of 1916, around 1,000 men a day were required simply to cover the losses. By early 1917, replacement soldiers were of quite different calibre to the volunteers of 1914–15. Most were recruited under the 1916 Conscription Act and their training was pitifully inadequate, having been given reduced training during 1916. Many reached the lines with little experience of anything, even shooting a service rifle, and they provided poor material when it came to finding snipers.

Meanwhile, some experienced soldiers who had been wounded, possibly more than once (an increasingly common breed), were looking for a means of escaping the routines of trench warfare:

> I asked to become a sniper as I reckoned my chances of survival were better than if I stayed in my company. I'd been wounded twice in two years and I reckoned I needed a break. So off I went.[214]

Whether this was a wise move was questionable of course, for at the other end of the spectrum were those snipers who had already survived over the odds. After three months recovering from wounds, Rifleman Tom Durst returned to duty in early November 1916, but knew almost no one in his old battalion:

> I came back from being wounded but our sniper section was full of fellows I didn't know. Most had gone during the Somme fighting, all killed or wounded. I suppose I was lucky to have missed all that, I don't think I would be here if I'd not got wounded.[215]

Germany, too, had suffered terribly, losing some 350,000 men at Verdun and between 400,000 and 600,000 on the Somme. Even Ludendorff commented that the fighting had almost bled the German Army white, and it was not a situation that could continue. Experienced snipers were now becoming a rare commodity, so Mannfried Gottleib was surprised one day to be ordered from the front lines:

I had not been there very long when an orderly arrived and ordered me back to a village near Péronne, where there was a sniping school. I was to become a sniper instructor, with the rank of *Gefreiter* [corporal]. I needed no encouragement and was the envy of my comrades, who all wished me good luck.[216]

For the majority of front-line soldiers, there was no such escape and they endured as best they could the shelling, sniping and appalling weather in the winter of 1916–17.

In January 1917, after all the desperate fighting of the Somme battles, the German Army abruptly abandoned their old trenches along the lifeless snow-covered landscape, handing over ten times the amount of ground that the British had won during the Somme fighting. They retreated to a new defensive position, the Hindenburg Line. Although few realised it, this was to mark a completely new phase of fighting, which was eventually to see the abandonment of the old static form of trench warfare and to herald a more mobile form of war, in which snipers would be playing an increasingly demanding role.

Chapter Eight

The Beginning of the End

Following the slaughter witnessed in the battles of attrition of 1915 and 1916, by 1917 a change was detectable in the manner campaigns were fought, both tactically and technologically. Some were immediate and significant, such as the increasing use of air power and the introduction of the tank, but the most important factor was the realisation at command level that these new forms of warfare really could break the trench stalemate. Germany's use of fast-moving, well armed *Sturmtruppen* in 1916 had been an important innovation, as was the more effective use of artillery. Short, sharp artillery bombardments replaced the week-long pounding of earlier battles and shrapnel was phased out in favour of far more destructive high explosive.

Meanwhile, snipers began to be used as specific battlefield specialists, the Allies taking a leaf from the Germans, whose snipers had proven so effective that survivors of the battles of 1916/1917 often wrote of watching helplessly during attacks as entire platoons of men were shot as they cowered in shell-holes or in the remains of shell-blasted trenches:

> On my right an officer commanding a section had perished with all his men, except for one who came running towards me, the whole front of his face shot away. On my left two other sections had been killed to a man.[217]

Rarely was it possible for these snipers to be neutralised, for tactical doctrine of the time ensured that the British snipers were employed as ordinary line infantry:

When I went over the top, I was carrying my rifle without its telescope, which was slung over my shoulder. It wasn't until the second day that I was able to take cover in a German trench and start sniping. I shot the machine-gun crews but it was very dangerous work as the German snipers were so active. I was lucky to get away with it, so many of them [other British snipers] were just killed during the advance. It was a bloody waste of good trained men.[218]

Occasionally, a careless German sniper would be spotted and dealt with, as recounted by Captain Graham Seton-Hutchison during the fighting for High Wood in mid-July, 1916: 'I raised a rifle to the trees and took deliberate aim, observing my target crash through the foliage and into the undergrowth beneath.'[219] But such instances were rare indeed. Mostly, the British and Commonwealth troops were at the mercy of the Germans and powerless to retaliate:

We were in a shell-hole on the slope in front of Trones Wood. The sergeant, myself and two others, I didn't know them. We decided to stay put because the sniper fire was appalling, you couldn't so much as peek over the lip of the crater. Some Jerry must have managed to get on our flank though, for 'crack' the chap next to me slid down, with a hole in the top of his helmet. Then he got our sergeant in the neck and we sunk as low as we could but all the rest of the day this bloody Jerry tried to get us. 'Crack, crack', we couldn't even roll over to get our water bottles. It was the longest day I ever spent and it took days to get the smell of blood out of my nostrils. It woke me up at nights for years afterwards.[220]

In the wake of the introduction of the reprinted British *Training and Employment of Divisions* manual of early 1917, there filtered down a series of improvements in the way troops and snipers were employed. It was a new type of war, which the manual described as: 'progressive battle, with limited objectives [. . .] leading up by gradual stages to an attack on deep objectives'.

Much had been gleaned from French and German tactics at Verdun and on the Somme, where, despite ferocious barrages, attacking troops failed to take their objectives and were pinned down by a withering hail of machine-gun and sniper fire. Clearly men advancing in extended lines with their rifles at the port were going to achieve little on the modern battlefield. Instead, it was decided they should advance in two flexible waves of skirmishers, followed by platoons backed up by third and fourth waves which consolidated the ground. Specifically, the manual of *Training and Employment of Platoons* asserted that the leading infantry sections (comprising about thirty to forty men) should have 'at least two scout snipers on their flanks' and the *Scouting and Patrolling* manual of December 1917 explained in greater detail that a sniper's duty during an attack was to 'place himself in advantageous positions, such as shellholes and trenches', where he would take advantage of any 'suitable targets'. That this paid dividends was unquestionable, Private Thomas Barrett[221] gaining the first and only British sniper's VC of the war for his work in hunting down and killing German snipers holding up an advance in 1917, thus enabling the attack to continue.

While the majority of casualties in an attack (around 80 per cent) were due to effective machine-gun fire, in the more fluid fighting that began to take place in 1917/1918 the Germans were, on occasion, pushed back into territory that had formerly been behind their front lines. They began to adopt defensive tactics that took a heavy toll on the advancing Commonwealth forces. Indeed, Allied casualties for 1918 were higher than any other year of the war. Their tactics would stand them in good stead in the latter part of the war, relying on sparsely manned, well-sited defensive positions (in cellars or well-concealed positions in open ground), held only by machine-gunners and snipers, normally working in conjunction. When in danger of being overrun, they would abandon their positions and fall back, leaving the defence to other teams already in position behind them. This tactic used few men but could be kept up almost indefinitely, and was a highly efficient form of fighting retreat that slowed any advance to a crawl, for each sniper and machine-gunner had to be found and dealt with.

Set piece battles began to take on a new form, as witnessed by the early 1917 campaigns around Arras, and the successful battle for Messines, for which, for the first time, troops were to be fully informed as to what was expected and even shown scale models of their objectives. It was also to lead to a more open form of warfare, although the desperate, awful slogging match known as Passchendaele in 1917 proved that not all of the lessons of 1915 and 1916 had been learned.

A serious problem in Flanders, which was to be duplicated on the Hindenburg Line, was the Germans' widespread use of pillboxes, for the waterlogged ground conditions in the north had made digging trenches almost impossible. Thus, concrete fortifications were commonplace and finding a means of dealing with them was challenging, for most were invulnerable to shellfire. They also had interlocking fields of fire, making frontal attack impossibly costly, as they housed not only machine-gun teams but also snipers, who often operated in hides or shell-holes outside the pillboxes but connected by means of trenches or tunnels to the entrance.

In the wake of the Germans' retreat in January 1917 to the heavily defended lines around Arras, these concrete forts became an even greater thorn in the side of the Allies, for it was a form of fighting that the soldiers there had little experience of. However, the French had been facing the problem since 1915 and had found a solution that involved not so much a sledgehammer as a toothpick, for the most effective tactics to overcome these strongpoints involved the use of snipers. The French had determined the best solution was initially to use artillery firing gas and smoke to blind the enemy, while sending fighting platoons forward under heavy covering fire from light machine guns. Once close enough, they would use sniper teams to shoot into the slits of the pillboxes and pick off enemy snipers, while grenade men crawled close enough to drop their deadly bombs inside. Once within range, the snipers had to engage in a slow and dangerous duel with the Germans. It was a slow business, as the British discovered:

> The first few yards we went over were churned up by weeks of shellfire and unburied and half buried fragments of men simply littered the ground. We passed Geoff with a few men and a Lewis gun stuck in a shell-hole. The Germans were streaming machine-gun fire from the top of the pillbox. We picked off the snipers and machine-gunners one by one, until

only one grey rat remained. He had two shots at me. I had one and missed him. He had another which was pretty close and, thinking he had made a bull, he showed his white face cautiously over the rim of a trench round the pillbox. I was waiting for it and made no mistake that time. Puckrin crept up and dropped a bomb through a loophole. We counted six round the pillbox, all shot through the head.[222]

A new method of dealing with the ubiquitous Maxim guns had also been adopted:

We would shoot the guns, not the gunners. It was quite sensible because killing the gunner meant it was only a matter of time before another replaced him. What we'd do [. . .] was shoot into the jacket or mechanism of the guns because that would knock them out completely. Often the crews would surrender when they realised they couldn't use their guns.[223]

In response to this sniping, the vulnerable water jackets of the Maxim guns were routinely equipped with an armoured barrel jacket and frontal plate to prevent bullets penetrating, and from spring 1917 German gunners were issued with an armoured helmet browplate and a breastplate, adding to their already medieval look. It was a small indicator of the seriousness with which the German command viewed the casualties being inflicted on the machine guns and their crews by snipers.

Effectiveness of Sniping

The publication of the new *Scouting and Patrolling* manual was something of a watershed in the history of sniping, for at last it was officially acknowledged that the employment of snipers had a far broader tactical remit than the simple ideas of 1915. Back then, the main concern had been simply to make No Man's Land a safer place by killing German snipers; but two years on it was understood that, apart from inflicting casualties on the enemy, snipers also contributed to the intelligence-gathering properties of the Army, as well as improving morale and reducing the Germans' will to fight. Even the most ostrich-like generals could not help but accept that the casualty returns from front-line sniper sections made impressive reading (particularly once the problems of providing sufficient scoped rifles and proper training had been addressed) and that snipers were contributing to the war effort in a manner out of all proportion to their numbers.

As a prime example of their value, in purely numerical terms, the Canadian records for 1 January to 5 April 1916 are informative. Allowing for the fact that this was relatively early in the war and sniper training was still being properly formulated, their tally is quite impressive. It should also be borne in mind that these are confirmed hits: that is, those observed by a second person, and it would be reasonable to calculate that the actual tally would be double these figures:

Hits claimed by snipers from 1st, 2nd and 3rd Canadian Divisions.

1st Division	48
2nd Division	96
3rd Division	262
Total	**406**

During this period prisoners captured by the Canadians stated that twenty-six German soldiers had been killed by direct shots to the head in one company alone, and that, on average, each infantry company suffered between ten and fourteen men killed by Canadian snipers for every two-week tour in the front line – roughly averaging out at one man per day per company. The Canadian report went on the hypothesis that:

> Assuming that a German company held a line of 400 yards and the Canadian Corps held a line of 2,000 yards, approximately fifty German companies would be necessary to hold the line opposite to us [. . .] and if the average held good for the Corps, it seems fifty Germans were killed per day, and a complete German battalion wiped out in twenty days.[224]

While this can, perhaps, be considered a slight exaggeration of the facts, even if the kill ratio were halved to twenty-five men per day, this would still be a larger number than could be achieved by any means but the heaviest (and most costly) shellfire, and certainly not by machine guns, trench mortars or any other alternative means of waging war.

Clearly the sniping war was being fought at a level inconceivable two years previously, but what of the quality of men who were now passing through the sniping schools? Where the Allies were concerned, shortage of manpower was a serious issue by 1917. Australia, New Zealand, Canada and South Africa had suffered grievously in 1915 and 1916, and recruitment in countries that had relatively small populations to start with was slow indeed. Britain's losses had become so severe that, in the long term, even the Conscription Act would fail to provide enough men to prosecute the war at previous levels of intensity. Furthermore, by mid-1917, it was apparent that those sent to the front arrived with so little training, finding someone who knew how to shoot a rifle properly was something of a miracle:

> I was eighteen when I was conscripted and after we done [*sic*] basic training, drill and suchlike – I think it was three weeks – then we was [*sic*] sent to France, to Etaples, where we done more drilling and bayonet practice. I never shot me [*sic*] rifle at all until we went into the trenches at Monchy in 1917. I had sharp eyes though and got put into the sniper section as an observer but I never did shoot a rifle again.[225]

With a dearth of experienced soldiers, officers desperately needed the good men they still had to help instil confidence and discipline in the recruits, and they were reluctant to see veterans lost via transfer to other duties, such as sniping.

But a few old sweats took the opposite view, some, like Private Tom Durst, abandoning their sniping in favour of less dangerous methods of fighting. Having been wounded a third time, Tom decided to apply for a commission. Being one of the regiment's longest serving snipers, he was a great loss to his section, for his experience was invaluable, but he surmised: 'You couldn't keep going at that game for ever and I knew my number would soon be up, it was just a matter of time.'[226]

Attitudes

After four long years of war, it had become apparent there was a change in attitude among front-line soldiers. Men had developed a deep-rooted cynicism about the war and its politics and they no longer fought for the 1914 ideals of King and Country. War had become a matter of surviving and looking after their immediate chums, for it was death on an industrial scale. By 1917 it had simply become a job to be fought to the finish:

> I see no excuse for war, unless it is in defence of home and dear ones. Otherwise it is just legalised murder conducted on a large scale. No one excuses individual murder [. . .] while in war you murder a man you have never seen, who has never done you an injury. But of course we are fighting for national honour. How absurd! A soldier when he bayonets a man does not nurse the nation's wrongs in his breast.[227]

Despite official acknowledgement of their abilities and value, the job of snipers in the Commonwealth Army was regarded as necessary but dirty and there was little love for them. After weary years of hard fighting, men had lost their innate curiosity about their enemy and developed a fatalistic attitude, which often showed itself in a paradoxical way, sometimes in the openly cold-blooded killing of snipers:

> We had been under fire from Jerry snipers and we had got most of them. We were standing round waiting to move up when one stood up not 10 yards away with his hands in the air. 'Kamerad,' he said, 'Kamerad.' My mate George said 'Bugger that for a game!' and turned his Lewis gun on him. I don't suppose he was the first to do it, but that Jerry had been killing our mates ten minutes before hadn't he?[228]

Of course, all who engaged in sniping knew their lives were forfeit in the event of surrender, with a bayonet or bullet the usual end, although such treatment was not solely meted out to snipers: machine-gunners, too, were equally detested. Often, anger would rise to the point of public execution, as one British officer laconically noted in his diary:

> 16 July 1916. Royal Scots catch and hang one sniper. Shelling and a great deal of sniping.[229]

Unsurprisingly, the official history of the Royal Scots makes no mention of such incidents. Whatever the moral arguments, the fact was that summary execution of snipers was routine on the battlefields of Gallipoli, France, Italy and Palestine. No snipers on any side wore any distinguishing insignia, and in the event of capture, they would try to dispose of their rifles and scopes as quickly as possible. It was not a guarantee of survival but it raised the odds slightly, and any chance was better than none.

And yet, occasionally, there would be surprising acts of humanity. One veteran corporal recalled clearing a German trench very late in the war and finding a young German sniper, aged not more than seventeen, in a hide. His sergeant was clutching a Mills grenade with the pin out, and the crouching German was wild-eyed with terror:

> My sergeant had his arm raised to throw the grenade but he said 'Christ [. . .] he's just a bloody kid, the bastards are using bloody kids' and pulled him out by the scruff of his neck, then sent him to the rear.[230]

The more experienced soldiers understood that the enemy were now fighting a losing battle and they had developed a degree of empathy with their foe:

> I was asked to find a German sniper who was causing a nuisance and it took some time [. . .] we found him in a ruined cottage just behind the German lines but he was very careful. I watched him for hours and the other lads would ask 'Have you got him yet?' Eventually we saw him fire, he was in the

roof space behind the tiles and I shot back, quickly. It all went quiet like and Jack, my observer says 'There he goes.' He was out the back of the cottage, heading for their trenches but he was running slowly, limping, so I was sure I'd hit him. Jack said 'shoot the bastard,' but I didn't, I let him go. I reckoned his war was finished and the armistice came two weeks later. I was always glad I didn't kill that Jerry.[231]

Because it was, for the most part, an invisible war waged from concealed positions often well in front of, or behind, the lines, the work of snipers remained mysterious. Despite the fact that the sniper was there to save the lives of his comrades, antipathy toward them – certainly from the Allied perspective – seems to have grown as the war progressed: not only because few infantrymen understood what they did, but also because they appeared to take few visible risks. Their ability to appear and vanish at will made them few friends in the front lines, as many misunderstood their purpose and believed (with some justification) that their sniping only attracted enemy retaliation, both from snipers and artillery, which the Poor Bloody Infantry had to put up with:

I never liked them [snipers] they would shoot some poor Hun and bugger off then we'd get it in the neck. Our officer often used to chase them out, telling them to ply their murderous bloody trade somewhere else.[232]

The reasons for this are not hard to understand, for even late in the war, the deliberate killing of an enemy soldier was, in an emotive way, still regarded by many as tantamount to murder. The logic of this attitude was, of course, insupportable in the face of modern warfare, with gas, flame-throwers and artillery shells killing in their thousands. Those Queens of the Battlefield, the machine guns, were responsible for the deaths of tens of thousands of soldiers, but even their hated crews stood at least a slight chance of surviving surrender – depending on circumstances. The actual statistics for sniper casualty rates are difficult to estimate, as snipers were simply listed as infantry if killed or wounded, but in British units, 50 per cent casualties among snipers through 1918 seems to have been normal:

April 19th. Our snipers did not get into their hides until it was
light – so they were seen. Already half of them have been hit.[233]

Yet, despite their losses, the sniping war was still somehow deemed
morally unacceptable, even by those who waged it. After seventy-odd
years many of the snipers I interviewed were at pains to tell me they
had never deliberately shot anyone, and were discomfited by what
they had done.

The Final Push

The last year of the war saw something of a role reversal on the part of
the British and Commonwealth snipers, upon whose shoulders fell
much of the defensive fighting during Germany's last-gasp attempt at
victory, the *Kaiserschlacht* offensive of March 1918. The British
snipers had fortuitously been advised in the *Manual* of 1917 that in
defence, their tactics were to find 'battle positions' in any suitable
ground, and then delay the enemy advance for as long as possible.
During the offensive many of them did exactly that, to the extent of
sacrificing their own lives to enable their comrades to escape. How
many died is unknown, as there are very few surviving accounts of the
fighting during what was a very confused period. It was to prove
Private Huxford's last fight:

The Jerries came over so quickly they just overran our lines.
We were in rest and were told to get up [to the front] double-
quick. My mate Sam and I grabbed our rifles and as much
ammunition as we could carry and found a small sap off the
reserve lines that had a good view of our front. There was a
little wood that we could see Jerries gathering in, it was only
400 yards away and we opened up on them. We must have got
several then their artillery started dropping shells on us and we
hopped it [. . .] we were heading back to our reserve lines when
a shell landed slap bang between us. Next thing I knew I was
on a stretcher staring up at the sky. I don't think any of our old
sniper section came out of that fight.[234]

It was a tale repeated over and over along the old Somme front lines, as Commonwealth troops tried to stem the advance. Although the Germans were eventually stopped at Villers-Bretonneux on 4/5 April 1918, the losses inflicted on the British Army were severe and many irreplaceable scouts and snipers had been lost. However, in gambling all on the offensive, Germany had dealt its final card, and it was only a matter of time before some form of peace would have to be agreed.

In the interim, Germany was having its own problems in continuing to wage war on such a massive scale. By 1918 shortages of raw materials meant that rubber, leather and cotton were unobtainable. As a consequence, jackboots were phased out in favour of short, British-style laced ankle boots, and bandages were made of paper. Copper, iron and steel were also hard to source, as too were the basic ores for the manufacture of alloys. Steel, rather than brass, was being tried for shell and cartridge cases and new forms of explosive were being invented as the normal forms of TNT and glycerine-based chemicals were proving harder and harder to find. Food was always in short supply, not only for the families at home, but also for the front-line soldiers who devoured captured British rations with glee. Indeed, the vast quantities of food and drink captured by the German troops in the *Kaiserschlacht* contributed materially to the slowing down of the advance, as men were confronted with unimaginable luxuries such as tinned meats, chocolate and whisky, all of which they felt morally obliged to stop and consume.

With regard to the issue of sniping rifles and optics, the manufacture of glass did not pose an immediate problem, but there had been a move towards reducing the size of telescopic sights, in part as a means of saving materials but also to make them lighter. Hensoldt, for example, produced an excellent, compact telescopic sight that was to set a new benchmark in size and weight, and which was to have a profound effect on British thinking in the near future.

As the war moved from the trenches to open country, fighting retreats became commonplace and the use of snipers to delay and harass served the German Army well:

The Australian advance was halted by a German sniper at the crossroads near Bray who pinned down the men for an hour.

Eventually one of our own snipers found him and despatched him with one shot. The advance then proceeded again as planned.[235]

But life for the Germans was getting steadily more difficult as trained Commonwealth snipers appeared with increasing frequency along the front. German sniper training had reached its apogee by 1917, with men being passed through one of thirty sniper schools set up behind the lines on a two-week course of instruction. The German snipers were still being used in a primary role of hunter-killer, with observation and intelligence-gathering coming second, but there was no shortage of suitable men. As far as the raw material for sniper training went, many of the new German recruits were no more than boys barely out of school:

> We had recruits at our school who were sixteen, seventeen years of age [. . .] many had only basic rifle training and we had to teach them how to shoot before we could begin on sniper instruction. But after 1917 we also had many men who had served as sharpshooters on the Eastern Front and had gained a great deal of experience. I recall one who said he had shot over three hundred Russians.[236]

These men would wreak havoc on the Allies as they began their slow advance through France from August 1918, the enemy snipers turning each hedgerow and village into a defensive position that had to be bitterly contested, in a precursor to the fighting a generation later after D-Day. In 1918 most German sniper sections comprised at least twenty-four men but this was insufficient to deal with the ascending level of Allied sniping superiority. For the beleaguered Germans, life had become even more difficult, for in November 1917, the first American troops had arrived in the trenches.

The American Sniper

The American Expeditionary Force comprised elements of both the US Marines and US Army, and while all ultimately answered to the same Commander-in-Chief, General Pershing, each was subject to different command structures. Where the training of snipers was concerned there was something of a dichotomy, for although the Army had entered the war with an issue sniping rifle, they had no training programme and no accredited snipers. The Marine Corps, on the other hand – which prided itself on the expertise of its riflemen – had plenty of good sharpshooters but no sniping rifles. The Army used the standard (and very competent) Springfield Model 1903 .30–06-calibre rifle, and sniper variants were equipped with an almost identical version of the Model 1913 Warner and Swasey scope, which was used by the Canadian Army. The Marines had been looking for some time at adopting a telescopic sight for fitting to their Springfields, but had decided against the Warner, in part because the US Department of Ordnance had re-evaluated it in 1913, and had been fairly damning about its performance, stating its deficiencies as:

> With the eyepiece offset [. . .] the shooter is forced to assume an uncomfortable position.
> There is insufficient eye relief.
> The magnification is higher than necessary, and the field of view correspondingly smaller than desirable.
> Too small an exit pupil limits the sight's effectiveness at night.
> Excessive weight and bulk.
> The glass reticle was easily obscured by film and moisture.
> Lost motion (that is play) in the windage and elevation adjustments made them subject to error.[237]

The American Warner varied slightly from that of the Canadian model in being range-calibrated differently, to allow for the different weight of the .30-calibre bullet, the range drum being marked to a highly optimistic 3,000 yards instead of the 2,400 yards of the Ross, plus the receiver mounting bracket was different. The US Army had some 1,530 Model 1903/Warner combinations, but its adoption was, in many respects, a curious choice for the Army, as there existed several other makes of scope that were lighter, more efficient and undoubtedly cheaper. Arguably, there was no available optical sight that could have been adopted by the US military that did not have *some* shortcomings, but there were certainly better choices available. Indeed, the Ordnance had examined a number of alternatives during tests undertaken in 1913–14. These included a 5 x Stevens sight, Frankford Arsenal No. 7 and No. 10 scopes (both of 2.5 x), a 2.8 x Casey prismatic (similar to the commercial Zeiss) and a number of German-supplied scopes, of which the 3.2 x Goerz proved of particular interest. After extensive tests in 1913 and 1914 the Goerz was recommended for adoption in December 1915. The report of the US School of Musketry stated that, in its opinion:

> The C.P. Goerz sight possesses all the essential requirements [. . .] such as adjustment, simplicity, strength, rigidity and convenience to the user, and that for military use it is as such superior to the Warner & Swasey type as the latter is to the Winchester A5 model. The School's recommendation is:
> That the Goerz Telescopic Sight be adopted for issue, replacing the Warner and Swasey sight.
> That they be issued at the rate of two to each organisation of the mobile Army armed with the rifle.[238]

In order to facilitate manufacture under licence in the US, Frankford Arsenal prepared drawings of the Goerz, calling it the 'Telescopic Musket Sight Model 1916, No. 1'. However, according to a contemporary Ordnance report, work did not progress as it should have done:

> On account of the pressure of more essential work, and the apparent lack of further demand on the part of the service for musket sights, little action toward producing the Goerz type was taken until March 1917. At this time a representative of the Winchester Company stated that he believed his concern was in a position to develop an improved sight which would equal the Goerz optically and would be an improvement [. . .] in certain respects, and which could be produced more readily in quantity.[239]

The US Ordnance Department therefore commissioned Winchester to design and build the new scope, designated the Telescopic Musket Sight, M1918. It was an overbore pattern, short-bodied, and used sliding ring mounts similar to that of the A5, necessitating the scope be manually pulled back after each shot. It was of 2.6 x with a useful 8.5-degree field of view, and the Board recommended it be put into production forthwith.

Orders for 32,000 Model 1918 sights were placed with Winchester in July 1918, and lens manufacture was subcontracted to the Eastman-Kodak Company of Rochester, New York, which was asked to supply 42,607 sets of lenses. But by November 1918 none had been supplied and most of the order was then cancelled, although by late 1919 three completed examples had been sent to the Infantry School at Fort Benning. Perhaps it was as well the order was never fulfilled, for subsequent testing showed that:

> The optical lenses worked loose and the lenses themselves became uncemented, rendering it impossible to use the sight.
> The rear mounting bracket fractured from recoil.
> If the sight were not drawn back into the firing position each time, the shooter was liable to injury from the rebound of the telescope.[240]

Allowing for the fact that none of these alternative scopes were in large-scale production, the only serious competitor to the Warner was the Winchester A5, which was in commercial production and which had already been adopted by Britain and Canada. But it was a scope the US Army did not rate particularly highly. When tested against competitors in late 1915, the Department of Ordnance commented that it suffered from:

> The field of view is so small on account of the excessive power as to affect its usefulness, except for slow fire at fixed targets for which work it was considered excellent.
> The spacing of the brackets only 6 inches apart on such a long telescope is considered a source of weakness.

The bolt of the rifle cannot be operated unless the telescope is pushed forwards [. . .] this fact and the necessity of drawing it back to the firing position after each shot materially increases the time of firing.

The exit pupil is so small that the sight is of no use in poor light.[241]

Because of this report, the Marine Corps chose to eschew the Winchester scope, but in the wake of serious casualties inflicted on them by German snipers, they realised, belatedly, that they needed to adopt some form of optical sight and opted for the A5.

Marine pattern Winchester scopes had improved mounts, as neither the dovetail blocks originally supplied nor the micrometer-adjusted mounting ring system were considered robust enough. Both were modified for Marine use but alas, it was too little, too late, for of the 500 A5 scopes and mounts ordered virtually none reached the Front before the cessation of hostilities in November 1918.

Prior to the cancellation of the order for the Model 1918 scope, the Department of Ordnance had also taken a momentous decision to fit them, not to the Springfield Model 1903 rifle, but to a British design, the Model 1917 Enfield rifle. This was officially designated the US Telescopic sight Rifle, Caliber .30 Model of 1918, and it was interesting for several reasons. The stock was one piece and had a commercial-type pistol grip, slotted finger rests and was of 'special construction, with no barrel guard, nor upper bands, while the lower band is of special design', which was tacit acknowledgement of one of the major problems besetting all Great War sniping rifles – the swelling of the wood causing loss of accuracy. It was an early example of a 'free floating' barrel, where no part of the barrel touches any part of the stock forwards of the breech. It was to be issued with a special heavy barrel, having a twist of 1 in 10,[242] which had proved more accurate and durable in tests. Neither did the Model 1918 have provision for iron sights – a serious omission repeated on the issue Springfield Model 1903-A4 sniping rifle of the Second World War. But it mattered little, for it seems that few of these weapons were ever produced, (although there is mention of one appearing during a long-range target shoot near Washington in early April 1918).[243] Certainly, none ever arrived in France and it seems unlikely more than a handful were ever completed.

Sniper Training

None of this really made much difference to the Marine and Army snipers, who, despite the lack of suitable equipment, used their rifles with issue iron sights to very good effect. As with the Canadian troops, there was no shortage of hunters in the ranks, and by early 1918 this was of crucial importance, as Hesketh-Prichard commented:

> When first the Americans began to come to the school we were delighted because we expected an influx of really good shots. So many of our best men, British, Canadian and Australian had been killed or wounded, and we were well aware that for this particular job of sniping, America must have an inexhaustible supply of the right material among her frontiersmen. Nor were we disappointed.[244]

The Americans had learned to select men on the basis of both shooting and hunting ability, understanding that few target shooters made good snipers. Their enthusiasm was a surprise and joy to the weary instructors at the British and Canadian sniping schools:

> When the Americans arrived a large number of their officers and men passed through our schools and were distinguished by their passionate desire to learn all that they could, in order, as one said to me, 'to make up for lost time.' They started schools of their own, modelled on ours, and in most cases partly staffed by British instructors.[245]

Even at the earliest stages, there was friendly rivalry between the American and Commonwealth snipers, in particular the Canadians, who lost no time in reminding the Americans that they had witnessed four long years of war and had learned a great deal. This experience was something the young American snipers lacked, and it would cost them dearly. Once in the lines, they were subjected to a level of sniping beyond anything they could have imagined. Colonel F. Wise, commanding the 60th Infantry Battalion in the Argonne, had seen what the Germans were capable of during the bitter fighting for Belleau Wood, and he organised the best shots in his unit into impromptu counter-sniping teams. Using them as an offensive force, he placed them 100 yards behind his advancing troops with orders to find and eliminate any German snipers, and by the end of the fighting his scratch-built sniper teams had accounted for fifty Germans. As Marine Elton Mackin recounted:

> A sniper fired – ours, he had a rifle with a telescopic sight. The leading man went down hard, his comrades jumped for cover. The snipers kept up the fire.[246]

But if the soldiers lacked the sniping technology to deal with the Germans, they certainly didn't lack the skills, and the mountain boys of Arkansas, Tennessee, Kentucky and other states soon put their hunting skills to good use.

Colonel Wise was fortunate in being able to form such a unit from the many hunters within the ranks, but there were some who fought the Germans at a more individual level. Doubtless the most singular story of one man's approach to the sniping war was that of Sergeant Alvin York, who used a service Model 1917 Enfield rifle and iron sights to silence four machine-gun nests by shooting twenty-five German gun crewmen through the head at a range of 300 yards. This understandably encouraged the surrender of some 132 others and gained York a richly deserved Congressional Medal of Honor.

However, he was merely one of many, most of whom received no recognition for their deeds. Herman Davis, a native of Arkansas, only received official acknowledgement for his sniping feats by accident. He was a passionate hunter and outdoorsman, but at 5'3" he was physically undersized, as well as being 30 years old. Initially, Davis was rejected for military service in favour of younger, fitter men but eventually managed to enlist and arrived in France in July 1918 with the 113th Infantry Battalion. On arrival in the trenches he enquired why a troublesome German machine gun was not being shot at. Upon being told that the 1,000-yard distance was beyond practical rifle range, he shrugged and commented: 'That's jest a good shootin' distance' and proceeded to shoot four of the enemy gunners. His backwoods skills and extraordinarily precise shooting ensured he was appointed company scout/sniper and he began a solo campaign to eliminate all of the Germans he came across. Quite what he achieved will never be known, as he mostly worked alone, but the few events that he mentioned to friends after the war were remarkable enough. During an advance, Davis moved through the German lines to within 50 yards of their position and proceeded to shoot eleven Germans who emerged from a dugout to man their machine guns. Later, when his company came under heavy machine-gun fire near Verdun, he crawled into No Man's Land until he found a vantage point from where he could see the Germans, then coolly shot every member of the crew. Unlike most of his shooting feats, this particular incident happened to be witnessed by an American artillery officer who reported it and Davis was awarded the US Distinguished Service Cross. During the continuing advance he shot at least another twenty-six enemy, mostly machine-gunners, whom he seemed to have a particular dislike of, and his medal collection expanded with the award of the Medaille Militaire and Croix de Guerre with Palm Leaf and Silver Star.

Like most of his sniping contemporaries, Davis did not want or relish publicity, and when he returned to Arkansas in 1919 he almost never mentioned his war service, details only coming to light when General Pershing placed him number four in his list of the '100 Greatest Heroes of World War One'. His medals remained unworn in his beloved fishing tackle box, and when asked about them he once said he got them 'simply as a part of my duties'. Sadly, he died in poverty in January 1923 as a result of complications brought on by gas inhalation during the war, but a monument to him was erected by proud citizens at Manila, Arkansas, in 1925. Despite their dearth of proper sniping rifles, and lack of cohesive training, there seems little doubt that the snipers of the AEF managed to give as good as they got, one German writing in his regimental history that:

> We had great trouble from the [American] riflemen who were very accurate shots. Three of our troop of machine-gunners were shot down one after the other and no one was prepared to

take their place. With no fire support from the [machine] guns we were soon overrun and forced to surrender. It was a bitter blow to us who had fought so hard and so well.[247]

The Best for Last: The Pattern 1914 Sniping Rifle

While Britain and its Commonwealth allies had almost exclusively used the SMLE rifle in various modified guises for sniping, it had never been designed as such, and while it performed adequately, there were always complaints about its shortcomings. The offset scopes were difficult to use, awkward to adjust and unnecessarily big and heavy. The thin-walled barrels of the Enfield did not promote long-range accuracy and barrel wear was too rapid, Hesketh-Prichard estimating that 500 rounds being sufficient to render a sniping rifle too inaccurate for use. It could not be argued that in pre-war tests the Mauser-inspired Enfield Pattern 1914 rifle had done well, even if its .276-calibre ammunition had proved problematic, but in the wake of the Enfield factory's commitment to supplying the British government with as many SMLEs as possible, its production could not be undertaken. It had not vanished from sight though, for contracts had been given to Winchester and Remington for a total of 3,400,000 Pattern 1914 rifles, to be supplied in .303 calibre at $30 (£6) each. The first batch of P14s arrived in England in May 1916 (only to be promptly rejected by British inspectors!) but after hasty modifications to the design, some 1,235,298 rifles were eventually supplied.

During late 1916 P14s began arriving at the School of Musketry at Hythe, where it was found that they were considerably more accurate than the Enfield, aided, to no small extent, by the adoption of a special rearsight that incorporated a micro-adjustment of one minute of angle, or 1 inch at 100 yards, similar in type to those fitted to the Ross rifle. And so, by mid-1917, the sniper schools were being supplied with P14 rifles that proved as effective at shorter ranges (up to 300 yards) with these iron sights as the extant scoped SMLEs. Thus, by 1918, they were being issued without telescopes to sniper sections on the basis of three per battalion. At longer ranges, testing was carried out on P14s mounted with Aldis as well as captured German scopes, including the new short Hensoldt. Comparison testing showed the

Aldis to be inferior, so it was decided to manufacture a new telescope, the Pattern 1918, which was a shameless copy of the Hensoldt. On 11 April 1918 it was approved to be fitted to a new sniping rifle, a modified Pattern 14 designated the Pattern 1914 Mk I W(T) the 'T' meaning telescopic. The mounting system was the tried and tested German front double claw system, with a single claw at the rear retained by a thumb latch, and 2,000 rifles were to be set up by the Periscopic Prism Company.

All of these rifles were supplied by Winchester and all scopes were marked with the rifle serial number and a W prefix. (A few rifles were apparently fitted with Aldis scopes but no information exists as to the possible number.) It was to prove an excellent combination, but alas, the rifle was not approved for production until 31 December 1918 and the first examples did not come off the production line until long after the Armistice had been signed. Perhaps it was fortunate for the Germans that these new weapons did not see service in the war.

The Finale

By August 1918, the Kaiser's army was being forced onto the back foot. The Germans could no longer sustain the effort of waging war in the face of a determined Allied advance across the Western Front and south through the Argonne and Champagne regions. It was, at last, a war of movement, and one in which the Allied snipers could work on their own terms. Moving with advanced patrols, they spied on German positions, reporting the sites of artillery batteries and machine-gun posts. They would move silently into No Man's Land during the night and wait patiently for targets to show themselves, forcing the Germans to take cover while Allied troops advanced, and it is interesting to note that more gallantry awards to snipers were made in 1918 than at any other period during the war.

Examples of the success of such tactics are legion – at Mont St Quentin, near Péronne, on 1 September 1918, an Australian sniper, Sergeant Alby Lowerson of the 21st Infantry Battalion, rallied a few men and stalked, then killed, the crews of several German machine-gun positions, winning the Victoria Cross in the process. At Arras, in August, three snipers of the 4th Canadian Mounted Rifles advanced to deal with four machine guns, whose crews they shot. They finished off the day by forcing the remaining fourteen Germans to surrender and made them carry their guns back to Canadian lines.

It was not all one-sided though, for the Germans were, by now, expert at fighting retreats, and their light MG/08–15 Maxim guns (more portable than the heavy version), combined with the use of snipers, made life extremely uncomfortable for the Allies, as the Canadian history recorded:

> At Le Quesnel, one Boche sniper did more damage than four machine guns which were firing from the same locality. The guns were located, the sniper was not.[248]

Working through the villages and towns was possibly the most exacting of all duties for the troops, for they were perfect places in which a sniper could conceal himself, shoot, then escape with little chance of detection. The dangers were well summed up by Sergeant E. Cook of the 1st Somerset Light Infantry, who was leading mopping-up parties to root out stubborn German defenders in the final weeks of the war:

> We hurried forwards [. . .] and started mopping up the houses. Now, this is a dangerous and thankless task. You are an exposed target from all angles. Snipers began to pick off the men, these are very difficult to locate and dislodge. Several shots were certainly meant for me, a sniper does not usually miss. One man came out of a house 20 yards away and fired – a miss – my turn – a bull. And so we worked our way around, death lurking at every corner.[249]

Cook eventually received a sniper's bullet in the leg, finishing his war just nine days before the Armistice. He was probably one of the lucky ones, for as the war came to its end, most of the final casualties were the result of sniping, and the last man killed, Canadian Private George Lawrence Price,[250] was shot in the head by a sniper just two minutes before 11 o'clock on 11 November.

In retrospect, there was little doubt that the sniper had become a vital factor in waging modern war. While Germany had understood the value of sniping from the beginning, it took the British and their allies two years to catch up, and another year before their snipers were acknowledged as the battlefield specialists that they had become.

And yet, despite the wealth of experience gained during the war, none of the combatants saw any reason to continue sniper training post-1918. Britain withdrew all its sniping rifles and placed them in store, subsequently stripping them of their telescopes, which were sold off into the commercial gun trade in 1925. Much the same happened to the rifles of other countries: France stored their Lebels and Berthiers until the 1930s, before eventually selling them off as surplus to colonial powers – minus their scopes of course (lest they be turned on their former owners). The United States, too, seemed to forget all it had learned from the war and the US Army never did instigate a sniper training programme, leading to a severe shortage of suitable men upon their entry into the Second World War in 1941. While the Marines continued to train their riflemen to a very high standard, encouraging competitive shooting, even they did not adopt a dedicated sniping rifle, having to utilise hastily converted target rifles when they went to war in the Pacific in 1942.

Neither was there any interest in retaining the expertise of men who had worked so hard to become snipers. The British government was soon under pressure to scale down the Army, and there were huge post-war defence cuts. Snipers ceased to be retained as part of the Army establishment, although scouts were kept as part of each infantry battalion. However, no special sniper training was given.

In reality, most of the snipers had had enough of war and were content to walk away and resume normal lives, although this was often difficult. The understanding of post-traumatic stress was in its infancy, and men were simply expected to keep their problems to themselves and get on with things:

> After the last time I was wounded I put in for a commission [in the Machine Gun Corps] which meant that by the time I had got through OTC [Officer Training] it was October 1918 and the war was almost over. I was glad though, I don't mind admitting it, I had been wounded three times as a sniper, and

I knew it was just a matter of time [. . .] I don't think any of our sniper section came through the war, they were all killed or wounded. For years after the war I used to wake in the early hours and get up and go walking, to try and forget some of things I'd seen and done. There were lots of men like me, some of them would be walking all night but we never talked about it, though sometimes you'd get in conversation with someone and they'd ask if you'd been 'over there' and you'd say yes and you'd ask each other where you'd served, but that was about it. I never, ever told anyone I had been a sniper, not even my wife. They wouldn't have understood.[251]

For many of the German snipers, their war was not to end in 1918, for the Army returned home undefeated, still carrying its weapons, to a heroes' welcome. A large number of German soldiers immediately became embroiled in the Spartacists' revolt, which broke out between pro-Communist groups and loyal soldiers, resulting in fierce street fighting across many major cities. Although not widely reported at the time, it was, for many German soldiers, almost a continuation of the war, albeit with a more local enemy. Fighting was very bitter indeed:

When the ceasefire was announced, I was teaching sniper recruits and my officer called out to us, 'You are lucky men, the war has ended!' I was so tired, I could not really understand what it meant to stop fighting. We returned to Munich in December 1918 and were immediately asked to join the *Freikorps* in defeating the Communists. I had learned so much in the trenches that the fighting for me was easy and we did much street sniping but shooting fellow German soldiers who had been in the trenches like me sickened me. One day I went home and threw my rifle in the river then burned my uniform and I never picked up another rifle from that day. In 1931, I was by then married with a family, there was such discontent in Germany [. . .] I could see it all happening again and so I took my family to America.[252]

In Germany, the employment of snipers ceased following the Treaty of Versailles, which severely restricted the size of its Army, as well as the type and number of weapons it could retain. Snipers and scoped rifles were high on the prohibited list and hundreds of rifles were confiscated and destroyed. Although some clandestine training was undertaken, it was not until the rise of the NAZI party in the 1930s that the Army, and the SS in particular, began to equip and train snipers, although it was on a very limited basis.

Perhaps the final words on the subject should be left to the man who had probably done more than any other individual to promote sniping in the British Army, Vernon Hesketh-Prichard:

> After all, what is the good of all my big game shooting, if it did not culminate in this? To spend thirty years, all of them since my earliest days, in the hunter's craft, and then use one's knowledge in the greatest war in history and in such a job as mine, may well be – is – glorious.[253]

He returned home, his health broken, and died at Gorhambury on 14 June 1922. He was buried in the Grimston vault in St Michael's church, St Albans: no floral tributes or representatives were sent by the Army.

SNIPER SANDY

(to the tune 'Sister Susie's sewing shirts for soldiers'

Sandy Mac the sniper is a-sniping from his loophole
With a telescopic rifle he is looking for the Hun
If he sees a sniper lurking or a working party working
At once he opens fire on them and bags them every one
And when you come into our trench, by night-time or by day
We take you to his loop-hole, and we point to him and say

*Sniper Sandy's slaying Saxon soldiers
And Saxon soldiers seldom show but Sandy bags a few
And every day the Bosches put up little wooden crosses
In the cemetery for Saxon soldiers Sniper Sandy slew*

Now in the German trenches there's a sniper they call Hermann
A stout and solid Saxon with a healthy growth of beard
And Hermann with his rifle is the pride of every German
Until our Sandy gets on him, and Hermann gets afeared
For when he hears the bullets come he slides down to the
                                              ground
And trembling, he gasps out to his comrades all around

*Sniper Sandy's slaying Saxon soldiers
And Saxon soldiers seldom show but Sandy bags a few
And every day the Bosches put up little wooden crosses
In the cemetery for Saxon soldiers Sniper Sandy slew*

The Seaforths got so proud of Sandy's prowess with his rifle
They drew up a report on him and sent it to the Corps
And ninety seven was his bag – it doesn't seem a trifle
But Sandy isn't certain that it wasn't even more
And when Sir Douglas heard of it he broke into a laugh
And rubbed his hands and chuckled to the Chief of General
                                              Staff

*Sniper Sandy's slaying Saxon soldiers
And Saxon soldiers seldom show but Sandy bags a few
And every day the Bosches put up little wooden crosses
In the cemetery for Saxon soldiers Sniper Sandy slew.*

E.A. Macintosh
1893-1917

(killed Cambrai 21st Nov)

Notes

1. George Santayana 1863–1952.
2. Pegler, M., *Powder and Ball Small Arms*, Crowood Press, 1998.
3. Norbunov, Lieutenant G., *Russian Field Artillery*, quoted in Pegler, op. cit.
4. A double-barrelled percussion rifle invented by John Jacob (1812–58) using both conical and a specially developed explosive bullet and capable of accurate shooting to 2,000 yards.
5. H. Green, from a letter quoted by H.T. Lambrick in *John Jacob of Jacobabad*, Cassel & Co., London, 1940.
6. *The Army and Navy Journal*, August 1874.
7. Keegan, J., *The Face of Battle*, J. Cape, London, 1976.
8. Ray, F.L., *Shock Troops of the Confederacy*, CFS Press, N.C., 2006.
9. Stevens, op. cit.
10. Trepp, C., Papers & Letters from Captain Isler, 24 September 1862, New York Historical Society.
11. Inspection report of the 1st USSS, 1 November 1862, 19 December 1862, National Archives, Washington.
12. Ripley, W.Y.W., *A History of Company F, 1st United States Sharpshooters*, Rutland, Vermont, 1883.
13. Morrow, J.A., *The Confederate Whitworth Sharpshooters*, private publication, 2002.
14. Stevens, C.A., *Berdan's United States Sharpshooters in the Army of Minnesota*, 1882.
15. US Patent No. 52,818, 27 February 1866 (UK Patent 3253, 10 December 1866).
16. UK Patent No. 137, 15 January 1865, Henry Mounier Boxer.
17. Crum, Lieutenant F.M., *Memoirs of a Rifleman Scout*, private publication, Stirling, 1950.
18. *Memoirs of a Boer Kommando*, London, 1905.
19. Ibid.

20. Crum, op. cit.
21. Churchill, W.S., *London to Ladysmith via Pretoria*, W.W. Norton, New York, 1989.
22. Major Patrick Ferguson, 1744–80.
23. Grenfell, Captain J., Royal Dragoons, DOW 25 May 1915, buried Boulogne Eastern Cemetery.
24. Richards, F., Old Soldiers Never Die, *Naval and Military Press*, Sussex, undated.
25. Pusch, Lieutenant F.L., Irish Guards, KIA 27 June 1916, buried Essex Farm Cemetery.
26. *The War Diary of the 1st Battalion Irish Guards in the Great War*, PRO WO/95.
27. *The Royal West Kent Regiment in the Great War*, Cassell, London, 1926.
28. Fairall, CSM J.H., Queen Victoria's Rifles, The London Regiment, KIA 24 August 1915, buried at Carnoy Military Cemetery.
29. Blessing, Lance Corporal P., Royal Inniskilling Fusiliers, KIA 30 November 1917, commemorated on Tyne Cot memorial.
30. Forbes, Sergeant J.K., Gordon Highlanders, KIA 25 September 1915, commemorated on Menin Gate Memorial.
31. The common term for infantrymen. The British equivalent was 'foot-sloggers'.
32. Document dated 23 January, 1915, Der Konigliche Landrat II.494.u.495, Bundesarchiv.
33. *Instructions for the use of S.m.K Cartridges and Rifles With Telescopic Sights*, German instructional pamphlet, dated 1915.
34. Hesketh-Prichard, Major H., *Sniping in France*, Pen & Sword, Barnsley, 1994 (reissue).
35. Scott, Sergeant R., Royal Irish Fusiliers, DOW 28 October 1914, buried Cité Bonjean Military Cemetery.
36. Sergeant H. Wilson, Royal Irish Fusiliers, quoted in *Angels and Heroes*, compiled by A. Moreno and D. Truesdale Pubs., Royal Irish Fusiliers Museum, Armagh 2004.
37. Feuss, Bock, Busch, Gerard, Goerz, Hensoldt, Kahles, Oigee, Voigtlander, Zeiss.
38. Tests quoted in Kent, D.W., *German 7.9mm Military Ammunition 1888–1945*. Kent Pubs., Ann Arbor, 1990.
39. Skipp, W., quoted in Arthur, M., *Forgotten Voices of the Great War*, Ebury Press, London, 2002.
40. Mannfried Gossen, 163rd Infantry Regiment, personal correspondence.

41. Ibid.
42. Ibid.
43. 'Short' in the nomenclature actually refers to its reduced barrel length and not, as many suppose, its magazine.
44. *Munitions of War: A War Record of the BSA Factory*, Frost, G.H., Birmingham, undated.
45. Report to the Small Arms Committee, 29 August 1904, library of the National Firearms Centre, Leeds.
46. List of Changes, No. 15629, dated 1 October 1911.
47. Philips, R., Duplus, F., Chadwick, J., *The Ross Rifle of Canada*, Chadwick Pubs., Nova Scotia, 1984.
48. Greener, Captain L.L., Royal Warwickshire Regiment, KIA 5 December 1917, commemorated on Cambrai Memorial.
49. McBride, H., *A Rifleman Went to War*, Lancer, Arkansas, 1993.
50. Trumpeter J. Naylor, Royal Field Artillery, BEF.
51. Stevens, Private P.J., Royal Welsh Fusiliers, KIA 25 January 1915, buried Bois Grenier Communal Cemetery.
52. Hesketh-Prichard, *Sniping in France*.
53. Richards, op. cit.
54. Dunn, Captain J.C., *The War the Infantry Knew*, King Ltd., London, 1938.
55. Hesketh-Prichard, op. cit.
56. Ibid.
57. Passiful, Private L., Essex Yeomanry, DOW 2 February 1916, buried Béthune Town Cemetery.
58. Marshall, A., quoted in Arthur, Max, *The Last Post*, Weidenfeld & Nicolson, London, 2005.
59. Barraclough, Private A., quoted in Van Emden, R., *The Trench*, Transworld, London, 2002.
60. Butler, Major P., DSO, *A Galloper at Ypres*, Fisher-Unwin, London, 1920.
61. Ibid.
62. Hesketh-Prichard, op. cit.
63. Gossen, op. cit.
64. Sleath, F., *Sniper Jackson*, Herbert Jenkins, London, 1919.
65. Dunn, op. cit.
66. Barraclough, op. cit.
67. Blessing, op. cit.

68. Richards, op. cit.
69. Hesketh-Prichard, *A Memoir*, (Ed. E. Parker), Fisher Unwin, London, 1924.
70. Ibid.
71. Private A. Huxted, Royal Berkshire Regiment, interview with the author.
72. Ibid.
73. Forbes, op. cit.
74. *Student and Sniper Sergeant: A Memoir of J.K. Forbes*, privately published, 1917.
75. Crum, Major F.M., *Scouts and Sniping in Trench Warfare*, private publication, August 1916.
76. Dunn, op. cit.
77. Hesketh-Prichard, *A Memoir*.
78. Cusak, J. MM., *Scarlet Fever*, Cassell & Co., London, 1972.
79. Ibid.
80. Sleath, op. cit.
81. Richards, op. cit.
82. Gossen, op. cit.
83. McBride, op. cit.
84. Union Metallic Cartridge Company.
85. United States Cartridge Company.
86. McBride, op. cit.
87. Cloete, S., *A Victorian Son*, Collins, London, 1972.
88. Affectionately known as the 'Smellie'.
89. Fremantle, Captain T.F., *Notes of Lectures and Practices in Sniping*, Crumble Ltd., Leicester, 1916.
90. Penberthy, op. cit.
91. War Office Contracts, Ministry of Munitions weekly reports up to July 1915, National Archives, Kew.
92. Goldsmith, D.L., *The Grand Old Lady of No Man's Land*, Collector Grade Publications, Ontario, 1994.
93. In *The British Sniper* (Skennerton Margate Australia, 1983). Skennerton calculated 9,788 but a number were produced prior to the official specification SA 390 being introduced. The exact number is probably somewhat in excess of 10,000.
94. Hesketh-Prichard, *Sniping in France*.
95. Specification, Small Arms No. 390, 4 May 1915, MOD Pattern Room/National Firearms Collection, Leeds.

96. Hesketh-Prichard, *Sniping in France*.
97. Huxford, A., personal interview.
98. Hesketh-Prichard, op. cit.
99. Ibid.
100. Durst, T., personal interview.
101. Ibid.
102. Ibid.
103. Hesketh-Prichard, op. cit.
104. McBride, op. cit.
105. Durst, op. cit.
106. Huxford, op. cit.
107. Ibid.
108. Alvan Clarke, 1804–87.
109. William Malcolm, 1823–90.
110. Stroebel, N., *Old Rifle Scopes*, Krause Publications, Wisconsin, 2000.
111. Huxford, op. cit.
112. Watts and Company are still resident at 67 St James's St, London.
113. Casalla, C. F., *Surveying and Drawing Instruments and Appliances*, London, 1942.
114. Hesketh-Prichard, *A Memoir*.
115. Ibid.
116. Ommundsen, Lieutenant H., Honourable Artillery Company, KIA 19 September 1915, buried Brandhoek Military Cemetery.
117. Fremantle, Major T.F., *The Book of the Rifle*, London 1901.
118. Fremantle, Lieutenant T.F.H., Ox and Bucks Light Infantry, DOW 17 October 1915, buried Etaples Military Cemetery.
119. Hesketh-Prichard, *A Memoir*.
120. Ibid.
121. Ibid.
122. Hesketh-Prichard, *Sniping in France*.
123. Ibid.
124. Ibid.
125. Hesketh-Prichard, *A Memoir*.
126. Ibid.
127. Richards, op. cit.
128. Edmund Gottlieb, correspondence with the author.
129. Hesketh-Prichard, op. cit.
130. Fremantle, op. cit.
131. Patent No. 24,687, 28 December 1914.

132. Sines G. & Sakellarakis Y., 'Lenses in Antiquity', *American Journal of Archaeology*, Issue 91 (1987), pp. 191–6.
133. Ibid.
134. Fremantle, op. cit.
135. A number exist in the collection of the Royal Armouries Museum, Leeds.
136. McBride, op. cit.
137. Information from translated documents kindly supplied by Ibrahim Attalik.
138. Idriess, I.L., *The Desert Column*, Angus & Robertson, Sydney, 1951.
139. Ibid.
140. Herbert, A.P., *The Secret Battle*, Chatto & Windus, London, 1970.
141. Dean, T.C., Royal Naval Division, correspondence with the author.
142. Idriess, op. cit.
143. Ibid.
144. Ibid.
145. Ibid.
146. Gilbert, Corporal G., quoted in Macdonald, Lyn, *1915, The Death of Innocence*, Headline Press, London, 1993.
147. Idriess, op. cit.
148. *The Times*, 16 July 1915, p. 4.
149. Dean, op. cit.
150. Ibid.
151. Crutchley, C.E. (ed.), *Machine Gunner 1914–1918*, London, 1975.
152. Melville, M.L., *The Story of the Lovat Scouts, 1900–1980*, St Andrew's Press, Scotland, 1984.
153. Armstrong, Major N.A., *Fieldcraft, Sniping and Intelligence*, Canadian Official Publication, 1933.
154. Penberthy, op. cit.
155. Crum, op. cit.
156. Huxford, op. cit.
157. Armstrong, op. cit.
158. Durst, op. cit.
159. Ibid.
160. Hesketh-Prichard, *Sniping in France*.
161. Durst, op. cit.
162. Hesketh-Prichard, *A Memoir*.
163. Hesketh-Prichard, *Sniping in France*.
164. Ibid.

165. Ibid.

166. Ibid.

167. Hesketh-Prichard, *A Memoir*.

168. Ibid.

169. Guirand de Scevola, 1871–1950.

170. Ibid.

171. Hesketh-Prichard, *Sniping in France*.

172. Harvey, Private A., 2nd Duke of Cornwall's Light Infantry, correspondence with the author.

173. Ibid.

174. Huxford, op. cit.

175. Hesketh-Prichard, *Sniping in France*.

176. Ibid.

177. Hesketh-Prichard, *A Memoir*.

178. 'Training for Snipers', First Army School of Sniping and Scouting, December 1916.

179. Huxford, op. cit.

180. Hesketh-Prichard, *Sniping in France*.

181. Huxford, op. cit.

182. Knight, J., *The Civil Service Rifles in the Great War*, Pen and Sword, Barnsley, 2004.

183. Crum, op. cit.

184. Hesketh-Prichard, *A Memoir*.

185. Gottlieb, op. cit.

186. Solomon J. Solomon, 1860–1927.

187. Crum, op. cit.

188. 'Sniping in Trench Warfare', National Archives of Canada, Manuscript MG30 Accession: E2 Vol. 1. Armstrong papers.

189. Ibid.

190. McBride, op. cit.

191. Report to the OC 31st Battalion, dated 4 September 1915, from the Staff 6th Canadian Infantry brigade, Canadian National Archives A6.272.

192. Francis Peghamagabow, 1891–1952.

193. Now called the Wasauking First Nation tribe.

194. Wheeler, V., *The 50th Battalion in No Man's Land*, Quebec, undated.

195. Walton, Private A., Durham Light Infantry, KIA 23 April 1917, buried Wancourt Military Cemetery.

196. Hesketh-Prichard, *A Memoir*.

197. Norwest, Private H.L., 50th Infantry Regiment, KIA 18 August 1918, buried Warvillers Cemetery extension.

198. Gossen, op. cit.

199. Idriess, I.L., *The Australian Guerrilla: Sniping*, Paladin, Colorado, 1978.

200. Idriess, *The Desert Column*.

201. Ibid.

202. Idriess, *The Australian Guerrilla*.

203. James, Private L., correspondence with the author.

204. Courtesy of the South African Museum of Military History.

205. Methven, N.W., published in the *Journal of the Military Medal Society of South Africa*, December 1984.

206. Friedrich Schultze (ex-Lieutenant, 24th Brandenburg Regiment).

207. Ibid.

208. *Infantry Regiment No. 70 in the Great War*, private publication, 1924.

209. The diary of Henri Debray, privately owned.

210. Jünger, E., *Copse 125*, Zimmerman & Zimmerman, 1985.

211. Ottavio Bottecchia 1894–1927, winner of the Tour de France 1924 and 1925.

212. *History of the 142nd Infantry Regiment 1914–1918*, Berlin, 1923.

213. Hesketh-Prichard, *Sniping in France*.

214. Herritt, Private C., Middlesex Regiment, interview with the author.

215. Ibid.

216. Gottlieb, op. cit.

217. Hutchison, G.S., *Pilgrimage*, Rich and Cowan, London, 1935.

218. Durst, op. cit.

219. Ibid.

220. Dennis, Private A., Royal Fusiliers, interview with the author.

221. Barratt, Private T., VC, South Staffordshire Regiment, KIA 27 July 1917, buried Essex Farm Cemetery.

222. Private R. Lawrence, 3rd South African Infantry, quoted in Macdonald, L., *Voices and Images of the Great War*, Michael Joseph, London, 1988.

223. Huxford, op. cit.

224. National Archives of Canada, AG9 Series III Vol. 4143.

225. Egan, Private Frank, York and Lancaster Regiment, correspondence with the author.

226. Durst, op. cit.

227. Lawrence, op. cit.

228. Personal account supplied to the author.

229. Shingleton, Lieutenant S.F., RFA, *Reminiscences of the War 1914–1919*, typescript, London, 1923.

230. James, H., ex-Corporal Royal Fusiliers, *My War*, typescript, private collection, undated.

231. Huxford, op. cit.

232. Private A.E. Sparks, Royal West Kent Regiment.

233. Dunn, op. cit.

234. Huxford, op. cit.

235. *Official History of Australia in the Great War*, Bean, C.E.W., Melbourne, 1983.

236. Schultze, op. cit.

237. Report by the US Board of Ordnance to the Chief Inspector of Ordnance, October 1914, National Archives, Washington.

238. Report of the School of Musketry to the US Board of Ordnance, 18 December 1915, National Archives, Washington.

239. Rutherford H.K., *Ordnance Magazine*, July–August 1921 and January–February 1924.

240. Ibid.

241. Ibid.

242. Specified in the *Handbook of Ordnance Data*, published by the Department of the Office of the Chief of Ordnance, November 1918.

243. *Arms and the Man* magazine, 13 April 1918.

244. Hesketh-Prichard, *A Memoir*.

245. Hesketh-Prichard, *Sniping in France*.

246. Mackin, Marine E., 2/5th Marines, *Fighting Leathernecks: The Marine Corps in WW1*.

247. *A History of the 174th Infantry Regiment*, Berlin, 1922.

248. *The Official History of Canada in the Great War, 1914–1919*, A. Fortescue Duiguid, Ottawa, undated.

249. Account by Yeoman Warder E. Cook, Royal Armouries Library, Tower of London.

250. Price, Private G.L., Saskatchewan Regiment, KIA 11 November 1918, buried St Symphorian Cemetery.

251. Durst, op. cit.

252. Schultze, op. cit.

253. Hesketh-Prichard, *A Memoir*.

Index